HEALTH

FOUNTAINHEAD PRESS V SERIES

Edited by
Sujata Iyengar and Allison K. Lenhardt

FOUNTAINHEAD
PRESS

Our green initiatives include:

Electronic Products
We deliver products in non-paper form whenever possible. This includes pdf downloadables, flash drives, & CDs.

Electronic Samples
We use Xample, a new electronic sampling system. Instructor samples are sent via a personalized web page that links to pdf downloads.

FSC Certified Printers
All of our printers are certified by the Forest Service Council which promotes environmentally and socially responsible management of the world's forests. This program allows consumer groups, individual consumers, and businesses to work together hand-in-hand to promote responsible use of the world's forests as a renewable and sustainable resource.

Recycled Paper
Most of our products are printed on a minimum of 30% post-consumer waste recycled paper.

Support of Green Causes
When we do print, we donate a portion of our revenue to green causes. Listed below are a few of the organizations that have received donations from Fountainhead Press. We welcome your feedback and suggestions for contributions, as we are always searching for worthy initiatives.
Rainforest 2 Reef
Environmental Working Group

For information, please call or write:

1-800-586-0330

Fountainhead Press
Southlake, TX 76092

Web Site: www.fountainheadpress.com
E-mail: customerservice@fountainheadpress.com

First Edition

ISBN: 978-1-59871-632-0

Printed in the United States of America

INTRODUCTION TO THE FOUNTAINHEAD PRESS V SERIES

By Brooke Rollins and Lee Bauknight
Series Editors

The *Fountainhead Press V Series* is a new collection of single-topic readers that take a unique look at some of today's most pressing issues. Designed to give writing students a more nuanced introduction to public discourse—on the environment, on food, and on digital life, to name a few of the topics—the books feature writing, research, and invention prompts that can be adapted to nearly any kind of college writing class. Each *V Series* textbook focuses on a single issue and includes multi-genre and multimodal readings and assignments that move the discourse beyond the most familiar patterns of debate—patterns usually fettered by entrenched positions and often obsessed with "winning."

The ultimate goal of the series is to help writing students—who tend to hover on the periphery of public discourse—think, explore, find their voices, and skillfully compose texts in a variety of media and genres. Not only do the books help students think about compelling issues and how they might address them, they also give students the practice they need to develop their research, rhetorical, and writing skills. Together, the readings, prompts, and longer assignments show students how to add their voices to the conversations about these issues in meaningful and productive ways.

With enough readings and composing tasks to sustain an entire quarter or semester, and inexpensive enough to be used in combination with other rhetorics and readers, the *Fountainhead Press V Series* provides instructors with the flexibility to build the writing courses they want and need to teach. An instructor interested in deeply exploring environmental issues, for example, could design a semester- or quarter-long course using *Green*, the first of the *V Series* texts. On the other hand, an instructor who wanted to teach discrete units on different issues could use two or more of the *V Series* books. In either case, the texts would give students ample opportunity—and a variety of ways—to engage with the issues at hand.

The *V Series* uses the term "composition" in its broadest sense. Of course, the textbooks provide students plenty of opportunities to write, but they also include assignments that take students beyond the page. Books in the series encourage students to explore other modes of communication by prompting them to design web sites, for example; to produce videos, posters, and presentations; to conduct primary and secondary research; and to develop projects with community partners that might incorporate any number of these skills. Ultimately, we have designed the *Fountainhead Press V Series* to work for teachers and students. With their carefully chosen readings, built-in flexibility, and sound rhetorical grounding, the *V Series* books would be a dynamic and user-friendly addition to any writing class.

TABLE OF CONTENTS

Introduction: **Healing Writing**   **1**
By Sujata Iyengar and Allison Kellar Lenhardt

excerpt from **The Spirit Catches You and You Fall Down: A Hmong Child, Her American Doctors, and the Collision of Two Cultures**   **7**
By Anne Fadiman

excerpt from **A Life in Smoke**   **23**
By Julia Hansen

'You Look Great' and Other Lies   **41**
By Bruce Feiler

excerpt from **Bright-Sided**   **47**
By Barbara Ehrenreich

A Life Beyond Reason   **53**
By Dwight Christopher Gabbard

Surgeons III   **61**
By Lamar Dodd

What Are the Public Health Effects of Direct-to-Consumer Drug Advertising?   **63**
By Elizabeth A Almasi, Randall S Stafford, Richard L Kravitz, Peter R Mansfield

The Names Project AIDS Memorial Quilt   **73**

An Immune System Trained to Kill Cancer   **75**
By Denise Grady

How to Save a Life   **83**
By The Fray

excerpt from **Cracked: Putting Broken Lives Back Together Again: A Doctor's Story**   **85**
By Drew Pinsky, M.D. with Todd Gold

How to Fix the Obesity Crisis   **101**
By David H. Freedman

excerpt from What to Eat   115
    By Marion Nestle

excerpt from Sweetness Follows: The Story of Sam and the Treat
    of the Week   125
    By Katy Houston

excerpt from Stumbling on Happiness   127
    By Daniel Gilbert

Weather and Language Lessons   141
    By Kartik Chandaria

Preparedness 101: Zombie Apocalypse   145
    By Ali S. Khan

RU Healthy? Public Health Efforts Take On Text Messaging   151
    By Kim Krisberg

My Milk: On Becoming a Mother   155
    By Anne Enright

Are You Mom Enough?   163

The Case Against Breastfeeding   165
    By Hanna Rosin

A Drug for Down Syndrome   179
    By Dan Hurley

House of Commons Debates, 30 April 1946   191
    By Aneurin Bevan

Healing Life's Traumas   207
    By Denise Kersten Wills

How Yoga Can Wreck Your Body   213
    By William J. Broad

excerpt from Overtreated: Why Too Much Medicine is Making
    Us Sicker and Poorer   223
    By Shannon Brownlee

Major Assignments   241

Filmography   251

Works Cited   261

INTRODUCTION: HEALING WRITING

BY SUJATA IYENGAR AND ALLISON K. LENHARDT

The word *health* comes from the ancient language of Old High German, where it meant wholeness, the state of not being broken or incomplete. In English, the word has come to mean wholeness of body or mind. But what would this *wholeness* mean? Is health merely the absence of sickness, or is it a positive quality in its own right? If *health* exists on its own, how would you describe it? Is it the act of caring for ourselves as well as for others, or does *health* mean the process of curing or treating disease? Does *the best of health* mean the state of being youthful, athletic, good looking, confident, intelligent, and sane, or may one enjoy excellent health without possessing all of these qualities? Can we be happy if we have what some would consider mediocre or poor health? How much can we really control about our health? The essays, images, and excerpts in this reader, and the assignments alongside them, will take you through different ways of understanding your own health, the health of the nation, and the health of those who are dear to you.

Schools, workplaces, magazines, newspapers, and digital media surround us with advice on how to be healthy, how to stay in shape, how to stay well, and how to remain sound in mind and body. Sometimes, however, no matter how healthy our habits, we become ill; sometimes our bodies are genetically predisposed to develop a disorder or disease. In addition, when we search for cures or treatment, we might not be able to reconcile the conflicting advice that we encounter. Will yoga exercises relieve post-traumatic stress and uncoil tense or injured muscles, or will they exacerbate existing weaknesses? Is cancer the inevitable result of a bad card in the genetic lottery, or can we protect ourselves through diet, exercise, alternative medicine, and meditation? How can we evaluate this overwhelming, contradictory mass of information about health?

Working through the readings and assignments in this book will help you to reflect on our assumptions about what twenty-first century medicine considers to be a healthy body or mind and what present-day Americans choose as their preferred therapies for disease and illness. The readings encourage you to consider your relationship to traditional medical treatment and healthy bodies in order to help you reevaluate your concepts of health, illness, well-being, and medicine. We include readings that describe health in its standard terms— youth, vigor, beauty, ability—along with essays that expand our notion of what health or well-being might mean. We begin with excerpts from Anne Fadiman's *The Spirit Catches You and You Fall Down*, a thoughtful nonfiction novel about the contrast between the American medical establishment and Hmong shamanism, and its consequences for the health and life of a young girl caught in the middle of the culture clash. We conclude with excerpts from Shannon Brownlee's *Overtreated*, which argues (in the words of its subtitle) that American medicine as practiced at this point in the twenty-first century is "making us sicker and poorer." Our excerpt from psychologist Daniel Gilbert's *Stumbling on Happiness* reframes the generally accepted combination of "health and happiness," as he describes how people who have bodies or lives that most of us would describe as unhealthy or broken return to an inborn set point of happiness. Likewise, Dwight Christopher Gabbard's reflective essay about the contentment of his severely disabled son encourages us to imagine the experiences and abilities of those in bodies that differ profoundly from what we consider to be "normal" or healthy.

At the same time, those who experience sickness—psychological or physical— need care and support in order to return to well-being or find ways to thrive in a world that prizes physical vigor, independence, and cheerfulness. Etymologically, the Latin word for *care*, or *management*, *cura*, gives us our word *cure*. Some readings, therefore, examine the agents accountable for care and health; in particular, they discuss the extent to which individuals can control their health. Do recent discoveries in neuroscience, genetics, and behavioral health mitigate patients' responsibility for their health? The research summarized and discussed by David H. Freedman on obesity and by

Drew Pinsky on addiction encourages us to evaluate the complex relationships among individual factors that can contribute to disease or poor health, such as environmental cues, inherited predispositions, and personal choices. At the same time, the *care* in *health care* involves other persons or groups in addition to the patient or health-seeker. To what extent are families, mothers, employers, caretakers, and government officials—among other parties—obliged to care for the health of citizens and residents of the nation-state? Aneurin Bevan's 1946 speech establishing Britain's National Health Service provides some historical perspective on a very different medical system from that of twenty-first century America. Should a health care system offer citizens the opportunity to achieve good or excellent health or should it restrict itself to healing catastrophic illness? Is good health a right, a benefit, an entitlement, or a privilege? As we write these words, America's health care system is in transition. As you work through this reader, we hope that the breadth of our readings will enable you to take an informed position on current debates.

While we were putting together these readings, developing these assignments, and talking to our students, we realized that writing and healing in some ways mirror each other. Readers often describe *good* writing as intelligent, elegant, witty, and beautiful. In some ways, we define *good* writing according to qualities that we also use to describe *healthy* bodies and minds. We talk about *strong* and *weak* drafts or thesis statements, or *fleshing out* an argument. Both good writing and good health, however, are not attributes that are innate or unchanging. While some persons might have better *writing genes*, just as some have genes that predispose them to physical vigor, persuasive, graceful writing often develops through good habits, just as a robust, sound body and mind can flourish through consistent nurturing.

We can also imagine health as a metaphor for the writing process: like your health, writing is not always linear and takes time to improve. Your drafts might suffer setbacks as you struggle to define your argument, but they might also undergo amazing changes, sometimes because of how those earlier setbacks have changed your perspective. You can think of your first draft, or prewrite, as your initial *diagnosis*, where you examine the evidence and record your first reactions to the topic. Your diagnosis could change, however, depending upon what you discovered during the process of researching your topic and further examining your draft. As you continue to add to your draft, you might request the help of other writers such as your instructor or your peers—who will take on the imaginary role of surgeon, physical trainer, or therapist—in repairing the awkward places or to reconstruct a paper that began incoherently. Advice from your instructor and your peers can help you *treat* your ailing draft.

Even with their advice, however, you must be the one to perform the surgery, conduct the exercises, or undergo the therapy to heal your draft. As the due date approaches, you might feel that you are performing what nurses call *triage* (the process of evaluating and prioritizing tasks) on your writing, as you race against time to strengthen your claims, evidence, and organization. Ideally, you will have reserved enough time for final edits, so that you spend the days and hours before your due date making cosmetic changes (editing for style, tone, and diction) rather than dramatic interventions (changing your thesis completely). As you finish your draft, you stitch, or suture, the paper together carefully, editing for style and checking over your work for errors.

Strong writing and healthy papers thrive through consistent care. Just as we might try to maintain our health, well-being, and happiness through our way of life, so we can still nourish and nurture our writing to better health, even after we complete final drafts or finish a composition class. Moreover, we might enjoy better results if we commited our attention to regular habits rather than to briefly fashionable fads in order to maintain good health and good writing.

Finally, what we discover in the process of writing is much more important than striving to achieve a perfected or completed piece of work. Writing, regardless of its quality, can be a healing process. For some persons, the act of writing is therapy, a way to express emotions and work out problems. But even if you choose a topic distant from your personal experience, or if you do not find the act of writing therapeutic, writing will exercise your mind, as you develop your thoughts about a particular topic by writing about your ideas. We hope that these readings and the assignments will help you develop a healthy and balanced diet of reading and exercises for healing or enhancing your writing and that you enjoy them as much as our own students have.

Look for news items and features about health, illness, and wellness in a variety of mass media: magazines (print and digital), newspapers, television programs or channels, yyys and podcasts, and your social media networks. Make a list of at least ten headlines that you see. Write a brief (one-sentence) summary of the pieces you find beneath the headlines. Do any of them offer conflicting advice or information? Do any particular health issues dominate the conversation?

Our student Caroline Baughman inspired our comparison of the writing process to the healing process. How do you imagine your writing process? Is there a particular metaphor that you prefer? Can you extend this metaphor to different aspects of your writing process?

With a group of your classmates, talk about your reading "diet." What kind of texts and information do you consume, and in what forms? Do you read print books for pleasure or school? Do you watch or listen to broadcast media? Do you spend time on social media? Take a look at the government's current guidelines on nutrition (http://www. choosemyplate.gov/). Draw a "plate" to represent your reading habits. Present your "plate" to the class.

Nonfiction writer Anne Fadiman spent months interviewing and getting to know the family of Lia Lee, the young girl whose tragedy she investigated and ultimately concluded was the result not of Lia's sickness but of the clash between two belief systems: Western allopathic medicine and Hmong shamanic faith healing. Fadiman's 1997 book, from which this excerpt comes, won the National Book Award.

excerpt from

THE SPIRIT CATCHES YOU AND YOU FALL DOWN: A HMONG CHILD, HER AMERICAN DOCTORS, AND THE COLLISION OF TWO CULTURES

BY ANNE FADIMAN

When Lia was about three months old, her older sister Yer slammed the front door of the Lees' apartment. A few moments later, Lia's eyes rolled up, her arms jerked over her head, and she fainted. The Lees had little doubt what had happened. Despite the careful installation of Lia's soul during the *hu plig* ceremony, the noise of the door had been so profoundly frightening that her soul had fled her body and become lost. They recognized the resulting symptoms as *qaug dab peg*, which means "the spirit catches you and you fall down." The spirit referred to in this phrase is a soul-stealing *dab*; *peg* means to catch or hit; and *qaug* means to fall over with one's roots still in the ground, as grain might be beaten down by wind or rain.

In Hmong-English dictionaries, *qaug dab peg* is generally translated as epilepsy. It is an illness well known to the Hmong, who regard it with ambivalence. On the one hand, it is acknowledged to be a serious and potentially dangerous condition. Tony Coelho, who was Merced's congressman from 1979 to 1989, is an epileptic. Coelho is a popular figure among the Hmong, and a few years ago, some local Hmong men were sufficiently concerned when they learned he suffered from *qaug dab peg* that they volunteered the services of a shaman, a *txiv neeb*, to perform a ceremony that would retrieve Coelho's errant soul. The Hmong leader to whom they made this proposition politely discouraged them, suspecting that Coelho, who is a Catholic of Portugese descent, might not appreciate having chickens, and maybe a pig as well, sacrificed on his behalf.

On the other hand, the Hmong consider *qaug dab peg* to be an illness of some distinction. This fact might have surprised Tony Coelho no less than the dead chickens would have. Before he entered politics, Coelho planned to become a Jesuit priest, but was barred by a canon forbidding the ordination of epileptics. What was considered a disqualifying impairment by Coelho's church might have been seen by the Hmong as a sign that he was particularly fit for divine office. Hmong epileptics often become shamans. Their seizures are thought to be evidence that they have the power to perceive things other people cannot see, as well as facilitating their entry into trances, a prerequisite for their journeys into the realm of the unseen. The fact that they have been ill themselves gives them an intuitive sympathy for the suffering of others and lends them emotional credibility as healers. Becoming a *txiv neeb* is not a choice; it is a vocation. The calling is revealed when a person falls sick, either with *qaug dab peg* or with some other illness whose symptoms similarly include shivering and pain. An established *txiv neeb*, summoned to diagnose the problem, may conclude from these symptoms that the person (who is usually but not always male) has been chosen to be the host of a healing spirit, a *neeb*. (*Txiv neeb* means "person with a healing spirit.") It is an offer that the sick person cannot refuse, since if he rejects his vocation, he will die. In any case, few Hmong would choose to decline. Although shamanism is an arduous calling that requires years of training with a master in order to learn the ritual techniques and chants, it confers an enormous amount of social status in the community and publicly marks the *txiv neeb* as a person of high moral character, since a healing spirit would never choose a no-account host. Even if an epileptic turns out not to be elected to host a *neeb*, his illness, with its thrilling aura of the supramundane, singles him out as a person of consequence.

In their attitude toward Lia's seizures, the Lees reflected this mixture of concern and pride. The Hmong are known for the gentleness with which they treat their children. Hugo Adolf Bernatzik, a German ethnographer who lived with the Hmong of Thailand for several years during the 1930s, wrote that the Hmong he had studied regarded a child as "the most treasured possession a person can have." In Laos, a baby was never apart from its mother, sleeping in her arms all night and riding on her back all day. Small children were rarely abused; it was believed that a *dab* who witnessed mistreatment might take the child, assuming it was not wanted. The Hmong who live in the United States have continued to be unusually attentive parents. A study conducted at the University of Minnesota found Hmong infants in the first month of life to be less irritable and more securely attached to their mothers than Caucasian infants, a difference the researcher attributed to the fact that the Hmong mothers were, without exception, more sensitive, more accepting, and more responsive, as well as "exquisitely attuned" to their children's signals. Another study, conducted in Portland, Oregon, found that Hmong mothers held and touched their babies far more frequently than Caucasian mothers. In a third study, conducted at the Hennepin County Medical Center in Minnesota, a group of Hmong mothers of toddlers surpassed a group of Caucasian mothers of similar socioeconomic status in every one of fourteen categories selected from the Egeland Mother-Child Rating Scale, ranging from "Speed of Responsiveness to Fussing and Crying" to "Delight."

Foua and Nao Kao had nurtured Lia in typical Hmong fashion (on the Egeland Scale, they would have scored especially high in Delight), and they were naturally distressed to think that anything might compromise her health and happiness. They therefore hoped, at least most of the time, that the *qaug dab peg* could be healed. Yet they also considered the illness an honor. Jeanine Hilt, a social worker who knew the Lees well, told me, "They felt Lia was kind of an anointed one, like a member of royalty. She was a very special person in their culture because she had these spirits in her and she might grow up to be a shaman, and so sometimes their thinking was that this was not so much a medical problem as it was a blessing." (Of the forty or so American doctors, nurses, and Merced County agency employees I spoke with who had dealt with Lia and her family, several had a vague idea that "spirits" were somehow involved, but Jeanine Hilt was the only one who had actually asked the Lees what they thought was the cause of their daughter's illness.)

Within the Lee family, in one of those unconscious processes of selection that are as mysterious as any other form of falling in love, it was obvious that Lia was her parents' favorite, the child they considered the most beautiful, the one who was most extravagantly hugged and kissed, the one who was dressed in the most exquisite garments (embroidered by Foua, wearing dime-store glasses to work her almost microscopic stitches). Whether Lia occupied this position from the moment of her birth, whether it was a result of her spiritually distinguished illness, or whether it came from the special tenderness any parent feels for a sick child, is not a matter Foua and Nao Kao wish, or are able, to analyze. One thing that is clear is that for many years, the cost of that extra love was partially borne by her sister Yer. "They blamed Yer for slamming the door," said Jeanine Hilt. "I tried many times to explain that the door had nothing to do with it, but they didn't believe me. Lia's illness made them so sad that I think for a long time they treated Yer differently from their other children."

During the next few months of her life, Lia had at least twenty more seizures. On two occasions, Foua and Nao Kao were worried enough to carry her in their arms to the emergency room at Merced Community Medical Center, which was three blocks from their apartment. Like most Hmong refugees, they had their doubts about the efficacy of Western medical techniques. However, when they were living in the Mae Jarim refugee camp in Thailand, their only surviving son, Cheng, and three of their six surviving daughters, Ge, May, and True, had been seriously ill. Ge died. They took Cheng, May, and True to the camp hospital; Cheng and May recovered rapidly, and True was sent to another, larger hospital, where she eventually recovered as well. (The Lees also concurrently addressed the possible spiritual origins of their children's illnesses by moving to a new hut. A dead person had been buried beneath their old one, and his soul might have wished to harm the new residents.) This experience did nothing to shake their faith in traditional Hmong beliefs about the causes and cures of illness, but it did convince them that on some occasions Western doctors could be of additional help, and that it would do no harm to hedge their bets.

County hospitals have a reputation for being crowded, dilapidated, and dingy. Merced's county hospital, with which the Lees would become all too familiar over the next few years, is none of these. The MCMC complex includes a modern, 42,000-square-foot wing—it looks sort of like an art moderne ocean liner—that houses coronary care, intensive care, and transitional care units; 154 medical and surgical beds; medical and radiology laboratories outfitted with state-of-the-art diagnostic equipment; and a blood bank. The waiting rooms in the hospital and its attached clinic have unshredded magazines, unsmelly bathrooms, and floors that have been scrubbed to an aseptic gloss. MCMC is a teaching hospital, staffed in part by the faculty and residents of the Family Practice Residency, which is affiliated with the University of California at Davis. The residency program is nationally known, and receives at least 150 applications annually for its six first-year positions.

Like many other rural county hospitals, which were likely to feel the health care crunch before it reached urban hospitals, MCMC has been plagued with financial problems throughout the last twenty years. It accepts all patients, whether or not they can pay; only twenty percent are privately insured, with most of the rest receiving aid from California's Medi-Cal, Medicare, or Medically Indigent Adult programs, and a small (but to the hospital, costly) percentage neither insured nor covered by any federal or state program. The hospital receives reimbursements from the public programs, but many of those reimbursements have been lowered or restricted in recent years. Although the private patients are far more profitable, MCMC's efforts to attract what its administrator has called "an improved payer mix" have not been very successful. (Merced's wealthier residents often choose either a private Catholic hospital three miles north of MCMC or a larger hospital in a nearby city such as Fresno.) MCMC went through a particularly rough period during the late eighties, hitting bottom in 1988, when it had a $3.1 million deficit.

During this same period, MCMC also experienced an expensive change in its patient population. Starting in the late seventies, Southeast Asian refugees began to move to Merced in large numbers. The city of Merced, which has a population of about 61,000, now has just over 12,000 Hmong. That is to say, one in five residents of Merced is Hmong. Because many Hmong fear and shun the hospital, MCMC's patient rolls reflect a somewhat lower ratio, but on any given day there are still Hmong patients in almost every unit. Not only do the Hmong fail resoundingly to improve the payer mix—more than eighty percent are on Medi-Cal—but they have proved even more costly than other indigent patients, because they generally require more time and attention, and because there are so many of them that MCMC has had to hire bilingual staff members to mediate between patients and providers.

There are no funds in the hospital budget specifically earmarked for interpreters, so the administration has detoured around that technicality by hiring Hmong lab assistants, nurse's aides, and transporters, who are called upon to translate in the scarce interstices between analyzing blood, emptying bedpans, and rolling postoperative patients around on gurneys. In 1991, a short-term federal grant enabled MCMC to put skilled interpreters on call around the clock, but the program expired the following year. Except during that brief hiatus, there have often been no Hmong-speaking employees of any kind present in the hospital at night. Obstetricians have had to obtain consent for cesarean sections or episiotomies using embarrassed teenaged sons, who have learned English in school, as translators. Ten-year-old girls have had to translate discussions of whether or not a dying family member should be resuscitated. Sometimes not even a child is available. Doctors on the late shift in the emergency room have often had no way of taking a patient's medical history, or of asking such questions as Where do you hurt? How long have you been hurting? What does it feel like? Have you had an accident? Have you vomited? Have you had a fever? Have you lost consciousness? Are you pregnant? Have you taken any medications? Are you allergic to any medications? Have you recently eaten? (The last question is of great importance if emergency surgery is being contemplated, since anesthetized patients with full stomachs can aspirate the partially digested food into their lungs, and may die if they choke or if their bronchial linings are badly burned by stomach acid.) I asked one doctor what he did in such cases. He said, "Practice veterinary medicine."

On October 24, 1982, the first time that Foua and Nao Kao carried Lia to the emergency room, MCMC had not yet hired any interpreters, de jure or de facto, for any shift. At that time, the only hospital employee who sometimes translated for Hmong patients was a janitor, a Laotian immigrant fluent in his own language, Lao, which few Hmong understand; halting in Hmong; and even more halting in English. On that day either the janitor was unavailable or the emergency room staff didn't think of calling him. The resident on duty practiced veterinary medicine. Foua and Nao Kao had no way of explaining what had happened, since Lia's seizures had stopped by the time they reached the hospital. Her only obvious symptoms were a cough and a congested chest. The resident ordered an X ray, which led the radiologist to conclude that Lia had "early bronchiopneumonia or tracheobronchitis." As he had no way of knowing that the bronchial congestion was probably caused by aspiration of saliva or vomit during her seizure (a common problem for epileptics), she was routinely dismissed with a prescription for ampicillin, an antibiotic. Her emergency room Registration Record lists her father's last name as Yang, her mother's maiden name as Foua, and her "primary spoken language" as "Mong." When Lia was discharged, Nao Kao (who knows the alphabet but does not speak or read English) signed a piece of paper that said, "I hereby acknowledge receipt of the instructions indicated above," to wit:

"Take ampicillin as directed. Vaporizer at cribside. Clinic reached as needed 383–7007 ten days." The "ten days" meant that Nao Kao was supposed to call the Family Practice Center in ten days for a follow-up appointment. Not surprisingly, since he had no idea what he had agreed to, he didn't. But when Lia had another bad seizure on November 11, he and Foua carried her to the emergency room again, where the same scene was repeated, and the same misdiagnosis made.

On March 3, 1983, Foua and Nao Kao carried Lia to the emergency room a third time. On this occasion, three circumstances were different: Lia was still seizing when they arrived, they were accompanied by a cousin who spoke some English, and one of the doctors on duty was a family practice resident named Dan Murphy. Of all the doctors who have worked at MCMC, Dan Murphy is generally acknowledged to be the one most interested in and knowledgeable about the Hmong. At that time, he had been living in Merced for only seven months, so his interest still exceeded his knowledge. When he and his wife, Cindy, moved to Merced, they had never heard the word "Hmong." Several years later, Cindy was teaching English to Hmong adults and Dan was inviting Hmong leaders to the hospital to tell the residents about their experiences as refugees. Most important, the Murphys counted a Hmong family, the Xiongs, among their closest friends. When one of the Xiong daughters wanted to spend the summer working in Yosemite National Park, Chaly Xiong, her father, initially refused because he was afraid she might get eaten by a lion. Dan personally escorted Chaly to Yosemite to verify the absence of lions, and persuaded him the job would do his daughter good. Four months later, Chaly was killed in an automobile accident. Cindy Murphy arranged the funeral, calling around until she found a funeral parlor that was willing to accommodate three days of incense burning, drum beating, and *qeej* playing. She also bought several live chickens, which were sacrificed in the parking lot of the funeral parlor, as well as a calf and a pig, which were sacrificed elsewhere. When Dan first saw the Lees, he instantly registered that they were Hmong, and he thought to himself, "This won't be boring."

Many years later, Dan, who is a short, genial man with an Amish-style beard and an incandescent smile, recalled the encounter. "I have this memory of Lia's parents standing just inside the door to the ER, holding a chubby little round-faced baby. She was having a generalized seizure. Her eyes were rolled back, she was unconscious, her arms and legs were kind of jerking back and forth, and she didn't breathe much—every once in a while, there would be no movement of the chest wall and you couldn't hear any breath sounds. That was definitely anxiety-producing. She was the youngest patient I had ever dealt with who was seizing. The parents seemed frightened, not terribly frightened though, not as frightened as I would have been if it was my kid. I thought it might be meningitis, so Lia had to have a spinal tap, and the parents were real resistant to that. I don't remember how I convinced them. I remember feeling very anxious because they had a real sick kid and I felt a big need to explain to these people, through their relative who was a not-very-good translator, what was going on, but I felt like I had no time, because we had to put an IV in her scalp with Valium to stop the seizures, but then Lia started seizing again and the IV went into the skin instead of the vein, and I had a hard time getting another one started. Later on, when I figured out what had happened, or not happened, on the earlier visits to the ER, I felt good. It's kind of a thrill to find something someone else has missed, especially when you're a resident and you are looking for excuses to make yourself feel smarter than the other physicians."

Among Dan's notes in Lia's History and Physical Examination record were:

> HISTORY OF PRESENT ILLNESS: The patient is an 8 month, Hmong female, whose family brought her to the emergency room after they had noticed her shaking and not breathing very well for a 20-minute period of time. According to the family the patient has had multiple like episodes in the past, but have never been able to communicate this to emergency room doctors on previous visits secondary to a language barrier. An english speaking relative available tonight, stated that the patient had had intermittent fever and cough for 2–3 days prior to being admitted.

> FAMILY & SOCIAL HISTORY: Unobtainable secondary to language difficulties.

> NEUROLOGICAL: The child was unresponsive to pain or sound. The head was held to the left with intermittent tonic-clonic [first rigid, then jerking] movements of the upper extremities. Respirations were suppressed during these periods of clonic movement. Grunting respirations persisted until the patient was given 3 mg. of Valium I.V.

Dan had no way of knowing that Foua and Nao Kao had already diagnosed their daughter's problem as the illness where the spirit catches you and you fall down. Foua and Nao Kao had no way of knowing that Dan had diagnosed it as epilepsy, the most common of all neurological disorders. Each had accurately noted the same symptoms, but Dan would have been surprised to hear that they were caused by soul loss, and Lia's parents would have been surprised to hear that they were caused by an electrochemical storm inside their daughter's head that had been stirred up by the misfiring of aberrant brain cells.

Dan had learned in medical school that epilepsy is a sporadic malfunction of the brain, sometimes mild and sometimes severe, sometimes progressive and sometimes self-limiting, which can be traced to oxygen deprivation during gestation, labor, or birth; a head injury; a tumor; an infection; a high fever; a stroke; a metabolic disturbance; a drug allergy; a toxic reaction to a poison. Sometimes the source is obvious—the patient had a brain tumor or swallowed strychnine or crashed through a windshield—but in about seven out of ten cases, the cause is never determined. During an epileptic episode, instead of following their usual orderly protocol, the damaged cells in the cerebral cortex transmit neural impulses simultaneously and chaotically. When only a small area of the brain is involved—in a "focal" seizure—an epileptic may hallucinate or twitch or tingle but retain consciousness. When the electrical disturbance extends to a wide area—in a "generalized" seizure—consciousness is lost, either for the brief episodes called petit mal or "absence" seizures, or for the full-blown attacks known as grand mal. Except through surgery, whose risks consign it to the category of last resort, epilepsy cannot be cured, but it can be completely or partially controlled in most cases by anticonvulsant drugs.

The Hmong are not the only people who might have good reason to feel ambivalent about suppressing the symptoms. The Greeks called epilepsy "the sacred disease." Dan Murphy's diagnosis added Lia Lee to a distinguished line of epileptics that has included Søren Kierkegaard, Vincent van Gogh, Gustave Flaubert, Lewis Carroll, and Fyodor Dostoyevsky, all of whom, like many Hmong shamans, experienced powerful senses of grandeur and spiritual passion during their seizures, and powerful creative urges in their wake. As Dostoyevsky's Prince Myshkin asked, "What if it is a disease? What does it matter that it is an abnormal tension, if the result, if the moment of sensation, remembered and analysed in a state of health, turns out to be harmony and beauty brought to their highest point of perfection, and gives a feeling, undivined and undreamt of till then, of completeness, proportion, reconciliation, and an ecstatic and prayerful fusion in the highest synthesis of life?"

Although the inklings Dan had gathered of the transcendental Hmong worldview seemed to him to possess both power and beauty, his own view of medicine in general, and of epilepsy in particular, was, like that of his colleagues at MCMC, essentially rationalist. Hippocrates' skeptical commentary on the nature of epilepsy, made around 400 B.C., pretty much sums up Dan's own frame of reference: "It seems to me that the disease is no more divine than any other. It has a natural cause just as other diseases have. Men think it is divine merely because they don't understand it. But if they called everything divine which they do not understand, why, there would be no end of divine things."[1]

Lia's seizure was a grand mal episode, and Dan had no desire to do anything but stop it. He admitted her to MCMC as an inpatient. Among the tests she had during the three days she spent there were a spinal tap, a CT scan, an EEG, a chest X ray, and extensive blood work. Foua and Nao Kao signed "Authorization for and Consent to Surgery or Special Diagnostic or Therapeutic Procedures" forms, each several hundred words long, for the first two of these. It is not known whether anyone attempted to translate them, or, if so, how "Your physician has requested a brain scan utilizing computerized tomography" was rendered in Hmong. None of the tests revealed any apparent cause for the seizures. The doctors classified Lia's epilepsy as "idiopathic": cause unknown. Lia was found to have consolidation in her right lung, which this time was correctly diagnosed as aspiration pneumonia resulting from the seizure. Foua and Nao Kao alternated nights at the hospital, sleeping in a cot next to Lia's

1 Despite this early attempt by Hippocrates (or perhaps by one of the anonymous physicians whose writings are attributed to Hippocrates) to remove the "divine" label, epilepsy continued, more than any other disease, to be ascribed to supernatural causes. The medical historian Owsei Temkin has noted that epilepsy has held a key position historically in "the struggle between magic and the scientific conception." Many treatments for epilepsy have had occult associations. Greek magicians forbade epileptics to eat mint, garlic, and onion, as well as the flesh of goats, pigs, deer, dogs, cocks, turtledoves, bustards, mullets, and eels; to wear black garments and goatskins; and to cross their hands and feet: taboos that were all connected, in various ways, with chthonic deities. Roman epileptics were advised to swallow morsels cut from the livers of stabbed gladiators. During the Middle Ages, when epilepsy was attributed to demonic possession, treatments included prayer, fasting, wearing amulets, lighting candles, visiting the graves of saints, and writing the names of the Three Wise Men with blood taken from the patient's little finger. These spiritual remedies were far safer than the "medical" therapies of the time—still practiced as late as the seventeenth century—which included cauterizing the head with a hot iron and boring a hole in the skull to release peccant vapors.

bed. Among the Nurse's Notes for Lia's last night at the hospital were: "0001. Skin cool and dry to touch, color good & pink. Mom is with babe at this time & is breastfeeding. Mom informed to keep babe covered with a blanket for the babe is a little cool." "0400. Babe resting quietly with no acute distress noted. Mom breast feeds off & on." "0600. Sleeping." "0730. Awake, color good. Mother fed." "1200. Held by mother."

Lia was discharged on March 11, 1983. Her parents were instructed, via an English-speaking relative, to give her 250 milligrams of ampicillin twice a day, to clear up her aspiration pneumonia, and twenty milligrams of Dilantin elixir, an anticonvulsant, twice a day, to suppress any further grand mal seizures.

NOTES ON SOURCES

Delores J. Cabezut-Ortiz, *Merced County: The Golden Harvest*, recounts how Tony Coelho was rejected by the Jesuits because of his epilepsy. Blia Yao Moua told me about the offer to perform a Hmong healing ceremony for Coelho in Merced.

On becoming a *txiv neeb*: Dwight Conquergood, *I Am a Shaman*; Jacques Lemoine, "Shamanism in the Context of Hmong Resettlement"; Bruce Thowpaou Bliatout, "Traditional Hmong Beliefs"; and Kathleen Ann Culhane-Pera, "Description and Interpretation of a Hmong Shaman in St. Paul."

On how Hmong parents treat their children: Hugo Adolf Bernatzik, *Akha and Miao*; Nusit Chindarsi, *The Religion of the Hmong Njua*; Brenda Jean Cumming, "The Development of Attachment in Two Groups of Economically Disadvantaged Infants and Their Mothers: Hmong Refugee and Caucasian-American"; E.M. Newlin-Haus, "A Comparison of Proxemic and Selected Communication Behavior of Anglo-American and Hmong Refugee Mother-Infant Pairs"; Charles N. Oberg et al., "A Cross-Cultural Assessment of Maternal-Child Interaction: Links to Health and Development"; and Wendy Walker-Moffat, *The Other Side of the Asian American Success Story*.

The information on Merced Community Medical Center was provided by Vi Colunga, Arthur DeNio, Doreen Faiello, Ed Hughell, Liz Lorenzi, Betty Maddalena, Marilyn Mochel, Dan Murphy, Theresa Schill, Bill Selvidge, Betty Wetters, and Janice Wilkerson.

The Hmong population of Merced City is an estimate based on projections from the 1990 census. It attempts to take into account new refugees from Thailand, secondary migrants from other parts of the United States, and births (using Hmong, not American, birthrates). The Demographic Research Unit of the California Department of Finance and Rhonda Walton at the Merced Human Services Agency provided assistance.

Much of the information here and elsewhere on the medical aspects of epilepsy is drawn from conversations with neurologist Elizabeth Engle of Boston Children's Hospital and with Neil Ernst and Peggy Philp of Merced Community Medical Center. I also found these works helpful: Owen B. Evans, *Manual of Child Neurology*; Orrin Devinsky, *A Guide to Understanding and Living with Epilepsy*; Robert Berkow, ed., *The Merck Manual of Diagnosis and Therapy*; Alan Newman, "Epilepsy: Light from the Mind's Dark Corner"; and Jane Brody, "Many People Still Do Not Understand Epilepsy." Eve LaPlante discusses the relationship between epilepsy and creativity in *Seized: Temporal Lobe Epilepsy as a Medical, Historical, and Artistic Phenomenon*. Owsei Temkin recounts the history of epilepsy in his fascinating work *The Falling Sickness: A History of Epilepsy from the Greeks to the Beginnings of Modern Neurology*. The Hippocrates quotation is from *On the Sacred Disease*, quoted in Richard Restak, *The Brain*; the Dostoyevsky quotation is from *The Idiot*.

NOTE ON HMONG ORTHOGRAPHY, PRONUNCIATION, AND QUOTATIONS

According to a folktale collected by anthropologist Robert Cooper and his colleagues, the Hmong language once had a written form, and many important things about life and about the journey between death and rebirth were written down in a great book. Unfortunately, the book was eaten by cows and rats. After its disappearance, no text was equal to the task of representing a culture as rich as that of the Hmong, and the Hmong language was therefore spoken but not written.

So matters remained until the end of the nineteenth century. Since then, more than two dozen Hmong writing systems have been devised by missionaries and linguists, based on Chinese characters as well as on Thai, Lao, Vietnamese, and Russian alphabets. There is also a fascinating eighty-one-symbol writing system called Pahawh Hmong—it looks a little like Sanskrit—that was developed in 1959 by Shong Lue Yang, a messianic Hmong leader who was not previously literate in any language. It is used by the Chao Fa, the resistance group that, in reduced numbers, is still waging a guerrilla war against the communist regime in Laos.

To represent the Hmong words in this book, I have used the writing system most generally accepted by both the Hmong people and by linguists: the Romanized Popular Alphabet. RPA, as it is usually called, was devised in 1953 in Laos by three missionary linguists, Linwood Barney, William Smalley, and Yves Bertrais. It represents all the sounds of the Hmong language with Roman letters, using no diacritical marks—a godsend for typists. RPA can be exasperating if you expect it to be phonetic. (For example, *txiv neeb*—a Hmong shaman—is, improbably enough, pronounced "tsi neng." What happened to the *v*? What happened to the *b*? Where did the *ng* come from?) However, if you view it as a kind of code, it is remarkably ingenious and not nearly as difficult as it looks.

The Hmong language is monosyllabic (except for compound words) and, like many Asian languages, tonal. That is, a word's meaning depends not only on its vowel and consonant sounds but on its pitch and on whether the voice rises, falls, or stays on the same level. The most unusual aspect of RPA is that these tones are represented by a word's final consonant. (Words spoken with a mid-tone that neither rises nor falls are the exception: they are spelled without a final consonant.) Most Hmong words end in vowel sounds, so final consonants are always tonal markers and are never pronounced.

For example, *dab*—a spirit—is pronounced "da." (The final *b* indicates the tone, in this case high and level. Because tones are hard to master without hearing them, I am ignoring them in my suggested pronunciations of the other words and phrases here.) *Paj ntaub*—literally, "flower cloth," an intricately worked textile—is pronounced "pa ndow." *Qaug dab peg*—literally, "the spirit catches you and you fall down," the Hmong term for epilepsy—is pronounced "kow da pay."

There are many other aspects of RPA pronunciation, most of them too complex to describe here. I will mention just three. One is that *x* sounds like *s*. Another is that a double vowel represents a nasal sound, like the *ng* in "sing." (These two oddities, along with the fact that the final consonants aren't sounded, explain why *txiv neeb* is pronounced "tsi neng.") A third is that *w* is a vowel, pronounced something like a French *u*. For example, the unlikely-looking word *txwv*—a children's game resembling jacks—is pronounced, roughly, "tsu."

In order to make their own names reasonably easy for Americans to pronounce, the Hmong in the United States do not use RPA for proper nouns. Capitalized words are pronounced more or less the way they are spelled. For example, the word "Hmong," which in RPA would be spelled *Hmoob*, is simply pronounced "Mong," with an almost inaudible aspiration at the beginning of the word. "Lia Lee," which in RPA would be spelled Liab Lis, is pronounced just as you would expect: "Leea Lee."

There are two principal groups of Hmong living in Laos and Thailand, the White Hmong and the Blue Hmong. (White and blue are the colors favored for each group's traditional skirts.) Their dialects are similar but vary slightly in pronunciation. I have used White Hmong spellings in this book.

I have quoted conversations with Hmong people in this book in the forms in which I heard them. That is to say, English-speaking Hmong are quoted verbatim, and non-English-speaking Hmong are quoted in the words my interpreter, May Ying Xiong, used as she translated their comments sentence by sentence. This has the paradoxical effect that highly educated Hmong such as Jonas Vangay and Blia Yao Moua, because of the grammatical idiosyncrasies of their English, seem to speak less "perfectly" than, say, Nao Kao Lee and Foua Yang, whose speech is filtered through an American-educated, and therefore grammatically conventional, interpreter. However, the alternatives—messing up May Ying's translations or cleaning up the speech of English-speaking Hmong—seemed to me far worse. The first was out of the question, and the second would rob the reader of the rich texture of English underlain by Hmong, French, and other languages, as well as removing him or her one further step from my own experience as a listener.

Watch this video of anthropologist Dwight Conquergood (mentioned in Fadiman's account) undergoing a Hmong healing ceremony (http://www.youtube.com/watch?v=bYm0c5yM8J4) or the documentaries *Between Two Worlds* and *The Split Horn*. Notice how present-day Hmong families struggle to combine spiritual and physical health. What sorts of resources best helped you understand the controversy surrounding Lia's health? Can you think of other cultures or religions that integrate spiritual, mental, and physical health, and other problems these groups encounter within the U.S. medical establishment?

Fadiman's account grips the reader because she moves between multiple points of view—from that of Lia's family to her doctors' and to the author's own perspective. Remember the last time that you or someone you know well experienced a health event and write about it from at least two different points of view.

This assignment will help you prepare for Major Assignment #1: Write a Health Memoir. With a group of your classmates, identify a single health care situation that you have all, or nearly all, encountered (such as a physical examination, immunizations, or having someone bandage a childhood cut or scrape). Make a list of events, beliefs, and feelings that informed that situation (you could begin with the simple questions: who, what, where, why, and when?) and compare your answers.

Fadiman's "Notes on Pronunciation" explain to a reader trained to read English words in the Roman alphabet how to pronounce Hmong words. The Hmong language also uses the Roman alphabet, but in it, particular letters and combinations of letters represent different sounds from the ones they stand for in English. Lia's story happened more than twenty years ago, when the Hmong were a little-known group in North America. Since that time, many educated Hmong have developed web resources to help those from different backgrounds to understand their language and beliefs. Investigate some of these resources, such as http://www.hmongdictionary.com/learntospeakhmong.php or http://www.hmongcc.org. Write a short note for a Hmong reader on how to pronounce the American words that you think might prove most crucial to obtaining health care in the United States.

Longtime smoker, recovering alcoholic, and health editor Julia Hansen found herself so addicted to cigarettes that the only way she could imagine breaking free was, paradoxically, to demand bondage: she asked her husband to chain her to the radiator during the day for a week while he went to work so that she could try to quit her two-packs-a-day habit. She memorialized her experience in A Life in Smoke, which came out in 2006; the following excerpt describes both Julie's present problems and her past ones and how she seeks out nicotine— among other substances—to numb the pain.

excerpt from

A LIFE IN SMOKE

By Julia Hansen

6:26 a.m.

I lean over John's broad back to peer at the clock. Flopping back on my pillow, I pull the heavy quilt up to my chin and stare at the ceiling.

I am not ready for this. Who quits smoking on four hours of sleep?

Last night I'd wandered the house until 2:30 a.m., smoking cigarette after cigarette, trying to commit the act to memory. A taste: hot, a drought in the mouth. A smell: stale, like poverty. The way cigarette smoke ribbons, turns to cloud and drifts sullenly to the ceiling. I grieved the satisfying snap! *of a lighter. The first stinging lungful of smoke over morning coffee or after a good meal. Scraping the ash from a lit cigarette to lay bare its hot glowing heart.*

Having smoked almost a pack in the three hours before I went to bed, I was wired; nicotine triggers a rush of adrenaline into the blood. Adrenaline is the hormone of cokeheads, skydivers, women who lift cars off their children. So minutes after I settled between the sheets, my heart began to hurl itself against my chest like a guard dog against a chain-link fence. The palpitations had plagued me almost every night for two years, and each night I was sure my heart would explode as my husband snored peacefully beside me. In the past year, I'd developed sleep apnea, too, so all in all, I dreaded going to bed. I knew I would drift off, over and over, only to start awake, gasping for air like a fish on the end of a hook.

There's no way I'm getting back to sleep. I shrug into my bathrobe and head downstairs. My pack of Basic Menthol Lights waits on the kitchen table. It holds one last cigarette, forlorn, bent. Any other morning, a fresh pack would have awaited me, neat and glossy in its cellophane wrapper. To me, a new pack of cigarettes is as pretty as a party invitation, to be opened with the same small thrill of pleasure.

I brew coffee, and then it's time. The clock reads 6:32. The Last Cigarette is a momentous event. It deserves respect, even if it's commemorated every other day. So I smoke with the solemnity of a pallbearer, paying my last respects to a beloved friend. I throw my mini-Bic into the trash, a gesture I've made more times than I care to admit, and a wave of sadness breaks over my head. When I think of living without cigarettes for the rest of my life, the world goes gray.

An executioner's drum roll sounds in my head, crescendos, and I put my cigarette to death.

I smoked my first cigarette at age nineteen, in my freshman year of college. Why so late? I have no good answer. Though no weed fiend, my mother enjoyed the occasional Camel Light, and I'd spent high school eyeing the popular kids, fantasizing that, with the flick of a Bic, I could join their ranks of smoky cool. Perhaps, as a girl, I even sneaked a puff with friends, and turned green—I don't recall. But that first retch-producing, eye-flooding Benson & Hedges Menthol Light 100 was worth waiting for. Smoking was perfect, one more billboard on the self-destructive road I traveled. I was drinking then, and cutting, and in comparison, smoking felt benign and even fun, another facet of my life to withhold from my parents.

During the summer of 1982, home on summer break, I hid my packs of Newport Lights and books of matches in the glove compartment of my VW Bug. I hadn't yet started to use lighters. I became a true smoker when I stopped using matches—which feel flimsy and temporary and, in smokers, provoke a certain anxiety—and started to buy lighters, smooth and solid and dependable. To a smoker, hell is a cigarette and no fire.

Every Friday night that summer, I made the forty-five-minute drive from my parents' home in Burlington, Connecticut—then a hick town, not the upper-class enclave it is now—to the Lit Club in Hartford, which booked punk bands on the weekends; it was the oasis in my suburban desert. I had discovered punk music in Washington, D.C., where I attended college, and its bellowing rage eased my surly self-consciousness.

I was interning for the rinky-dink local newspaper. All week, as I filed my stories and photographed scenes of summer revelry around the city, I thought about the drive to Hartford. On some level, it wasn't the music that drew me. It was the trip itself. With every mile I put between me and my parents, the bigger and brighter and more *me* I became. The pack of Newports was a totem that conjured the embryonic self I'd so painfully cobbled together.

And yet, as the week wore on, the thought of that drive made my stomach clench. A nervous driver, I drove a matronly fifty miles an hour and could not bring myself to venture into the passing lane.

I was afraid behind the wheel—of what, I didn't know. Fear was just a part of me, always had been, like the birthmark on my back, and the rage with which I covered it was a bandage too small for its wound. But my will to outrun my life—a life that was already too complicated—was stronger than my fear of rolling down the dark highway, alone, pursued by the silver stream of headlights in my rearview mirror.

Smoking helped me make that trip and the many others that mark the map of my life—alcoholism and recovery, failed relationships, marriage and divorce, the birth of my son. Cigarettes were my constant and unwavering companion on those dark, twisting roads. I'm still not sure whether I found them or they found me.

I've been locked up most of my life. First, I was shackled to my mother's love, chains of sadness and anger and guilt. As I grew, the chains lengthened, rattling like Marley's ghost, each new link forged in depression and vodka and razor blades and obscured in a haze of cigarette smoke. It took me years to discover that it was only my emptiness that I dragged behind me, so heavy it made me stagger.

Maybe that's why in November 2003, when I chained myself in my Allentown, Pennsylvania, home for a week in a last, desperate attempt to quit smoking, the act felt strangely familiar, like a perfume you've smelled before or a person whose face you've forgotten but whom you once swore to love forever.

I was forty, with a beautiful seven-year-old son, a new husband I adored, and a successful career as a health editor at a large publishing house. A health editor. Who smoked. A decade ago, I'd found the irony amusing. As the years passed, however, I began to develop this sick feeling in my gut, an irrational certainty that I would die if I didn't stop. But I couldn't. Something inside me compelled me to keep lighting up, even when my eyes swelled and my lungs burned and my heart seemed ready to burst the muscle and bone that separated it from the outside world.

I wanted to quit, but I didn't want to stop smoking.

Ambivalence is the addict's root affliction. For five years before I finally quit, I bought nicotine patches but mostly didn't use them. I'd open the box, toss the cassette tape and booklet into the trash, and put the patches on the kitchen counter, next to my ashtray. They languished there, like birthday cards that you mean to mail, but never do.

I'd tried to quit countless times, and succeeded twice. The first time was in February of 1996, when, newly married to my first husband, Matt, I discovered that I was pregnant. I lasted until Daniel was about a year old. I quit again, for eight months, in January of 2002, a few months after meeting John, my second husband.

After that were the countless miniquits, when I'd slap on a patch for two or three days until I crumbled. My failures first shamed and then hardened me; I accepted the certainty of my untimely death with gallows humor and a calculator. I'd read somewhere that each cigarette you smoke knocks seven minutes off your time on the planet. To amuse myself, I multiplied the estimated number of cigarettes I'd smoked—a pack a day for twenty-one years, that's 153,300—and did the math.

153,300 x7 minutes = 1,073,100 minutes

= 17,885 hours

= 745.2 days

= 2.0416 years

Two years of my life, up in smoke.

I continued to forfeit my days, seven minutes at a time. I smoked in the house and in the car, snuck out of Daniel's third birthday party at Chuck E. Cheese's, closing my eyes as the nicotine entered my bloodstream and lit up my brain like a Fourth of July sparkler. I puffed apologetically at his soccer games under other mothers' accusing eyes.

I won't say that I loved cigarettes more than my son, but I did love them more than I loved myself. From 1998 to 2001, the years that encompassed an affair, my divorce, and another doomed relationship, I smoked up to two packs a day. I wanted to care that I could die and leave Daniel motherless, but I didn't. At least, not enough. When you're consumed by self-hatred, there's no room for anyone else. Not in any way that counts.

The Lockdown, as I call my voluntary house arrest, was a variation of an idea I'd given my mother in the summer of 2003, during one of our countless discussions about her weight. "You should chain yourself to your computer, set up a webcam, have Dad bring you water and cottage cheese, and share your weight-loss journey in streaming video," I'd said. "It's a metaphor for your addiction to food. You'd get a million hits a day. Oprah would flip."

"You're nuts," my mother said, and that was that, or so I thought. But the idea stuck in my head with the stubbornness of an advertising jingle. Months later, on a balmy Friday night in October, John and I and his parents sped up Route 476 from Philly on our way back to Allentown after a night out. I sat in the back next to my mother-in-law, and the smoke from John's father's cigarette filled my throat like a gag. So what. His smoke or mine, in twenty years I'd be breathing through plastic tubing anyway. I tried to imagine one of my lung cells at the very moment of its cancerous mutation. Would I feel its first murderous division, the way some women feel the moment they conceive?

Then, from nowhere, a thought illuminated the inside of my skull, blazing with the kind of light reserved for celestial visitations. I blinked.

"Yes," I said.

"What," John said, eyes on the road.

"I'm going to chain myself in the house for a week to quit smoking."

John Senior laughed. My husband said, "You're demented." Fair enough. But I was also desperate. The plan seemed like my last hope, and possessed a peculiar logic: If I couldn't control my impulse to smoke on my own, I'd impose that control.

On Monday, I put in for a week's vacation. Lockdown, a month away, began on Monday, November 17. The next Saturday, John and I went to Home Depot and bought a 72-foot length of chain—brushed-nickel finish, heavy steel, purchased off the roll at 69 cents per foot—and two small combination locks. We'd worked it all out. We'd use one lock to fasten the chain around my left ankle and snap the other to the radiator in the dining room. John would shackle me each morning before he left for work. I'd have the run of the first floor, my computer, and my cell phone. John would release me when he got home. (We decided against shackling me to the bed at night. I am a restless sleeper, and John said that the chain would rattle as I tossed and turned, keeping him awake.)

The chain was as unwieldy as a corpse. At Home Depot, when John gathered it up and heaved it on the scale, I noted its weight: forty pounds. But it was lighter than the weight of the habit I'd dragged behind me for twenty years.

My chain, to which I would be attached for up to eleven hours a day, was my addiction to nicotine. I could see it, hear it, hold it; it had heft and weight. Each link was a story, a story about cigarettes and me. Rasping across my wooden floors, its weight disabling my stride, the chain would narrate my life in smoke. [. . .]

DAY 2

6:20 a.m.

The smell of pancakes, all vanilla and burnt butter and contentment, drifts into the living room and penetrates its chill—the furnace kicked on only a few minutes ago. Frankie purrs beside me, eyes closed, paws tucked under. Wrapped in my blanket, I sip black coffee, muttering snide commentary on the morning's top stories. I've been flipping channels for almost two hours. At 4:28 a.m. my eyes snapped open like switchblades—nicotine withdrawal tends to disturb sleep—and I am agitated.

A wasp in a jar, trapped by the day ahead. When John came downstairs, pink and wet-headed from his shower, he took one look at my sneering, rumpled self and fired up his griddle. My husband believes in the restorative power of sugar and fat. But I chew the inside of my cheek, hungry only for smoke.

Headline News cuts to a commercial. A patrician-looking man behind a podium addresses a packed auditorium of employees. He tells them that he has an announcement that will brighten their day: He has ordered them new printers and copiers from a certain company. "Tell them why, Andy," he says. A man in the audience rises, grinning like a chimp, and burbles, "They're people-friendly!"

This ad runs every day on CNN. To John, it's about printers and copiers. To me, it's about the subjugation of the common man to Big Business. Why should Andy, who probably hasn't received a raise or a word of praise from his boss in years, have to fake enthusiasm about new copiers? I'll bet the elitist bastard at the podium didn't even buy American. As I'm swept along on a swift current of rage, I know my reaction is way out of proportion, even factoring in nicotine withdrawal and my antipathy for corporate America. Then it hits me.

John enters the darkened living room with plates of pancakes and bacon. Taking mine, I say, "I think I need to start my Wellbutrin again." Oh, shit. I haven't taken my anti-crazy pills for several months, but John didn't know that. I'd let my prescription lapse, telling myself I was too busy to meet with my psychiatrist to renew it.

At least, that was my excuse. The truth is, I've stopped and started my antidepressants dozens of times over the years, repeating a painful and predictable cycle: bridle at my dependency on the pill du jour (I've tried them all), convince myself that I don't need them, slip back into depression, crawl back to the pills for relief. Stupid, self-defeating behavior. Why do I do it to myself? I should have called my shrink weeks ago, when I conceived Lockdown. Not to take my antidepressant while I was smoking was bad enough. Not to take it while trying to quit is just stupid. Without nicotine to stabilize it, my mood is spinning like a gyroscope, and I need the Wellbutrin to make it stop. Of course, I've realized this too late.

John scowls at me. "You stopped taking it? When?"

"It's November, so…July, I think. I told you before."

"You did not." He cannot stand me when I'm off my medication. "Well, that explains a lot."

It's true that I've become even more irritable than usual. The week before, I'd asked Daniel to undress and get into the tub. Twice. The third time, I'd roared at him, my eyes shooting twin laser death rays of rage. Regarding me in hurt surprise, my son squinched his eyes shut, turned his face to the ceiling, and howled. Nor has John escaped my wrath. Lately, I find myself watching him with clenched teeth: Must you have your soda in a glass with ice? Can't you drink it out of the fucking can like everyone else?

"Why do you do this?" John asks, flooding his pancakes with sugar-free syrup. "You know what happens to you."

"I felt fine. Also, I hate taking off work to drive across town to his office. The guy only makes me come in so he can fleece Blue Cross."

I know that my accusation is unfair. I like this guy more than my last psychiatrist, who tented his fingers as he regarded me with the flat, dead gaze of a lizard. I always imagined him rubber-gloved, expectant, at a dissection table.

John sighs and spears a forkful of pancakes. "When will you get back on it?"

"I'm calling him today. I'm hoping he'll call in a prescription." My mood bucks again. Fighting tears, I place my hand over his. "I'm sorry. I swear, I'll never go off again."

He lays down his fork and draws me to him.

"Isn't it ironic," I say, my cheek against his chest. "Of all the people you know, who gets the most stressed out? Who most needs to relax?"

"You," says John, who knows his line.

"And here I am. Can't drink. Can't smoke."

I don't want him to chain me up and go away. I stay against his chest, my eyes closed. If I don't move, I will remain in this pocket of peace.

Gently, John pulls away and tips up my chin. "You okay?"

I nod.

"All right, come on. I've got to get to work."

Pulling myself together, I place my ankle on the coffee table. I remembered to wear socks. "How's your ankle?" John asks as he loops the chain around it.

"A little sore. Not too bad."

"Well, try to stay off your feet." He snaps on the lock. After rattling to the front door to see him off, I call my psychiatrist's office.

"He schedules his own appointments," says the receptionist, "but I'll take your name and number."

"Can you ask him to call in a prescription? For Wellbutrin—150 milligrams, twice a day. I know I haven't seen him in a while, but I'm not doing well. I think I should start it today."

"I'll give him the message," she says, unmoved.

When he calls three hours later, I describe my black mood, adding, "I quit smoking yesterday, too." I don't mention that I've chained myself in my house to do it.

"I'll call in the Wellbutrin, but I'd better see you in my office," he says. "December ninth."

"I'll be there." And I will. Quitting smoking could launch me into a major depression. My shrink knows it, too. That's why he's calling in the prescription without making me come in.

The metal around my ankle is a child's paper chain. How stupid to think it was a match for nicotine's invisible shackles. Nothing but a cigarette can fix what is broken.

Eric rented us an apartment in Queens, three subway stops from Shea Stadium. From the moment he double-parked in front of our building, I knew that the city—all relentless sirens and sour Dumpster odor and militant ugliness that melted into sudden moments of beauty—was my Oz. Each morning on my way to the 7 train, I picked up a *New York Post* at the newsstand outside the Jackson Heights stop and savored the headlines. My favorite: HEADLESS BODY IN TOPLESS BAR. By day, I sold art supplies on Lexington Avenue while Eric photographed wannabe models and actors. By night, we smoked and drank. I'd long since graduated from Heinz-flavored gin. Vodka was my poison. It tasted like a slap.

Actually, I did most of my drinking with my colleague Celeste, a failed actress ten years older than I who trailed the scent of gin like a feather boa. Every night after work, we headed for the nearby Blarney Stone and sat there for hours, drinking and smoking, cursing when we lit the wrong end of a cigarette. There's nothing worse than the taste of scorched filter—Bhopal, right there in your throat.

Celeste was not pretty. Her teeth were pearl gray, from years of cigarettes and booze; her hair was thin. But when she smiled, her chin tipped down, her eyes bright like a puppy's, so flawed and so real—she had you. Her hand on your arm, her desire to please, the way she waved her Eve Menthol Lights like batons, her audience her music—I couldn't touch her. I slumped at the bar beside her and watched her bewitch diplomats and captains of industry, charm even women into buying her drinks.

A year passed. I experienced my first panic attack and filled my first Xanax prescription. The *Challenger* burned in the sky. Eric returned to Connecticut, where his old job awaited him. His dream of becoming the next Scavullo hadn't panned out. Neither had our relationship. That was my fault. I drank too much and wouldn't wear his ring or set a wedding date. I went off with other men, lured by their cocaine.

Eric left me on a Sunday afternoon in June. His eyes shone with tears. Mine shone with Xanax. He gathered me in his arms and sobbed into my neck, his shoulders heaving. I patted his back, *Shh, shh. It's all right. Everything will be all right.* And it was. Alcohol and cigarettes and Xanax shoved the pain of his departure into the deepest part of me.

Soon after Eric left, my godmother died and left me some money, enough to live on for a few years if I was careful. I gritted my teeth, quit my job, and enrolled at Hunter College.

On my last day of work, Celeste and I went for a drink. "We'll never see each other," she said. She stared into her gin and tonic, stabbing her stirrer in and out of the cubes.

"Sure we will," I replied, but I was lying. A year ago, Celeste's drinking made me feel better about my own. Now it scared me. Her drinking had a relentless quality. As her charm settled to the bottom of her glass, trapped by melting ice and gnawed wedges of lime, her eyes glazed, like those of a pet put to sleep, and she developed an English accent, as if performing Evelyn Waugh. Her smile wobbled; her audiences drifted away. She bought her own gin and tonics now.

Occasionally, averting my eyes, I mentioned treatment centers and AA meetings—for her, of course, not for me. Celeste made excuses and continued to black out and wake in urine-soaked sheets. I gave up, smelling tragedy in her like dogs are said to smell cancer.

Celeste's tailspin into late-stage alcoholism didn't make me confront my own drinking, or even drink less. I just drank alone, after class. Somehow, I was graduated in 1988. I think. I didn't attend the ceremony, and Hunter didn't mail me my diploma. I didn't call to ask about it, either. I just let it slide.

Around that time, I lost my Connecticut driver's license. Literally lost it early one Sunday morning in a taxi, crossing over the Queensboro Bridge, on my way home after spending the night with a stranger. I remember my relief: *I'll never have to drive again.*

Like the chaos that defined my life, my smoking had assumed a consistent pattern, as familiar as a lover's imprint in the mattress. Now there was an ashtray on the milk crate beside my bed and a lighter in every room. I smoked my first cigarette of the day still wrapped in my blankets. The second with my first cup of coffee, the sour blend of nicotine and milky caffeine spreading like a stain in my mouth. The third outside, on my way to the F train. The next as I emerged from the station and walked the few blocks to work. Ten to twelve more during the work day, finishing the pack—or tearing into a new one—at night.

I smoked faster than anyone I knew: short puffs, a little catch in my breath, like a sob. Then the hard discharge, as if blowing out the candles on a birthday cake. Two or three seconds between each inhalation. Constantly tapping, flicking, rolling the ash, often knocking it off so I'd have to light it again. I smoked when I was hungry, tired, bored, angry, lonely, after sex, in the bathtub, on the toilet. When I couldn't smoke, I bit my lips or chewed the insides of my cheeks.

Like all compulsions, my smoking was tinged with anxiety and nerves, but the act soothed me. Muted a need I couldn't meet on my own: to belong somewhere, be a part of something. My yearning for connection shamed me; it was weakness, a boot on my chest. Preferring loneliness to rejection, I kept the world at arm's length. From a distance, behind a cigarette, I appeared attractive, intelligent, in control. Up close, I looked like what I was: an unlovable defective stain.

Men didn't seem to think so, however, and like cigarettes, they calmed me. Fortunately, I'd discovered they were as interchangeable as cigarette brands, merely variations of the same poison. I couldn't commit to any of them, of course. I couldn't even commit to an apartment. After Eric left, I moved every year. By 1989, I had left Queens and settled in Brooklyn Heights, the affluent neighborhood just across the East River at the lower tip of Manhattan, favored by artists and hip young professionals.

My apartment was as small as my life. The door opened into a kitchen the size of a large closet. In the bathroom, I could barely raise my arm to lift my blow dryer. But my bedroom was beautiful—light and airy, with a view of Court Street and the grocery store across the way where the cashiers ran up your bill if you didn't watch the register. My parents had given me a metal bed frame and headboard, but I left them on the street the last time I moved and bought a cheap futon bed. I spent a lot of time in it, passed out or in the company of men I didn't know and would never see again. Drunk or sober, I knew that love and happiness were beyond my reach. But cigarettes would always be there. Cigarettes, those small doors I closed gratefully, again and again, against the sadness and tedium of my days. […]

I always made it to work, though: I was an editor at *Playgirl*.

Housed in a Second Avenue high-rise, *Playgirl* was one of several porn magazines—including *High Society* and *Cheri*, for men—owned by a wealthy businessman. The men's magazines shared office space with *Playgirl*. Each morning, I rode the elevator to the thirty-second floor, passed through the mauve reception area, and opened the door to depravity.

My *Playgirl* colleagues were sweet young teetotalers with husbands and boyfriends. Of course, I befriended the editors of the men's magazines, who shared my fondness for alcohol. Somehow, when we drank together, one after-work cocktail took eight or more hours to finish. The next morning we crawled to our desks, pale and sick, to pore through manila folders bulging with transparencies of strippers—in my case, from Chippendales.

Most of my porn posse smoked, which made sense. Smoking and sex go together—the greedy rhythmic suck, the gush of creamy vapor over rouged lips. Now, Internet fetish sites show fully clothed women chain-smoking— "chaining," in the argot of devotees—French inhaling, or demonstrating "deep cone exhales," which look like tiny cyclones spinning out from between their thickly glossed lips. The popularity of these sites doesn't surprise me at all. In this culture of health hysteria, smoking is almost as depraved as porn— filthy, immoral, deviant.

If my colleagues and I deserved that characterization, it wasn't because we smoked. My friends plastered their offices with posters of nude women with the hard, slick, silicone-looking skin of dolls, images that commanded no more of my attention than their desk staplers. These same women—some of the sweetest girls you'd ever want to meet, all tanned skin and plunging cleavage—occasionally visited our floor, for reasons that I never understood. Each month, I sifted through snapshots of naked men, culling the best for publication in *Playgirl*'s back pages. (Alas, men one wouldn't want to see nude are those most eager to doff their clothing.) We hooted over our letters— pornographers get inordinate amounts of mail from people who believe that the CIA drugged them and implanted transistors in their molars. Once, a new editor at *High Society*—from the Midwest, I believe, and heartbreakingly innocent—was ambushed at his desk by his sobbing mother and tight-lipped father, who somehow had heard that their son worked in a den of iniquity. Hushed, embarrassed for the poor kid, we watched as they dragged him off, never to be seen again.

One morning soon after the fall of the Berlin Wall, I walked down the long carpeted hall to the art department. The publisher wanted *Playgirl* to run a special issue: Men of the Eastern Bloc. Normally, Freddie left it to me and my art director, Donna, to select the centerfold. But Men of the Eastern Bloc! Freddie smelled the sweet scent of publicity. He'd called me to his office the day before to review the aesthetic principles that should govern our choice.

The pickings were slim. While I don't remember specific flaws—an underbite, a lazy eye—their general unsightliness remains fixed in my memory. But

Freddie didn't care about their faces. As I recall, he leaned back in his plush office chair, his shrewd eyes caged behind aviator frames, gnawing on an unlit cigar the size of a turkey leg. His exact words are lost to me, but the gist was: Let the largest popo win.

Studying the manila folders in my lap, I chose my words carefully. "The thing is, sir, all of these guys are unattractive. I mean, *really* unattractive." I didn't add that they weren't from the Eastern Bloc. This was a detail, and Freddie was a man of vision.

Pick one, he said. And if his…member isn't big enough, airbrush it.

I'd told Donna about my meeting with Freddie a few days before. This morning, I had to break the news. At her desk, I silently placed several transparencies of my first choice on her light box and switched it on. Picking up her loupe, Donna examined them. After thirty seconds, she looked up at me.

"Did you see his *teeth*?"

"Oh, yeah. And it gets better. We have to retouch his wiener. Freddie wants it big. Halfway-down-his-leg big."

"At least it will draw attention away from his face." Then, this unpleasantness dispensed with, she looked at me and cocked an eyebrow.

"Let's go," I said.

This was the late 1980s, and a growing number of companies in the city were giving smokers their walking papers. Our banishment created a kind of perverse camaraderie. Fellow exiles from the nonsmoking world, we stood in a haze of brume, sharing the pleasure and pain of our compulsion as well as rain, snow, and unpleasant extremes of temperature.

Donna was my smoking buddy. Every hour, when the nudging need forced us to the elevator, we descended the thirty-two floors to the lobby and shuffled through the heavy revolving doors, clutching our cigarettes and lighters. We'd become almost like friends on our cigarette runs. Not clubbing-on-Saturday-night friends, although I would have liked that. She smoked like me—short hard puffs.

And once a week, I visited my therapist, Hannah. My weekly trip to her office on the Upper West Side, around the corner from the Dakota, where John Lennon lived and was shot, gave my chaotic life some small but comforting measure of predictability. She, too, had banned cigarettes from her office. I nicotine-loaded before and after our sessions.

Hannah was tiny, with luminous skin, wavy brown hair that reached halfway down her back, and a quick, brilliant smile. I was compelled to tell her things.

"I called Nick last night," I said at the start of one session. I still hadn't met my biological father, but I'd talked to him. In fact, I'd called him every six months for the past several years—late at night, after hours of swigging Smirnoff's. My mother had given me his number. She couldn't explain why she had it or how she knew that Nick lived alone in a large Midwestern city. He worked in a factory—doing what, she didn't know. I imagined him in a grim industrial setting, standing at a conveyor belt with black-hooded eyes, performing some repetitive, soul-numbing task.

"So what happened?" Hannah asked.

"The usual." Though sporadic, the conversations between Nick and me were as predictable as the pornography I wrote. They could last an hour or, like this one, minutes.

I sit on my bed, the only light from the neon-green buttons on the receiver. I punch in his number. *Ring-ring.*

"Hello."

"Nick," I say. "How's every little thing?"

"Who is this? It's almost midnight." His nasal Midwestern twang a mosquito's whine in the dark.

"It's me, the amazing invisible daughter. How long has it been?" My attempt to shame him fails, as usual.

"Julie, this business has gotta stop. You been drinkin'? Am I gonna have to call your mother again?"

I ignore him. "If Muhammad won't come to the mountain, the mountain must come to Muhammad. Wait, wait, I screwed that up. But it doesn't matter. I'm your mountain, Nick. Hold on."

I shove the Newport in my mouth and light it with shaky fingers. A moment of peace. Then the kaleidoscope pattern in my head shifts into a sodden sadness. Why do I bother to call him? There is nothing to say. He hasn't forgotten about me. I have never existed to him at all. I am a lone shoe in the road: How did *that* get here?

I drop the phone on the bed and hunch over, holding my stomach as if I'd been shot. I hear his voice, tinny and faint as if he were in Africa: "Hello? Hello?"

I rock in the dark, my eyes closed. My blood father has erased me from his life as cleanly as chalk from a blackboard.

When I was in the sixth grade, I'd looked up "tundra" in the dictionary. Its definition—a vast treeless plain in the arctic regions—intrigued me less than its etymology. In the language of the Inuit, it means "nothing."

The word took root in my brain. Eventually, when I pictured myself, I didn't see a petite, slender young woman with wavy black hair and dark eyes. I saw a stretch of cold, white, barren land. I wasn't in this image. I *was* this image.

I rock. See white sky darken, feel cold need whistle right through me.

After a while, I pick up the receiver and hold it to my ear. He must have heard me breathing.

"You there? Talk to me if you're there."

"Mail me a picture of you," I whisper. What a whiner I am, begging for scraps.

"Why?" he asks.

That's when I hang up.

I was crying by the time I finished the story. I hated tears; they advertised that you'd been caught wanting something. In every session, I played a game with myself: If I didn't reach for the box of Kleenex on the table beside my chair, my crying didn't count.

I kept my head low, but a tear fell on my wrist. I covered it with my other hand.

"Good girl," Hannah said, softly.

No, I wasn't. I'd cried. I hated her for her softness, myself for mine, and did not want to see the kindness in her eyes. Without looking up, I rose and walked out of her office, fumbling in the pocket of my leather jacket for my cigarettes.

Julia Hansen documents her self-destructive smoking and drinking and the extreme measures she feels compelled to deploy in order to bring these unhealthy behaviors under control. As a group, discuss what other sorts of habits you can imagine that could seriously damage one's health. Present your findings to the class.

Hansen blames herself bitterly for her continued addiction to cigarettes, but, as movies such as *The Insider* have dramatized, tobacco companies conspired to make cigarettes more addictive to consumers and to conceal their knowledge of tobacco's deleterious effects. Read the transcript or watch the broadcast of CBS's interview with whistle-blower Jeffrey Wigand (http://www.jeffreywigand.com/60minutes.php). Does knowing about the cover-up change your feelings about tobacco addiction? Contrast these transcripts to the CDC's anti-smoking campaign ads (use Google or Bing to search for the ads or go the CDC's Web site). The campaign's ads were described as graphic and shocking. Are the advertisements or the transcripts more effective in persuading someone not to start smoking? Or are neither the report nor the advertisement persuasive enough to stop you or someone you know from smoking?

In Book II of the *Nicomachean Ethics*, Aristotle discusses the connection between habit (*ethos*) and virtue (*ethike*). You can find a translation online at the Internet Classics Archive: <http://classics.mit.edu/Aristotle/nicomachaen.2.ii.html. Read sections 1 and 2, on habits. Have you ever taken extreme measures to break a habit? Are there habits or virtues that you would like to inculcate in yourself? What measures might you take in order to make your virtues into habits, or to turn your habits into virtues? Write yourself a list of resolutions.

Tumblr, the micro-blogging site; Pinterest, the social networking site; LiveJournal, the social blogging site; and Instagram, the social photo-sharing site have all banned or restricted posts that glorify unhealthful or dangerous practices such as bingeing and purging, starvation diets, or drug abuse. What are some of the risks and benefits of blogging about ill health, good health, and healthful practices? What are some of the ways that readers can evaluate the worth of some of the so-called *health* advice on popular blogs?

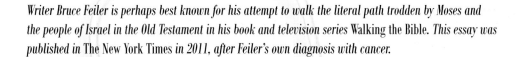

Writer Bruce Feiler is perhaps best known for his attempt to walk the literal path trodden by Moses and the people of Israel in the Old Testament in his book and television series Walking the Bible. *This essay was published in* The New York Times *in 2011, after Feiler's own diagnosis with cancer.*

'YOU LOOK GREAT' AND OTHER LIES

By Bruce Feiler

MY friend sat down and ordered a stiff drink. I didn't think of her as the stiff-drink kind. An hour later, after our spouses drifted off into conversation, she leaned over the table. "I need your help," she said. "My sister has a brain tumor. I don't know what to do."

Three years ago this month, I learned that I had a seven-inch osteosarcoma in my left femur. Put more directly: I had bone cancer. That diagnosis led me down a dark year that included nine months of chemotherapy and a 15-hour surgery to reconstruct my left leg.

At the time, my wife, Linda, and I were the parents of 3-year-old identical twin girls, and we were often overwhelmed with the everyday challenges of having a sick dad, a working mom and two preschoolers. We survived with help from many people. Our siblings organized an online casserole club, so friends could buy us dinner through a meal service. Grandparents rotated in and out of our basement. My high school classmates made a video at our reunion.

But as my friend's query suggested, some gestures were more helpful than others, and a few were downright annoying. So at the risk of offending some well-meaning people, here are Six Things You Should Never Say to a Friend (or Relative or Colleague) Who's Sick. And Four Things You Can Always Say.

First, the Nevers.

1. WHAT CAN I DO TO HELP? Most patients I know grow to hate this ubiquitous, if heartfelt question because it puts the burden back on them. As Doug Ulman, the chief executive of Livestrong and a three-time cancer survivor, explained: "The patient is never going to tell you. They don't want to feel vulnerable." Instead, just do something for the patient. And the more mundane the better, because those are the tasks that add up. Want to be really helpful? Clean out my fridge, replace my light bulbs, unpot my dead plants, change my oil.

2. MY THOUGHTS AND PRAYERS ARE WITH YOU. In my experience, some people think about you, which is nice. Others pray for you, which is equally comforting. But the majority of people who say they're sending "thoughts and prayers" are just falling back on a mindless cliché. It's time to retire this hackneyed expression to the final resting place of platitudes, alongside "I'm stepping down to spend more time with my family," or "It's not you, it's me."

3. DID YOU TRY THAT MANGO COLONIC I RECOMMENDED? I was stunned by the number of friends and strangers alike who inundated me with tips for miracle tonics, Chinese herbs or Swedish visualization exercises. At times, my in-box was like a Grand Ole Opry lineup of 1940s Appalachian black-magic potions. "If you put tumeric under your fingernails, and pepper on your neck, and take a grapefruit shower, you'll feel better. It cured my Uncle Louie."

Even worse, the recommenders follow up! Jennifer Goodman Linn, a former marketing executive who's survived seven recurrences of a sarcoma and is compiling a book, "I Know You Mean Well, but ...," was approached recently at a store.

"You don't know me, but you're friends with my wife," the man said, before asking Ms. Linn why she wasn't wearing the kabbalah bracelet they bought her in Israel.

4. EVERYTHING WILL BE O.K. Unsure what to say, many well-wishers fall back on chirpy feel-goodisms. But these banalities are more often designed to allay the fears of the caregiver than those of the patient. As one friend who recently had brain surgery complained: "I got a lot of 'chin ups,' 'you're going to get better.' I kept thinking: You haven't seen the scans. That's not what the doctor is saying." The simple truth is, unless you're a medical professional, resist playing Nostradamus.

5. HOW ARE WE TODAY? Every adult patient I know complains about being infantilized. The writer Letty Cottin Pogrebin, who had breast cancer, is working on a book, "How to Be a Friend to a Friend Who's Sick." It includes a list of "no-no's" that treat ailing grown-ups like children. When the adult patient has living parents, as I did, many mothers in particular fall back on old patterns, from overstepping their boundaries to making bologna sandwiches when the patient hasn't eaten them since childhood. "Just because someone is dealing with a physical illness," Mr. Ulman said, "doesn't diminish their mental capacity."

6. YOU LOOK GREAT. Nice try, but patients can see right through this chestnut. We know we're gaunt, our hair is falling out in clumps, our colostomy bag needs emptying. The only thing this hollow expression conveys is that you're focusing on how we appear. "When people comment on my appearance," Ms. Linn said, "it reminds me that I don't look good."

Next time you want to compliment a patient's appearance, keep this in mind: Vanity is the only part of the human anatomy that is immune to cancer.

So what do patients like to hear? Here are four suggestions.

1. DON'T WRITE ME BACK. All patients get overwhelmed with the burden of keeping everyone informed, coddled and feeling appreciated. Social networking, while offering some relief, often increases the expectation of round-the-clock updates.

To get around this problem, I appointed a "minister of information," whose job it was to disseminate news, deflect queries and generally be polite when I didn't have the energy or inclination to be. But you can do your part, too: If you do drop off a fruitcake or take the dog for a walk, insist the patient not write you a thank-you note. Chicken soup is not a wedding gift; it shouldn't come with added stress.

2. I SHOULD BE GOING NOW. You'll never go wrong by uttering these five words while visiting someone who's sick. As Ms. Pogrebin observes of such visits, don't overstay your welcome. She recommends 20 minutes, even less if the patient is tired or in pain. And while you're there, wash a few dishes or tidy up the room. And take out the trash when you leave.

3. WOULD YOU LIKE SOME GOSSIP? One surefire tip: a slight change of topic goes a long way. Patients are often sick of talking about their illness. We have to do that with our doctors, nurses and insurance henchmen. By all means, follow the lead of the individual, but sometimes ignoring the elephant in the room is just the right medicine. Even someone recovering from surgery has an opinion about the starlet's affair, the underdog in the playoffs or the big election around the corner.

4. I LOVE YOU. When all else fails, simple, direct emotion is the most powerful gift you can give a loved one going through pain. It doesn't need to be ornamented. It just needs to be real. "I'm sorry you have to go through this." "I hate to see you suffer." "You mean a lot to me." The fact that so few of us do this makes it even more meaningful.

Not long ago, I reached out to my friend's sister, Amy, who had endured three surgeries in the previous six months for a tumor in the thalamus. She was undergoing physical therapy and had just returned to work. What most annoyed her, I wondered?

"I liked having the family around," she said, referring to her six siblings and their five spouses. "But I had a lot of issues with my room seeming like a party and my not being in a place where I could be down if I wanted."

The most helpful tip she got? "People reminded me that I had a free 'No' clause whenever I needed it. Especially as someone who tends to please, that was helpful."

So in the end, what would she say to someone like her sister who leaned over and asked for advice?

"Fully embrace the vulnerability of the situation," she said. "I would never have gotten through it if I hadn't allowed people in."

That even included a new boyfriend, who became so intimately involved in her recovery that she allowed him access to her innermost self. The two became engaged in the I.C.U. and plan to marry next year.

Feiler mentioned that his family started an online casserole group to help his family function during his illness and treatment. Take a look at https://www.lotsahelpinghands.com/how-it-works and read about this community-building caregiving Web site. Or go to a similar group page on a social networking site such as Facebook. How have social media sites enabled us to help our friends and family? Are there any drawbacks to this kind of system?

Think about a time in your life where your friends, coworkers, or family members tried to comfort you, either because of an illness, the death of a loved one, or another tragic event. Some of the "don'ts" on Feiler's list might be seen as more of an individual response to a particular circumstance, while others you might strongly agree with as tenets for any situation in which a close friend or family member is suffering. What are some of your do's and don'ts for what to say to someone in this particular situation? Do you find that your list agrees or disagrees with Feiler's?

In a group, think about the challenges that a college student would face if he or she were diagnosed with a serious illness that required treatment during the school year. Research ways in which your health center, campus activities office, and/or student affairs office help students face this kind of crisis. Report your findings back to the class.

Write a plan for creating a group of caregivers on your campus. What would your group's objectives be? How would your group handle student needs and with what kinds of issues would you help for fellow students? How would you address issues of privacy and illness? Would you use a social media site such as Lotsa Helping Hands to organize your group's efforts?

Journalist Barbara Ehrenreich found herself both critiquing and chronicling the modern breast cancer awareness campaign when she herself was diagnosed with this illness. This chapter from her 2009 book, Bright-Sided, is a revised version of "Welcome to Cancerland," an essay she wrote for Harper's magazine in 2001.

excerpt from

BRIGHT-SIDED

BY BARBARA EHRENREICH

THE PINK RIBBON CULTURE

Fortunately, no one has to go through this alone. Forty years ago, before Betty Ford, Rose Kushner, Betty Rollin, and other pioneer patients spoke out, breast cancer was a dread secret, endured in silence and euphemized in obituaries as a "long illness." Something about the conjuncture of "breast," signifying sexuality and nurturance, and that other word, suggesting the claws of a devouring crustacean, spooked almost everyone. Today, however, it's the biggest disease on the cultural map, bigger than AIDS, cystic fibrosis, or spinal injury, bigger even than those more prolific killers of women—heart disease, lung cancer, and stroke. There are roughly hundreds of Web sites devoted to it, not to mention newsletters, support groups, a whole genre of first-person breast cancer books, even a glossy upper-middle-brow monthly magazine, *Mamm*. There are four major national breast cancer organizations, of which the mightiest, in financial terms, is the Susan G. Komen Foundation, headed by breast cancer survivor and Republican donor Nancy Brinker. Komen organizes the annual Race for the Cure®, which attracts about a million people—mostly survivors, friends, and family members. Its Web site provides a microcosm of the breast cancer culture, offering news of the races, message boards for accounts of individuals' struggles with the disease, and uplifting inspirational messages.

The first thing I discovered as I waded out into the relevant sites is that not everyone views the disease with horror and dread. Instead, the appropriate attitude is upbeat and even eagerly acquisitive. There are between two and three million American women in various stages of breast cancer treatment, who, along with anxious relatives, make up a significant market for all things breast cancer related. Bears, for example: I identified four distinct lines, or species, of these creatures, including Carol, the Remembrance Bear; Hope, the Breast Cancer Research Bear, which wore a pink turban as if to conceal chemotherapy-induced baldness; the Susan Bear, named for Nancy Brinker's deceased sister; and the Nick and Nora Wish Upon a Star Bear, which was available, along with the Susan Bear, at the Komen Foundation Web site's "marketplace."

And bears are only the tip, so to speak, of the cornucopia of pink-ribbon-themed breast cancer products. You can dress in pink-beribboned sweatshirts, denim shirts, pajamas, lingerie, aprons, loungewear, shoelaces, and socks; accessorize with pink rhinestone brooches, angel pins, scarves, caps, earrings, and bracelets; brighten up your home with breast cancer candles, stained glass pink-ribbon candleholders, coffee mugs, pendants, wind chimes, and night-lights; and pay your bills with Checks for the Cure™. "Awareness" beats secrecy and stigma, of course, but I couldn't help noticing that the existential space in which a friend had earnestly advised me to "confront [my] mortality" bore a striking resemblance to the mall.

This is not entirely, I should point out, a case of cynical merchants exploiting the sick. Some of the breast cancer tchotchkes and accessories are made by breast cancer survivors themselves, such as "Janice," creator of the Daisy Awareness Necklace, among other things, and in most cases a portion of the sales goes to breast cancer research. Virginia Davis of Aurora, Colorado, was inspired to create the Remembrance Bear by a friend's double mastectomy and told me she sees her work as more of a "crusade" than a business. When I interviewed her in 2001, she was expecting to ship ten thousand of these teddies, which are manufactured in China, and send part of the money to the Race for the Cure. If the bears are infantilizing—as I tried ever so tactfully to suggest was how they may, in rare cases, be perceived—so far no one had complained. "I just get love letters," she told me, "from people who say, 'God bless you for thinking of us.'"

The ultrafeminine theme of the breast cancer marketplace—the prominence, for example, of cosmetics and jewelry—could be understood as a response to the treatments' disastrous effects on one's looks. No doubt, too, all the prettiness and pinkness is meant to inspire a positive outlook. But the infantilizing trope is a little harder to account for, and teddy bears are not its only manifestation. A tote bag distributed to breast cancer patients by the Libby Ross Foundation (through places such as the Columbia-Presbyterian Medical Center) contained, among other items, a tube of Estée Lauder Perfumed Body Créme, a hot pink satin pillowcase, a small tin of peppermint pastilles, a set of three small, inexpensive rhinestone bracelets, a pink-striped "journal and sketch book," and—somewhat jarringly—a box of crayons. Marla Willner, one of the founders of the Libby Ross Foundation, told me that the crayons "go with the journal—for people to express different moods, different thoughts," though she admitted she has never tried to write with crayons herself. Possibly the idea was that regression to a state of childlike dependency puts one in the best frame of mind for enduring the prolonged and toxic treatments. Or it may be that, in some versions of the prevailing gender ideology, femininity is by its nature incompatible with full adulthood—a state of arrested development. Certainly men diagnosed with prostate cancer do not receive gifts of Matchbox cars.

But I, no less than the bear huggers, needed whatever help I could get and found myself searching obsessively for practical tips on hair loss, how to select a chemotherapy regimen, what to wear after surgery and eat when the scent of food sucks. There was, I soon discovered, far more than I could usefully absorb, for thousands of the afflicted have posted their stories, beginning with the lump or bad mammogram, proceeding through the agony of the treatments, pausing to mention the sustaining forces of family, humor, and religion, and ending, in almost all cases, with an upbeat message for the terrified neophyte. Some of these are no more than a paragraph long—brief waves from sister sufferers. Others offer almost hour-by-hour logs of breast-deprived, chemotherapized lives:

> Tuesday, August 15, 2000: Well, I survived my 4th chemo. Very, very dizzy today. Very nauseated, but no barfing! It's a first…. I break out in a cold sweat and my heart pounds if I stay up longer than 5 minutes.

> Friday, August 18, 2000: … By dinnertime, I was full out nauseated. I took some meds and ate a rice and vegetable bowl from Trader Joe's. It smelled and tasted awful to me, but I ate it anyway….Rick

brought home some Kern's nectars and I'm drinking that. Seems to
have settled my stomach a little bit.

I couldn't seem to get enough of these tales, reading on with panicky fascination
about everything that can go wrong—septicemia, ruptured implants, startling
recurrences a few years after the completion of treatments, "mets" (metastases)
to vital organs, and—what scared me most in the short term—"chemo brain,"
or the cognitive deterioration that sometimes accompanies chemotherapy.
I compared myself with everyone, selfishly impatient with those whose
conditions were less menacing, shivering over those who had reached Stage IV
("There is no Stage V," as the main character in the play *Wit*, who has ovarian
cancer, explains), constantly assessing my chances.

But, despite all the helpful information, the more fellow victims I discovered
and read, the greater my sense of isolation grew. No one among the bloggers
and book writers seemed to share my sense of outrage over the disease and
the available treatments. What causes it and why is it so common, especially
in industrialized societies?[1] Why don't we have treatments that distinguish
between different forms of breast cancer or between cancer cells and normal
dividing cells? In the mainstream of breast cancer culture, there is very
little anger, no mention of possible environmental causes, and few comments
about the fact that, in all but the more advanced, metastasized cases, it is the
"treatments," not the disease, that cause the immediate illness and pain. In
fact, the overall tone is almost universally upbeat. The Breast Friends Web site,
for example, featured a series of inspirational quotes: "Don't cry over anything
that can't cry over you," "I can't stop the birds of sorrow from circling my
head, but I can stop them from building a nest in my hair," "When life hands
out lemons, squeeze out a smile," "Don't wait for your ship to come in ... swim
out to meet it," and much more of that ilk. Even in the relatively sophisticated

---

1 "Bad" genes of the inherited variety are thought to account for less than 10 percent of breast cancers, and only 30 percent of women diagnosed with breast cancer have any known risk factor (such
as delaying childbearing or the late onset of menopause) at all. Bad lifestyle choices like a fatty diet
have, after brief popularity with the medical profession, been largely ruled out. Hence, groups like
Breast Cancer Action argue, suspicion should focus on environmental carcinogens, such as plastics,
pesticides (DDT and PCBs, for example, though banned in this country, are still used in many Third
World sources of the produce we eat), and the industrial runoff in our ground water. No carcinogen has
been linked definitely to human breast cancer yet, but many carcinogens have been found to cause the
disease in mice, and the inexorable increase of the disease in industrialized nations—about 1 percent
a year between the 1950s and the 1990s—further hints at environmental factors, as does the fact that
women migrants to industrialized countries quickly develop the same breast cancer rates as those who
are native-born.

Mamm, a columnist bemoaned not cancer or chemotherapy but the end of chemotherapy and humorously proposed to deal with her separation anxiety by pitching a tent outside her oncologist's office. Positive thinking seems to be mandatory in the breast cancer world, to the point that unhappiness requires a kind of apology, as when "Lucy," whose "long-term prognosis is not good," started her personal narrative on breastcancertalk.org by telling us that her story "is not the usual one, full of sweetness and hope, but true nevertheless."

Even the word "victim" is proscribed, leaving no single noun to describe a woman with breast cancer. As in the AIDS movement, upon which breast cancer activism is partly modeled, the words "patient" and "victim," with their aura of self-pity and passivity, have been ruled un-P.C. Instead, we get verbs: those who are in the midst of their treatments are described as "battling" or "fighting," sometimes intensified with "bravely" or "fiercely"— language suggestive of Katharine Hepburn with her face to the wind. Once the treatments are over, one achieves the status of "survivor," which is how the women in my local support group identified themselves, A.A.-style, when we convened to share war stories and rejoice in our "survivorhood": "Hi, I'm Kathy and I'm a three-year survivor." My support group seemed supportive enough, but some women have reported being expelled by their groups when their cancers metastasized and it became clear they would never graduate to the rank of "survivor."

For those who cease to be survivors and join the more than forty thousand American women who succumb to breast cancer each year—again, no noun applies. They are said to have "lost their battle" and may be memorialized by photographs carried at races for the cure—our lost brave sisters, our fallen soldiers. But in the overwhelmingly positive culture that has grown up around breast cancer, martyrs count for very little; it is the "survivors" who merit constant honor and acclaim. At a "Relay for Life" event in my town, sponsored by the American Cancer Society, the dead were present only in much diminished form. A series of paper bags, each about the right size for a junior burger and fries, lined the relay track. On them were the names of the dead, and inside each was a candle that was lit after dark, when the actual relay race began. The stars, though, were the runners, the "survivors," who seemed to offer living proof the disease isn't so bad after all.

This assignment will help you prepare for Major Assignment #4: Service-Learning Social Media Campaign. Using Google, Bing, or another search engine and the Web sites of CharityWatch and Wikipedia ("Cancer societies" entry), find the Web sites of major cancer organizations (such as the American Cancer Society, National Breast Cancer Coalition, Breast Cancer Alliance, Susan G. Komen For the Cure, Bone Cancer Research Trust, etc.). Can you identify in these sites the marketing strategies that Ehrenreich analyzes? How do these sites characterize different forms of cancer? Does each site personify cancer, as Ehrenreich suggests?

How ubiquitous is the "pink-ribbon" marketing? Start jotting down instances where you see the pink ribbon or hear the term used in daily life, for example on products in the grocery store, in social media, in advertisements, on pins or sweatshirts, or on bulletin boards and other venues on campus. Draft an argument about the kinds of places where you find the pink ribbon.

In a group of your classmates, at least one of you will have experienced or have been close to someone who has suffered from cancer or who has had a mammogram, biopsy, or other "pink-ribbon" experience. Many of these women may have found the "pink-ribbon culture" empowering or helpful. How would you summarize Ehrenreich's analysis for such a person? What are your own responses to this piece? If you were to characterize breast cancer with a different symbol, what would it be and why? Or do you think that the pink ribbon is effective? If so, why?

Dwight Christopher Gabbard teaches English at the University of North Florida. This reflective essay about his severely disabled son's ability to enjoy life appeared in The Chronicle of Higher Education *and the book* Papa, PhD *in 2010.*

A LIFE BEYOND REASON

By Dwight Christopher Gabbard

My son, August, has a number of quirks that distinguish him from the typically developing 10-year-old. He lives with cerebral palsy, is a spastic quadriplegic, has cortical visual impairment (meaning he is legally blind), is completely nonverbal and cognitively disabled, has a microcephalic head, and must wear a diaper. Moreover, he is immobile—he can't crawl or scoot around or hold himself up or even sit in a chair without being strapped in it. If someone were to put him on the floor and leave him there, he would be in the same location hours later, give or take a foot.

At home, in the eyes of my wife, Ilene; our 7-year-old daughter, Clio; and me, he seems merely a little eccentric, possessor of a few odd quirks, as I said. We don't think of him as being different; he is August, just another member of an already quirky family. Although he cannot play with his sister, she loves him. Without being prompted, she recently made pipe-cleaner wheelchairs for her dolls and rendered her wooden doll house ADA-compliant by retrofitting it with ramps. Now the dolls wheel freely in and out. For family bike rides, we have a specially built bicycle with a Tumble Forms chair attached to the front for him to ride in. I feed August his meals (he cannot feed himself), change his diapers, place him in the supersize jogger when I go running, and put him to bed. He and I have a good relationship: He laughs at my attempts at humor, which consist of making odd sounds or putting him face-up on the rug, holding his feet and legs up high, and rocking him swiftly back and forth. He seems to enjoy my company, and I most certainly enjoy his.

Outside of our home, my wife and I and Clio are constantly reminded of how unusual August must appear to other people. He elicits responses ranging from aversion to "the stare." We understand that his drooling stems from his cerebral palsy—the spasticity in the muscles of the mouth prevents him from being able to control saliva. No connection exists between mental disability and drooling, but, in the public imagination, this association has long been established.

In the eyes of some, August fits stereotypical images such as the comic-strip character Zippy the Pinhead. Yet likening my son, and other people who have microcephalic heads, to Zippy is about as relevant as likening African-Americans to blackface caricatures. In the eyes of others, August resembles Terri Schiavo, who, for the secular-educated, triggers the fearful response of "better off dead than disabled." Many such well-meaning people would like to put an end to August's suffering, but they do not stop to consider whether he actually is suffering. At times he is uncomfortable, yes, but the only real pain here seems to be the pain of those who cannot bear the thought that people like August exist. For many of those folks, someone with August's caliber of cognitive and physical disability raises the question of where humanity leaves off and animality begins. But that animal-human divide is spurious, a faulty either-or.

And then there are the Christians, who see in August a child of God. Given the educated alternative I just sketched out, that response seems a relief. Here in the South, they come up and say "God bless!," to which, depending on the occasion and the person, I sometimes respond, "This is my beloved son, in whom I am well pleased."

For almost everyone, August signifies one of the great tragedies that can befall a family.

After his birth, we ourselves lived in the tragic mode, but we soon grew tired of it. August brings us joy, as does his sister. Admittedly, the parenting commitment takes time from my career. And caring for August requires more time than does attending to Clio. Because August is a spastic quadriplegic, he requires the consuming regimen of daily full-body care.

Each morning I lift him from his bed, put him on a table, change his diaper, and wash and dress him. Next I carry him up to the breakfast room, strap him into his wheelchair, hand-feed him breakfast, wash his hands and face, brush his teeth, wheel him out to the van, and drive him to his school. On regular school days, this morning preparation can take up to two hours to perform. In the late afternoon and evenings, I follow a similar routine: I drive through heavy traffic from campus to the only after-school facility in Jacksonville, Fla., equipped to handle children like August. Once there, I lift him into the van, bring him home, hand-feed him dinner (his food must be puréed and otherwise specially prepared so that he won't choke on it), find something to occupy him after dinner, and finally prepare him for bed. All of this activity takes two to three hours.

Often in the evenings, my wife and I hire people to help us so that we can get our work done and take care of our daughter. However, we cannot just hire the 15-year-old down the street to babysit: To take care of August properly, a caregiver requires at least a week of training. On my campus we have had good luck finding nursing and physical-therapy students, but we must pay more than the customary $7 an hour.

On the days that I teach and August's school is out of session, or his after-school facility shuts down, my wife and I must scramble to cover him. We cannot afford for my wife, a self-employed physical therapist and Pilates instructor, to give up a day of patients and clients. Other types of day-care facilities and the usual programs for typically developing 10-year-olds cannot accommodate a boy with spastic quadriplegia. I used to take him with me to the university, but he has now grown too large for that, and besides, he can be temperamentally unpredictable, making teaching difficult.

Just recently our family experienced an additional ripple of difficulty. My wife suffered a herniated disk in her neck, brought on in part by lifting August. An artificial disk was inserted, and, once she is fully recovered, the new disk will limit her to lifting no more than 50 pounds. Unfortunately, August now weighs at least 70. Because we moved from San Francisco to Jacksonville so that I could take my tenure-track job, we have no family in the vicinity to help us. Even worse, we have no rich uncles. As a result, almost all of the caregiving responsibilities have fallen on me. My wife and I have plans—but at present not the money—to remedy the situation: Procure a lift (for inside the home) as well as a van with a wheelchair ramp. (Yes, August has a state Medicaid waiver, and we have health insurance through my university, but when we make requests for his needs, the wheels turn slowly and sometimes not at all.)

In the meantime, I cannot leave the house for more than about eight hours at a time. Every day, morning and evening, I must be on hand to perform the routines. In sum, I cannot travel at all, even overnight. Hence, in the near future, I do not foresee going to conferences, traveling to do research, or applying for those tempting academic opportunities that entail going abroad, or, for that matter, going anywhere. In a sense, I am as stranded as Robinson Crusoe on his island. Just a few weeks ago someone in the university offered me an additional job with a small pay increase. However, the job required spending three days' training in Orlando, so I had to turn it down.

While August has limited what I can accomplish in my academic career, he also has broadened my teaching and scholarship. In order to explain how he has done so, I have to go back to my grade-school years, in Palo Alto, Calif. For the most part, I was a good student and a nice boy—nice, that is, except when I was bullying Peter, the lone kid in the class who had learning disabilities. Perceiving him to be the bearer of stigma, my fellows and I trailed after Peter, calling him idiot, moron, imbecile, stupid, and cretin. Our *Lord of the Flies* vitriol at least respected the boundary of not physically harming him, though our psychological abuse must have damaged him.

As I grew older, I was inspired by Socrates' statement that "the unexamined life is not worth living." Similarly, Aristotle's dictum that man is the animal having "logos," the power of reasoning, impressed me. The notion that the human being is a rational animal made sense, and I internalized it as a basic assumption, as I did Socrates' pronouncement. At San Francisco State University, I became intrigued by the Enlightenment. John Locke, David Hume, and Immanuel Kant fascinated me. Who would not want to be enlightened? Who in his or her right mind would choose in favor of a benighted past of superstition, ignorance, and blind faith in custom? I put my faith in reason. Eventually I obtained my doctorate at Stanford in 18th-century British literature—the age of reason: Anne Finch, Alexander Pope, Jonathan Swift, Samuel Johnson.

In sum, I grew up prizing intellectual aptitude—not that I am a candidate for Mensa—and detesting "poor mental function." Perhaps what helped make me revere intelligence was growing up in Palo Alto, with Stanford less than half a mile away and a number of Nobel Prize winners and famous and wealthy technology innovators all around me. People in my immediate vicinity had good brains, and that meant money, respect, and international influence.

Given, then, my nearly metaphysical attachment to intelligence, imagine my surprise when in March 1999, at my first child's birth, he failed to breathe and consequently suffered severe brain damage. The delivery was taking place at a prestigious teaching hospital, one that, I later learned, was attempting to reduce the number of Caesarean sections because a belief had emerged that American medicine was relying too heavily on the procedure.

After his birth, as I entered the intensive-care nursery, I was deeply ambivalent, having been persuaded by the Princeton philosopher Peter Singer's advocacy of expanding reproductive choice to include infanticide. But there was my son, asleep or unconscious, on a ventilator, motionless under a heat lamp, tubes and wires everywhere, monitors alongside his steel and transparent-plastic crib. What most stirred me was the way he resembled me. Nothing had prepared me for this, the shock of recognition, for he was the boy in my own baby pictures, the image of me when I was an infant.

Eight months after the birth, a doctor commented, after viewing the results of a CT scan, that his brain looked like "Swiss cheese," it was so full of dead patches.

So from the start, I had to wrestle with the reality of his condition. Martin Luther held the opinion that, because a child such as August was a "changeling"—merely a mass of flesh, a *massa carnis,* with no soul—he should be drowned. And Singer reasonably would maintain that my son would not qualify as a "person," because he would have no consciousness of himself in time and space.

Days later, at the hospital consult, the doctors tried to explain what had gone awry but without yielding any information that might provide a basis for a malpractice suit. Because nothing significant was disclosed, my wife and I secured a lawyer to find out what had happened. A medical expert reviewing the records reported back that malpractice had occurred. In the meantime, we had discovered that the expense of caring for August over his lifetime would very likely exceed hundreds of thousands of dollars—a van with a lift, a lift in the house, thousands of hours of attendant care, lost wages, etc., all on the salaries of an educator and a physical therapist. Then the first lawyer mysteriously dropped out, and lawyer after lawyer looked over the records and passed on the case: A series of serious medical misjudgments had been made, but no single "smoking gun" instance of malpractice, certain to convince a jury, was likely to turn up.

My son's birth initially cast me into a wilderness of perplexity, doubt, and discontent. This was part of my wife's and my tragic mode. My formerly complacent assumptions began coming apart, and over the next few years they crumbled. I had seen the dark side of medicine—the quintessence of the Enlightenment—and firm ground slipped out from under me. Then came the culmination of the Terri Schiavo case, six years to the month after August's birth. That a Florida court would order the deliberate starvation and dehydration of a woman whose mental disability differed not that much from my son's struck me as what Gayatri Spivak terms "an enabling violation." Schiavo's death served as a turning point for me, and new interests, beliefs, and curiosities began to coalesce.

In my teaching and scholarship, I now interrogate some of the ideas that once informed my assumptions, and the questions that I ask fit awkwardly into the academic landscape. Is it really true that the unexamined life is not worth living? And is it accurate to say that only the possession of logos qualifies an entity for human status?

For me, Socrates' and Aristotle's monumental truths gave way to questions for which I still do not have answers. And yet I concluded that Martin Luther was wrong. I arrived at sufficient resolution to join a disability-rights group called Not Dead Yet and to pass out leaflets on its behalf when Singer spoke on my campus.

I do not know how far I wish to go in demystifying logos. After all, I would not want to encourage my students to make unintelligent choices, leave their potential unexplored, or write irrational essays. What I do want to do, though, is bring forward to my students, colleagues, and readers what should have been obvious to me all along: namely, that the Peters and Augusts of the world are as much members of our human tribe as any of us are.

Especially in an academic environment that rewards being smart, how do I broach the idea that people with intellectual disabilities are fully equal? We academics advance in our careers by demonstrating how clever we can be, and because so much depends on flaunting intelligence, it is harder for us than for most people to steer clear of prejudice. In posing my awkward questions, I have focused on teaching literature and disability-studies courses and writing articles that examine the rhetoric and representation of intellectual disability.

My commitment to bringing cognitive disability into the foreground in the humanities can be glimpsed in the way I teach Toni Morrison's short story, "Recitatif." I teach it every chance I get. Over all, the story illustrates how irrational frustration can well up even in sympathetic characters, compelling them to seek scapegoats. This story helped me begin to understand how my own troubles at home many years ago played a part in my abusive actions toward Peter. If I did not have August in my life, I probably never would have reconsidered my behavior toward Peter, or read Morrison's story carefully, let alone begun to teach it.

To admit how August has changed me is not to assert that what he has given me compensates for what he, my wife, my daughter, and I have lost on account of the poor decisions made by the hospital where he was born. There is no getting back what we have lost. Compensation is just a trope, and belief in compensation is as superstitious as belief in the medieval notion of correspondences. Besides, nothing can compensate for what all of us have had to give up. It would be better for everyone if August could run around and shout intelligible language.

And I agree with Rabbi Harold Kushner when he writes and talks about bad things happening to good people: August's disability does not form a part of "God's plan" and does not serve as a tool for God to teach me or anyone else wisdom. What kind of a God would it be, anyway, to deprive my boy of speech and movement just to instruct me? A cruel and arbitrary God. August's disabilities are not a blessing; but neither are they a divine curse. To traffic in a cosmic economy of blessings and curses is to revert to an ancient prejudice. Indeed, even though August's disabilities offer ample opportunity for public interpretation, they do not mean anything at all in and of themselves—they have no intrinsic significance. They simply are what they are.

That is not to deny that August, along with my daughter and my wife, is the most amazing and wonderful thing that has ever happened to me, for he has allowed me an additional opportunity to profoundly love another human being. A person such as Peter Singer well may conclude, reasonably, that I have become overpowered by parental sentiment. So be it. I can live with that. There are limits to reason.

Take a look at the arguments of disability advocate and lawyer Harriett McBryde Johnson in her essay "Unspeakable Conversations" (http://www.nytimes.com/2003/02/16/magazine/16DISABLED. html), an account of what it's like to be a gifted intellectual alive in a disabled body. Or visit the Web site of the advocacy group that supported McBryde, "Not Dead Yet" (http://www.notdeadyet.org/ Web site/). Have the readings changed your feelings about different kinds of bodies? Do you think that we overestimate the value of bodily autonomy, as McBryde suggests?

Pick a body part from among the following (hand, arm, leg, foot, neck, chest, knee) or a sense (sight, hearing, touch, smell, taste) and write down every time you use it and HOW you use it over a twenty-four-hour period. How you would complete those tasks if you no longer had the use of that organ or sense? What sort of help might you need from other persons? What kinds of tools or equipment? What kinds of technologies might you use?

With your classmates, write and disseminate a call for students on your campus to identify access issues for students and visitors with disabilities. Interview and, with your group, make a list of problem areas on campus, or areas where the environment is accessible to all (you may include online learning environments, too).

Artist Lamar Dodd obtained special permission to observe and sketch the cardiac surgeons who were operating on his wife Mary, who became ill in 1978. Through the 1980s Dodd developed a set of sixty vivid and colorful oil paintings called "The Heart series" that currently hang in the offices of the doctors who saved the life of his wife, but the hasty impression reproduced here reflects Dodd's real-time response to the rapid-fire action before his eyes.

SURGEONS III

BY LAMAR DODD

With a group of your classmates, try to figure out what is going on in Dodd's sketch. What objects or persons can you identify? Do you see a pair of hands, and can you find medical instruments? Why is the image difficult to understand? What emotion or mood does the sketch convey?

This assignment will help you to prepare for Major Assigment #3: Analyze an Advertisement for Prescription Medication. Many artists have explored health, illness, and the human body. Google's Art Project (http://www.googleartproject.com) allows students to explore works of art all over the world virtually through a web browser. Search for the term "heart" and select one of the images that appears. How is this image different from Dodd's? What is the function or role of the heart in Dodd's picture and in the one you've chosen? What is the relationship of the artist to the subject in each picture? What do you think is the purpose of each image?

Many surgeries must be concluded quickly, to protect the patient from losing too much blood and the heart from weakening under anesthesia. What signs of haste or urgency do you see in Dodd's sketch of his wife's heart operation? After obtaining permission where necessary, take a black marker or a pen with black ink, a clean sheet of drawing paper, a clipboard or lap desk, and a timer (the one on your cell phone will be fine!) with you to any place or event where people move or work quickly—a children's playground, a sporting event, a factory floor—and give yourself ten minutes to make a sketch of what is going on. Don't worry if you feel you cannot draw; do your best to indicate what you think is most important about what you see in front of you. After the timer goes off, stop sketching and look at your work. Do you remember what you were trying to capture?

Mindpop (http://www.mindpop.net) is an online "stroke comic book" by Nina Mitchell, a self-described "quirky young woman" who suffered a stroke in her mid-twenties and now blogs about her life, usually with a sentence or two in words and a well-chosen image. Many of Mitchell's examples dramatize the frustrations of living life with only one working arm. Write a couple of sentences describing an annoying or frustrating physical impediment that you encountered this week (a fender-bender, a stubbed toe, a cut finger, etc.). Find (or draw, or make digitally) an image that will enhance your sentences in a humorous, ironic, moving, or poignant way.

Elizabeth A. Almasi qualified at the Perelman School of Medicine in Philadelphia in 2011; Randall is Professor of Medicine at the Stanford Prevention Center, Stanford University School of Medicine; Richard Kravitz is co-vice chair of Internal Medicine at the University of California, David, and Peter R. Mansfield's Web site describes him as "the founder and is the Director of Healthy Skepticism Inc, an international organization aiming to improve health by reducing harm from misleading drug promotion: www.healthyskepticism.org."

WHAT ARE THE PUBLIC HEALTH EFFECTS OF DIRECT-TO-CONSUMER DRUG ADVERTISING?

By Elizabeth A. Almasi, Randall S. Stafford, Richard L. Kravitz, Peter R. Mansfield

Background to the debate: Only two industrialized countries, the United States and New Zealand, allow direct-to-consumer advertising (DTCA) of prescription medicines, although New Zealand is planning a ban. The challenge for these governments is ensuring that DTCA is more beneficial than harmful. Proponents of DTCA argue that it helps to inform the public about available treatments and stimulates appropriate use of drugs for high-priority illnesses (such as statin use in people with ischemic heart disease). Critics argue that the information in the adverts is often biased and misleading, and that DTCA raises prescribing costs without net evidence of health benefits.

ELIZABETH ALMASI AND RANDALL STAFFORD'S VIEWPOINT: PHARMACEUTICAL ADVERTISING MIGHT PRODUCE A VALUABLE PLACEBO EFFECT

The impact of DTCA on patient expectations has important implications for evaluating its role in the health-care system. While these expectations can lead to inappropriate and excessive prescribing, they also may induce a placebo effect that might increase the clinical effectiveness of the advertised products. This seldom-discussed effect of DTCA should be taken into account in discussion of policy approaches to this form of marketing.

The placebo effect can be triggered by an array of stimuli, such as pills, doctors, and devices. The effect is profound: about one-third of patients report relief from postoperative pain, cough, headache, depression, and other conditions when given a placebo. Surprisingly, the two models used to explain the placebo phenomenon are identical to the theories that lie behind the methodologies of consumer advertising.

The first model, classical conditioning, is based on Pavlovian conditioning theory. According to this theory, prior experiences with effective medical treatments "condition" the patient to associate pills, syringes, and authoritative medical opinions with imminent pain relief, eliciting a response similar to the active agents. Similarly, DTCA offers conditioned stimuli to associate each product with positive emotions: the joy of playing in beautiful fields for allergy sufferers (loratadine commercial) or the relief conveyed by elderly patients with arthritis participating in their favorite activities (rofecoxib commercial). Patients who take the advertised medication may be conditioned to elicit the positive feelings that were portrayed in the advertisement, which could enhance the medication's clinical effect.

The second theory to explain the placebo effect focuses on the expectancies formed from the information provided. According to the expectancy-value theory, individuals are receptive to signals confirming their initial expectancies after administration of a placebo treatment. The ability for information alone to produce a conditioned response explains why patients taking a placebo often report the same side effects as patients taking the active medication: the reported or observed experience of others can elicit a placebo effect by creating the expectancy of an effect. Likewise, many pharmaceutical advertisements teach viewers what to expect from the medication to capitalize on this conditioned response. Commercials for conditions such as high cholesterol and osteoporosis first assert that widely prevalent minor symptoms or unassessed biological parameters can have grave implications. Then, the promoted drug is introduced as the solution, and the relief associated with the drug is depicted in the advertisement, teaching the viewer what to expect.

These advertising strategies not only create consumer demand for the advertised products, but may also create the emotionally conditioned responses and expectancies instrumental to enhancing a placebo effect that occurs when the medication is taken. This conditioned response may increase the effectiveness of medications beyond that which is expected from their purely biological mechanisms.

Through the placebo effect, patients' positive expectations from DTCA may potentially reduce the amount of treatment requested or required. An enhanced placebo response also could improve patient adherence and outcomes. To the extent that advertisements "reward" patients for the same actions that physicians recommend, patients may be more likely to follow treatment instructions. In addition, physicians may facilitate a placebo response to the medications they prescribe by successfully borrowing strategies from DTCA. In fact, improved communication might result from personalizing the need for treatment, placing treatment benefits in perspective relative to drug side effects, and providing testimonial examples of past treatment successes. In addition, where a rationale for a class effect exists, physicians may enhance the effect of generic drugs by pointing out their inherent similarities to highly advertised, brand name medications.

Patients' heightened expectations also may motivate them to collaborate with their physicians, and thereby increase the quality of their care. Berger and colleagues suggest that patient expectation and physician perception of patient expectation for prescription medication correlate with the issuance of a prescription. Kravitz et al. confirmed this hypothesis. Assuming that the request for a prescription signals a patient's expectation, it is not surprising that in their study, standardized patients suffering from major depressive disorder who requested an antidepressant were much more likely to receive a prescription for antidepressants than patients who made no such request.

Yet these heightened expectations have been shown to increase treatment for all conditions, including those that may be marginally beneficial or even inappropriate. Kravitz et al. reported that standardized patients with adjustment disorder (a condition that is usually treated without medication) who made a request for a brand name antidepressant were five times more likely to receive a prescription for antidepressants, which, in this context, is "at the margin of clinical appropriateness." Heightened expectations may lead to inappropriate and costly demands for medications when evidence would dictate other medications or nonpharmacological interventions.

Optimal use of DTCA may require stricter guidelines on advertisements or more aggressive enforcement of current guidelines so that patients do not form unreasonable expectations. Diminishing the demand for inappropriate prescriptions would lessen the negative impacts of DTCA. Meanwhile, exposure to DTCA might, nonetheless, continue to improve health practices and outcomes through its ability to facilitate favorable clinical responses. By understanding the expectations that DTCA creates, physicians may limit the problems associated with DTCA, while harnessing this placebo effect to increase the effectiveness of prescribed treatment.

RICHARD KRAVITZ'S VIEWPOINT: REGULATE, DON'T BAN—THE POWER OF DTCA SHOULD BE HARNESSED FOR THE PUBLIC GOOD

The opposing positions on DTCA of prescription drugs are well known. Proponents tend to focus on DTCA's potential to educate consumers and encourage productive interchange between patients and physicians, while critics emphasize liabilities. In the US, reasoned discourse has nearly suffocated in an atmosphere thick with First Amendment objections (the First Amendment protects the right to free speech) served up by lawyers for Big Pharma and, on the opposing side, the occasional anticorporate rant.

A more dispassionate analysis would acknowledge three facts. First, prescription drug costs are rising rapidly—based on a confluence of increased prices, increased use of existing drugs, and introduction of new (more expensive) drugs, many of which are promoted directly to the consumer.

Second, some drugs are clearly overprescribed. (Overprescribing at the level of the individual implies that the benefits of taking the drug do not clearly outweigh the risks.) Overuse has been seen with antibiotics for viral upper respiratory track infections; antihistamines, benzodiazepines, and sedative-hypnotics in the elderly; inhaled beta-adrenergic agonists in children who are not taking "controller medications" for asthma; neuromodulators for chronic pain; and sildenafil and fluoxetine for augmentation of normal sexual and psychological functioning, respectively. The role of DTCA in promoting such overuse is unclear, although there is little question that advertising lowers the clinical threshold for prescribing.

Third, there is substantial underuse of some prescription drugs in the US. On a population basis, underuse of effective therapies may cause more deaths per year than overuse. Examples of underprescribed drugs include beta-blockers following myocardial infarction, angiotensin-converting enzyme inhibitors in congestive heart failure, adjuvant hormonal or chemotherapy following breast cancer surgery, prophylactic antibiotics prior to joint-replacement surgery, and warfarin in patients with atrial fibrillation.

Given that some drugs are underused and others overused, an intervention such as DTCA that increases prescribing could have beneficial effects, deleterious effects, or both. While logically coherent, this conclusion could not until recently claim much empirical support. A recent trial provides strong evidence that DTCA—like the prescription drugs it promotes—has both therapeutic and toxic effects.

The investigators trained actors ("standardized patients," [SPs]) to portray patients with major depression of moderate severity (a serious condition requiring treatment, referral, or close follow-up) or with adjustment disorder (a less serious condition in which supportive counseling and watchful waiting might suffice). SPs were randomly assigned to visit 152 primary-care physicians in three US cities (298 visits in all). In one-third of visits, the actresses (all non-Hispanic, white, middle-aged women) mentioned a TV advertisement and made a brand-specific request for Paxil (paroxetine); in another one-third of visits, they made a general request for "medicine that might help"; and in the rest of the visits they made no request.

There were two main findings. First, among SPs presenting with major depression, SPs making no request had only a 56% chance of receiving high-quality initial care (antidepressant prescription, mental health referral, or close follow-up). In contrast, SPs making a brand-specific or general request for medication were treated to this high standard of care in 90% of visits. That's good news, because it suggests that informed, motivated, and involved patients can dramatically improve the quality of their own care. Second, among SPs presenting with adjustment disorder, the proportion receiving an antidepressant prescription was 55% if a brand-specific request was made, 39% if a general request was made, and 10% if no request was made. That's not so good, because it means that requests associated with consumer drug advertisements could lead to lots of prescriptions at the very margins of clinical appropriateness.

In general, DTCA is most likely to deliver public health benefits when the condition to be treated is serious and when the treatment is safe, effective, and underused. DTCA will tend to deliver net harms when the condition is mild or trivial and when the treatment is potentially dangerous, marginally effective, or overused. DTCA—or a social marketing campaign modeled on it—could be an extremely effective way of encouraging patients with a recent myocardial infarction to take aspirin, beta-blockers, or an HMG-CoA-reductase inhibitor (statin). On the other hand, with health care costs spiraling out of control, it is hard to justify multimillion-dollar advertising campaigns touting drugs for baldness, toenail fungus, and overactive bladder. For obvious reasons, drug companies are not stepping forward with advertisements for the (often generic) medicines that are truly underused.

The question for US policymakers is not whether DTCA should be banned, but how can its benefits be maximized and risks minimized within our free enterprise system. Two policy initiatives hold special promise. A two-year moratorium on DTCA of new drugs, coupled with a requirement for systematic postmarketing surveillance, could avoid another Vioxx tragedy, in which drug marketing got well ahead of the science. In addition, the tax system could be used to create incentives for public–private consortia to produce mass media campaigns aimed at educating patients about common, serious medical conditions, and encouraging them to take evidence-based therapies.

DTCA is neither good nor evil; it is both. A little regulatory ingenuity could harness the enormous power of DTCA or DTCA-like public service announcements to improve the public health.

PETER MANSFIELD'S VIEWPOINT: THERE'S A BETTER WAY THAN DTCA

The collective evidence on DTCA suggests that it may have some benefits, but there is stronger evidence of harms (http://www.healthyskepticism. org/library/topics/dtca.php). Greater benefit could be gained, with less harm, from publicly funded health information and promotion DTCA is limited to drugs that are profitable to advertise: mostly expensive, new drugs for long-term use for common indications. Such advertising increases premature rapid uptake and overuse of new drugs before flaws, including safety problems, have been discovered and communicated to health professionals. Many new drugs are inferior to older treatments, and over two-thirds are no better but are often more expensive. Increased use of new drugs stimulated by DTCA can lead to adverse events directly (for example, cardiovascular events associated with COX-2 selective inhibitors, which were heavily advertised to the US public) or indirectly, by diverting resources from more cost-effective interventions.

DTCA rarely focuses on, and tends to drown out, high-priority public health messages about diet, exercise, addictions, social involvement, equity, pollution, climate change, and appropriate use of older drugs. Older drugs are less profitable to advertise because a share of the sales stimulated goes to generic competition. Consequently, DTCA for any currently advertised drug will become less profitable after expiry of patent protection from competition. When DTCA no longer provides competitive return on investment, it is stopped. Consequently, if there are any benefits from current DTCA (such as stimulating new requests for statins after a myocardial infarction), those benefits will be for a limited time only.

DTCA aims to persuade rather than to inform, and there is evidence that it is effective at persuasion. Content analyses of DTCA have found that the information provided is usually flawed and incomplete. Examples include a study of 320 drug advertisements in popular US magazines that found that the advertisements rarely provided information about success rates of treatment or alternative treatments, and a study of 23 US television advertisements for prescription drugs that found that the majority gave more time to benefits than to risks.

Such advertising can lead some people to falsely believe they are well informed, so it reduces their motivation to search for more reliable information. Finding reliable information is already difficult (like finding a needle in a haystack) and the "noise" of DTCA just makes the haystack larger.

Advertising drugs to the public often works by creating or exacerbating unhappiness or anxiety about symptoms or normal experiences (such as occasional erectile difficulties), and by creating high expectations of benefit from drugs. The combination of heightened unhappiness and high expectations can cause severe distress when a drug is unaffordable or when its effects are disappointing: for example, a qualitative study of men who used sildenafil for erectile dysfunction found that expectations raised by media hyperbole had an adverse effect on the morale of those for whom it was ineffective.

DTCA is often ambiguous and widens the indications beyond those for which the promoted drugs are worthwhile. For example, DTCA may have contributed to increasing unjustified use of antidepressants for young people.

DTCA may also have negative economic, social, and political consequences. For example, by increasing use of expensive drugs and increasing adverse events, DTCA increases taxpayer, insurance, and individual costs, which in turn can harm individual, familial, and national economies. The heavy costs of DTCA contribute to higher drug prices and are a hurdle for market entry of new competition. Revenue from DTCA creates a conflict of interest for media companies, because such advertising can undermine the media's freedom to report critically on the drug industry. DTCA can have a distorting effect on people's perceptions of health and disease, including promoting the medicalization of conditions that are within the spectrum of normality. DTCA sometimes persuades people to interpret distress as signifying individual illness rather than social or political problems to be solved. DTCA pushes a "Brave New World" where if "anything unpleasant should somehow happen, why, there's always [the sedative] soma to give you a holiday from the facts. And there's always soma to calm your anger, to reconcile you to your enemies, to make you patient and long-suffering."

There are two root causes of the problems with DTCA. The first is payment systems that reward drug companies for increasing sales of expensive drugs regardless of the impact on health. These systems should be redesigned. The second root cause is normal human vulnerability to being mislead. Few people have the time and advanced skills in drug evaluation, psychology, logic, economics, and semiotics, etc., required to evaluate drug promotion. Advertising can sneak in under the radar to influence even skeptical people without their awareness. Ideas that would be rejected if given attention get reinforced by repetition. More research is needed to test the hypothesis that it is possible to learn how to gain more benefit than harm when exposed to drug promotion.

Almost all government, health professional, and consumer inquiries into DTCA have concluded that it causes net public harm. It is too difficult to regulate DTCA, so I believe that the logical conclusion from the evidence is that the best option for improving overall health and wealth is to ban all types of DTCA, including "disease awareness" advertising. Drug company Web sites and media releases should be regulated carefully.

The public would benefit from reliable information and health promotion focused on public health priorities. Such information can be provided at no extra cost by copying, improving, and expanding policies and programs that are already successful in many countries. Governments and insurance companies who subsidize drugs currently pay for biased promotion indirectly via high drug prices. Instead, these agencies could fund information, education, and promotional services focused on public health needs. Such investments pay for themselves by reducing health care costs. Universities and nonprofit organizations are well placed to compete for this funding. These organizations are more trustworthy than drug companies because they don't gain from drug sales. Where behavior-change promotion is justified, these organizations could collaborate with advertising agencies. This collaborative approach has already been successful for many health-promotion campaigns—for example, promoting smoking cessation. These improvements would not achieve utopia, but would improve health and increase wealth overall.

To what extent does each author or set of authors answer or critique the assumptions of the others? Which section do you find most convincing? What do you notice about the ordering of the sections of the article? Re-order the article so that each author or set of authors directly answers the arguments or assertions of each other. For example: All three authors consider the effect of direct-to-consumer drug advertisements upon the relationship between doctors and patients. Almasi suggests that direct-to-consumer advertising might benefit patients by encouraging them to collaborate with their physicians and to ask for treatment, but Kravitz retorts that such patient requests sometimes lead to over-treatment for marginal conditions, and Mansfield adds that consumers susceptible to such advertising sometimes begin to consider normal, healthy variation as disordered and seek treatment that is completely unnecessary. After completing the exercise, think again about whose argument you find most convincing. Which organization (sequential or point-counter-point) was more effective?

Look for advertisements for prescription and over-the-counter medications in popular print and digital magazines such as *People*, *Time*, or *Men's Health*. Do you look at them differently after reading the findings of Almasi and her co-authors?

This assignment will help you prepare for Major Assignment #2: Analyzing a Drug Campaign. With a group of classmates, design a print commercial for an over-the-counter medication that you or people you know routinely use. Read the drug information on the insert (or online at the National Institutes of Health Web site: http://www.nlm. nih.gov/medlineplus/druginformation.html) carefully before you craft your advertisement. What will you emphasize? What, if anything, will you downplay?

Some say that the NAMES Project AIDS Memorial Quilt (often shortened simply to "the AIDS Quilt") is the largest community art project in the world. Over 46,000 individual panels, each the size of a gravestone, memorialize those who have died of AIDS since 1978. According to the Web site of the AIDS Memorial Quilt, "to see the entire Quilt, spending only one minute per panel, [would take] over 33 days."

THE NAMES PROJECT AIDS MEMORIAL QUILT

Can you identify the images and words in the panels reproduced above? What patterns appear in these panels? Take five minutes to freewrite about the associations and feelings that the quilt evokes in you.

Visit http://www.aidsquilt.org and read about the NAMES Project. Have you ever participated in a community art project, fabricated a group that made quilts or blankets, or organized a collaborative artistic work or event to memorialize a friend or family member? Why do you think that the founders of the NAMES Project chose a quilt to serve as this particular memorial?

With a group of your classmates, visit the NAMES Project Web site and have each person select a different panel and write, draw, or film a short response to it. Make a "quilt" or collage of your own by putting together your responses for the class.

Journalist Denise Grady has degrees in both Biology and English and has written extensively about health and medicine for Time, Scientific American *and* Reader's Digest *as well as for* The New York Times, *where she has worked since 1998 and where this article appeared in 2011.*

AN IMMUNE SYSTEM TRAINED TO KILL CANCER

BY DENISE GRADY

A year ago, when chemotherapy stopped working against his leukemia, William Ludwig signed up to be the first patient treated in a bold experiment at the University of Pennsylvania. Mr. Ludwig, then 65, a retired corrections officer from Bridgeton, N.J., felt his life draining away and thought he had nothing to lose.

Doctors removed a billion of his T-cells—a type of white blood cell that fights viruses and tumors—and gave them new genes that would program the cells to attack his cancer. Then the altered cells were dripped back into Mr. Ludwig's veins.

At first, nothing happened. But after 10 days, hell broke loose in his hospital room. He began shaking with chills. His temperature shot up. His blood pressure shot down. He became so ill that doctors moved him into intensive care and warned that he might die. His family gathered at the hospital, fearing the worst.

A few weeks later, the fevers were gone. And so was the leukemia.

There was no trace of it anywhere—no leukemic cells in his blood or bone marrow, no more bulging lymph nodes on his CT scan. His doctors calculated that the treatment had killed off two pounds of cancer cells.

A year later, Mr. Ludwig is still in complete remission. Before, there were days when he could barely get out of bed; now, he plays golf and does yard work.

"I have my life back," he said.

Mr. Ludwig's doctors have not claimed that he is cured—it is too soon to tell—nor have they declared victory over leukemia on the basis of this experiment, which involved only three patients. The research, they say, has far to go; the treatment is still experimental, not available outside of studies.

But scientists say the treatment that helped Mr. Ludwig, described recently in *The New England Journal of Medicine and Science Translational Medicine*, may signify a turning point in the long struggle to develop effective gene therapies against cancer. And not just for leukemia patients: other cancers may also be vulnerable to this novel approach—which employs a disabled form of H.I.V.-1, the virus that causes AIDS, to carry cancer-fighting genes into the patients' T-cells. In essence, the team is using gene therapy to accomplish something that researchers have hoped to do for decades: train a person's own immune system to kill cancer cells.

Two other patients have undergone the experimental treatment. One had a partial remission: his disease lessened but did not go away completely. Another had a complete remission. All three had had advanced chronic lymphocytic leukemia and had run out of chemotherapy options. Usually, the only hope for a remission in such cases is a bone-marrow transplant, but these patients were not candidates for it.

Dr. Carl June, who led the research and directs translational medicine in the Abramson Cancer Center at the University of Pennsylvania, said that the results stunned even him and his colleagues, Dr. David L. Porter, Bruce Levine and Michael Kalos. They had hoped to see some benefit but had not dared dream of complete, prolonged remissions. Indeed, when Mr. Ludwig began running fevers, the doctors did not realize at first that it was a sign that his T-cells were engaged in a furious battle with his cancer.

Other experts in the field said the results were a major advance.

"It's great work," said Dr. Walter J. Urba of the Providence Cancer Center and Earle A. Chiles Research Institute in Portland, Ore. He called the patients' recoveries remarkable, exciting and significant. "I feel very positive about this new technology. Conceptually, it's very, very big."

Dr. Urba said he thought the approach would ultimately be used against other types of cancer as well as leukemia and lymphoma. But he cautioned, "For patients today, we're not there yet." And he added the usual scientific caveat: To be considered valid, the results must be repeated in more patients, and by other research teams.

Dr. June called the techniques "a harvest of the information from the molecular biology revolution over the past two decades."

HITTING A GENETIC JACKPOT

To make T-cells search out and destroy cancer, researchers must equip them to do several tasks: recognize the cancer, attack it, multiply, and live on inside the patient. A number of research groups have been trying to do this, but the T-cells they engineered could not accomplish all the tasks. As a result, the cells' ability to fight tumors has generally been temporary.

The University of Pennsylvania team seems to have hit all the targets at once. Inside the patients, the T-cells modified by the researchers multiplied to 1,000 to 10,000 times the number infused, wiped out the cancer and then gradually diminished, leaving a population of "memory" cells that can quickly proliferate again if needed.

The researchers said they were not sure which parts of their strategy made it work—special cell-culturing techniques, the use of H.I.V.-1 to carry new genes into the T-cells, or the particular pieces of DNA that they selected to reprogram the T-cells.

The concept of doctoring T-cells genetically was first developed in the 1980s by Dr. Zelig Eshhar at the Weizmann Institute of Science in Rehovot, Israel. It involves adding gene sequences from different sources to enable the T-cells to produce what researchers call chimeric antigen receptors, or CARs—protein complexes that transform the cells into, in Dr. June's words, "serial killers."

Mr. Ludwig's disease, chronic lymphocytic leukemia is a cancer of B-cells, the part of the immune system that normally produces antibodies to fight infection. All B-cells, whether healthy or leukemic, have on their surfaces a protein called CD19. To treat patients with the disease, the researchers hoped to reprogram their T-cells to find CD19 and attack B-cells carrying it.

But which gene sequences should be used to reprogram the T-cells, from which sources? And how do you insert them?

Various research groups have used different methods. Viruses are often used as carriers (or vectors) to insert DNA into other cells because that kind of genetic sabotage is exactly what viruses normally specialize in doing. To modify their patients' T-cells, Dr. June and his colleagues tried a daring approach: they used a disabled form of H.I.V.-1. They are the first ever to use H.I.V.-1 as the vector in gene therapy for cancer patients (the virus has been used in other diseases).

The AIDS virus is a natural for this kind of treatment, Dr. June said, because it evolved to invade T-cells. The idea of putting any form of the AIDS virus into people sounds a bit frightening, he acknowledged, but the virus used by his team was "gutted" and was no longer harmful. Other researchers had altered and disabled the virus by adding DNA from humans, mice and cows, and from a virus that infects woodchucks and another that infects cows. Each bit was chosen for a particular trait, all pieced together into a vector that Dr. June called a "Rube Goldberg-like solution" and "truly a zoo."

"It incorporates the ability of H.I.V. to infect cells but not to reproduce itself," he said.

To administer the treatment, the researchers collected as many of the patients' T-cells as they could by passing their blood through a machine that removed the cells and returned the other blood components back into the patients' veins. The T-cells were exposed to the vector, which transformed them genetically, and then were frozen. Meanwhile, the patients were given chemotherapy to deplete any remaining T-cells, because the native T-cells might impede the growth of the altered ones. Finally, the T-cells were infused back into the patients.

Then, Dr. June said, "The patient becomes a bioreactor," as the T-cells proliferate, pouring out chemicals called cytokines that cause fever, chills, fatigue and other flulike symptoms.

The treatment wiped out all of the patients' B-cells, both healthy ones and leukemic ones, and will continue to do for as long as the new T-cells persist in the body, which could be forever (and ideally should be, to keep the leukemia at bay). The lack of B-cells means that the patients may be left vulnerable to infection, and they will need periodic infusions of a substance called intravenous immune globulin to protect them.

So far, the lack of B-cells has not caused problems for Mr. Ludwig. He receives the infusions every few months. He had been receiving them even before the experimental treatment because the leukemia had already knocked out his healthy B-cells.

One thing that is not clear is why Patient 1 and Patient 3 had complete remissions, and Patient 2 did not. The researchers said that when Patient 2 developed chills and fever, he was treated with steroids at another hospital, and the drugs may have halted the T-cells' activity. But they cannot be sure. It may also be that his disease was too severe.

The researchers wrote an entire scientific article about Patient 3, which was published in *The New England Journal of Medicine*. Like the other patients, he also ran fevers and felt ill, but the reaction took longer to set in, and he also developed kidney and liver trouble—a sign of tumor lysis syndrome, a condition that occurs when large numbers of cancer cells die off and dump their contents, which can clog the kidneys. He was given drugs to prevent kidney damage. He had a complete remission.

What the journal article did not mention was that Patient 3 was almost not treated.

Because of his illness and some production problems, the researchers said, they could not produce anywhere near as many altered T-cells for him as they had for the other two patients—only 14 million ("a mouse dose," Dr. Porter said), versus 1 billion for Mr. Ludwig and 580 million for Patient 2. After debate, they decided to treat him anyway.

Patient 3 declined to be interviewed, but he wrote anonymously about his experience for the University of Pennsylvania Web site. When he developed chills and a fever, he said, "I was sure the war was on—I was sure C.L.L. cells were dying."

He wrote that he was a scientist, and that when he was young had dreamed of someday making a discovery that would benefit mankind. But, he concluded, "I never imagined I would be part of the experiment."

When he told Patient 3 that he was remission, Dr. Porter said, they both had tears in their eyes.

NOT WITHOUT DANGER TO PATIENTS

While promising, the new techniques developed by the University of Pennsylvania researchers are not without danger to patients. Engineered T-cells have attacked healthy tissue in patients at other centers. Such a reaction killed a 39-year-old woman with advanced colon cancer in a study at the National Cancer Institute, researchers there reported last year in the journal *Molecular Therapy*.

She developed severe breathing trouble 15 minutes after receiving the T-cells, had to be put on a ventilator and died a few days later. Apparently, a protein target on the cancer cells was also present in her lungs, and the T-cells homed in on it.

Researchers at Memorial Sloan Kettering Cancer in New York also reported a death last year in a T-cell trial for leukemia (also published in Molecular Therapy). An autopsy found that the patient had apparently died from sepsis, not from the T-cells, but because he died just four days after the infusion, the researchers said they considered the treatment a possible factor.

Dr. June said his team hopes to use T-cells against solid tumors, including some that are very hard to treat, like mesothelioma and ovarian and pancreatic cancer. But possible adverse reactions are a real concern, he said, noting that one of the protein targets on the tumor cells is also found on membranes that line the chest and abdomen. T-cell attacks could cause serious inflammation in those membranes and mimic lupus, a serious autoimmune disease.

Even if the T-cells do not hit innocent targets, there are still risks. Proteins they release could cause a "cytokine storm"— high fevers, swelling, inflammation and dangerously low blood pressure—which can be fatal. Or, if the treatment rapidly kills billions of cancer cells, the debris can damage the kidney and cause other problems.

Even if the new T-cell treatment proves to work, the drug industry will be needed to mass produce it. But Dr. June said the research is being done only at universities, not at drug companies. For the drug industry to take interest, he said, there will have to be overwhelming proof that the treatment is far better than existing ones.

"Then I think they'll jump into it," he said. "My challenge now is to do this in a larger set of patients with randomization, and to show that we have the same effects."

Mr. Ludwig said that when entered the trial, he had no options left. Indeed, Dr. June said that Mr. Ludwig was "almost dead" from the leukemia, and the effort to treat him was a "Hail Mary."

Mr. Ludwig said: "I don't recall anybody saying there was going to be a remission. I don't think they were dreaming to that extent."

The trial was a Phase 1 study, meaning that its main goal was to find out whether the treatment was safe, and at what dose. Of course, doctors and patients always hope that there will be some benefit, but that was not an official endpoint.

Mr. Ludwig thought that if the trial could buy him six months or a year, it would be worth the gamble. But even if the study did not help him, he felt it would still be worthwhile if he could help the study.

When the fevers hit, he had no idea that might be a good sign. Instead, he assumed the treatment was not working. But a few weeks later, he said that his oncologist, Dr. Alison Loren, told him, "We can't find any cancer in your bone marrow."

Remembering the moment, Mr. Ludwig paused and said, "I got goose bumps just telling you those words."

"I feel wonderful," Mr. Ludwig said during a recent interview. "I walked 18 holes on the golf course this morning."

Before the study, he was weak, suffered repeated bouts of pneumonia and was wasting away. Now, he is full of energy. He has gained 40 pounds. He and his wife bought an R.V., in which they travel with their grandson and nephew. "I feel normal, like I did 10 years before I was diagnosed," Mr. Ludwig said. "This clinical trial saved my life."

Dr. Loren said in an interview, "I hate to say it in that dramatic way, but I do think it saved his life."

Mr. Ludwig said that Dr. Loren told him and his wife something he considered profound. "She said, 'We don't know how long it's going to last. Enjoy every day,' " Mr. Ludwig recalled.

"That's what we've done ever since."

This assignment will help you with Major Assignment #3: Explaining a Medical or Healthful Intervention. Does Grady do a good job of explaining in simple terms how researchers have helped the body to use its own immune system to cure cancer? How does she frame the story so that the technical details are easier to understand? Could you explain the process and procedures in your own words to a peer? To a school-age child? To a pre-schooler?

Grady's article discusses a miraculous cure delivered to the patient's cells by a defanged version of a deadly disease. In this case, scientists changed the gene for therapy, but there already exist in nature genes for life-threatening or painful disorders that also contain the potential to treat or protect against sickness. For example, inheriting two copies of a particular allele causes sickle-cell anemia, but a single copy of the gene confers protection against malaria. Watch the short video and read the resources about the beneficial mutation of sickle-cell at http://www.pbs.org/wgbh/evolution/library/01/2/l_012_02.html, and read about other examples of alleles that both cause disease and protect against illness here: http://www.pbs.org/wgbh/evolution/educators/course/session7/explain_b_pop1.html. Do you think that scientists may discover still more disease-causing alleles that, when inherited singly, can confer protection against other illnesses?

Write a short story in which a harmful inherited disorder turns out to confer a health benefit upon the sufferer under certain circumstances. If you like reading speculative fiction, take a look at Octavia Butler's dystopian space-opera sequence *Xenogenesis* to give you some ideas.

Indie-rock band The Fray's hit song from 2004, "How to Save a Life," from the album of the same name, has been used on several television shows (including the medical comedy Scrubs) and inspired the "Save a Life Campaign" to educate helpers, parents, and peers about teen suicide. The song came out of founder Isaac Slade's experience mentoring a suicidal young musician.

HOW TO SAVE A LIFE

BY THE FRAY

Step one you say we need to talk
He walks you say sit down it's just a talk
He smiles politely back at you
You stare politely right on through
Some sort of window to your right
As he goes left and you stay right
Between the lines of fear and blame
And you begin to wonder why you came

Where did I go wrong, I lost a friend
Somewhere along in the bitterness
And I would have stayed up with you all night
Had I known how to save a life

Let him know that you know best
Cause after all you do know best
Try to slip past his defense
Without granting innocence
Lay down a list of what is wrong
The things you've told him all along
And pray to God he hears you

Where did I go wrong, I lost a friend
Somewhere along in the bitterness
And I would have stayed up with you all night
Had I known how to save a life

As he begins to raise his voice
You lower yours and grant him one last choice
Drive until you lose the road
Or break with the ones you've followed
He will do one of two things
He will admit to everything
Or he'll say he's just not the same
And you'll begin to wonder why you came

Where did I go wrong, I lost a friend
Somewhere along in the bitterness
And I would have stayed up with you all night
Had I known how to save a life

Explore

Listen to a recording of The Fray performing "How to Save a Life" and then to two other performances of songs about health, illness, and wellness, such as Peggy Lee's "Fever" (1958), The Beatles' "When I'm 64" (1967), The Ramones' "I Wanna Be Sedated" (1979), The Smiths' "Still Ill" (1984), Blink-182's "Adam's Song" (1999), Rascal Flatts' "Skin" (2004), or Lady Gaga's "Born This Way" (2011). How do these songs define wellness, health, or disability? How do they recount traumatic medical events, chronic health concerns, or joyful well-being?

Collaborate

This assignment will help you prepare for Major Assignment #3: Explaining a Medical or Healthful Intervention. Visit the Save A Life Campaign Web site (http://www.savealifecampaign.com/). With a group of your classmates, discuss situations in which friends might have to intervene to save the health or life of a peer (such as preventing a friend from driving while intoxicated or from going home with a stranger). Can you write a how-to guide that outlines steps to help a friend in one of these situations? Be as specific as you can about your town or your campus.

Compose

The song "How to Save a Life" has inspired many video responses and school projects on YouTube and Vimeo. Watch the Fray's original video (http://www.vevo.com/watch/the-fray/how-to-save-a-life/USSM20601105) and look at one or two of the video responses (for example, here's a response made using clips from the *Twilight* films, which are based on the series by Stephenie Meyer: http://www.youtube.com/watch?v=1fq6dhmGkMs). Write a storyboard or a script for your own video to go with the song.

Dr. Drew Pinsky, well known as the radio host of the call-in sex advice show Loveline *and the television host of* Celebrity Rehab, *works at the Las Encinas Hospital in Pasadena, California as the Service Director of the Chemical Dependency Program and Residential Treatment Center. His book* Cracked, *from which we have selected this excerpt, came out in 2003.*

excerpt from

CRACKED: PUTTING BROKEN LIVES BACK TOGETHER AGAIN: A DOCTOR'S STORY

BY DREW PINSKY, M.D. WITH TODD GOLD

It's afternoon, and I'm in the conference room with a TV crew, taping a discussion I'm having with "Science Guy" Bill Nye about addiction. There's a loud commotion somewhere outside the hospital entrance, and we wait a long time for things to calm down. It sounds like a patient problem, though, so I excuse myself to go out and lend a hand.

Several people from the front-end admitting staff are out there, trying to calm down a woman I immediately recognize as a former patient named Rebecca. She is very thin, blonde, and flushed with anger. She's clearly on something, and she's screaming about being ripped off by the hospital.

"I want my money," she says.

I see several patients glance out their windows.

"What money?" I ask, closing the distance between us.

"The money I left in the hospital safe."

Rebecca's the poster girl for the notion that bad things happen to good people. At twenty-eight, she's attractive and smart as hell. She began to drink heavily while studying to be a dietician. After a year or two working in a hospital, she was struggling to keep it together. She soon went from alcohol to coke, and then into rehab at least twice. Though Rebecca would do the first of AA's twelve steps, admitting she was powerless and that her life had become unmanageable, she wouldn't capitulate to the process, and then she would come back for treatment.

Most recently she had spent a month at the unit, then six weeks at Sober Living, a halfway home where the structure from rehab is continued and reinforced in a less intensive setting. While in Sober Living, she continued to attend our day programs. She had followed instructions so well there that I thought she'd finally gotten it. In the midst of recovery, though, she was diagnosed with breast cancer. The blow sent her reeling back to the bottle, and then to the hospital.

I was crushed to see her back in the unit. Not by the fact that she'd relapsed: Her addiction was something we could deal with. The fear that had gripped her—that was something else.

Rebecca detoxed quickly, returned to Sober Living, and seemed buoyed by my repeated assurances that women her age with breast cancer did very well with the most aggressive treatment possible. The odds were in her favor. That was three weeks earlier.

Now Rebecca and I are standing in the sun on a warm afternoon. She appears to have lost at least twenty pounds since I last saw her. Her skin is chafed and sunburned. She's filthy.

"Hey, it's me here," I say. "We can talk."

I have trouble getting her to track and stay with me, but she calms down.

I try a different approach. "How's the cancer treatment going?" I say, knowing this is the heart of her relapse.

She looks up at me. Right in my eyes.

"Two of my lymph nodes tested positive," she says.

"Which we'd discussed as a possibility. And so?"

"My doctors recommended the most aggressive treatment, chemo and radiation."

"Again, we already knew this."

She adds a new wrinkle. Someday she wants to have children, and she's worried that the radiation and tamoxifen will make her infertile. Should she harvest her eggs, she asks, and save them? Or not? Should she just have the treatment?

These are good questions, and heavy issues for anyone. Still, I don't sense that we've touched on the real issue, the one that set her off.

"What happened right before you started using again?" I ask.

I'm quiet, willing to wait. I try never to let myself get in the way of my patients.

"I was getting an MRI, at least I was supposed to, but they couldn't get the IV hooked up," says Rebecca. What followed was a gut-wrenching debacle: When the X-ray techs were unable to find a vein, they cancelled her MRI and delayed her cancer treatment, which freaked her out and caused her to start drinking again. With that first drink she picked up where her disease had left off and got worse, ending up on the street.

"I can feel the cancer in me," she says, breaking down into tears. "I—I don't want to die. I'm scared."

"I understand," I say, taking some tissues off the counter and handing them to her. "It's a scary thing. But you aren't dying. You're trying to get treatment. Let's focus on that. You have to get through this."

Rebecca loses focus and grows agitated again. "I can't. I mean, I don't know how anymore."

I feel her frustration, fear, and the abyss of powerlessness, the deep, dark dungeon of pain that is at the core of so many addicts' use.

"You can. And for starters, you have to get back to Sober Living."

"I don't have any money," she cries.

Suddenly, Rebecca turns away and heads for the parking lot. She drives a black VW Jetta with a dent on the passenger door. The driver's seat is occupied by a friend of hers, who tells me that he's risking a lot to help Rebecca. He looks very frightened and overwhelmed. He's a former coke addict on probation, he says; he could go back to jail for being around a person using drugs or alcohol.

"But I didn't want to leave her," he says. "She's in a really bad place."

"Yeah," I agree.

I didn't anticipate someone else in the picture, but he could be an asset. At this point, the situation could go either way. As I explain to them, Rebecca could continue losing control until her deepest fears turn prophetic, or else she can get help. She needs to get back to Sober Living, where she had been doing well.

"Rebecca, will you go if your friend takes you there?" I ask.

She shrugs her shoulders and looks at the ground.

I can't imagine what's going on in her head. Her thoughts are so jumbled. This kind of resistance is something I have trouble coming to terms with.

She doesn't know where to turn. She needs someone else to provide the structure.

I look at her friend. "Will you take her there now, and promise me that you'll see her get checked in and situated?"

He nods.

I open the passenger door and help Rebecca into the car.

"This is going to be okay," I say. "You're going to be fine."

Then they drive off.

A few hours later Rebecca is back, defeated and desperate. She had been readmitted to the hospital after being turned away from Sober Living. When I ask why, she says they wanted her to detox before they let her back in. She stands in silence outside the nursing station, helpless, crying, waiting for me to tell her what to do. I don't always know what that should be. But then something happens.

Alexi turns the corner and talks to Rebecca.

"Just put her in a bed and we'll let her detox," says Alexi. "Then we'll send her back to Sober Living."

"But I don't have any money," says Rebecca.

"I'll figure something out," I say.

"Thank you," she says.

Rebecca stays for the next three days. By then her brain starts working again, and she is able to return to Sober Living. She requires hardly any withdrawal medication. Simply being in the hospital's safe environment enables her to reconstitute. She can't remember the scene she had outside the hospital. Before she leaves, we have a nice talk and agree that cancer sucks.

"But you deal with it head-on and, given the facts, you have a good chance of going into remission."

"I really have to get my shit together this time." She chuckles. "I would say the same thing to my patients at work. 'You have to get your shit together and decrease the animal fats and sodium.'"

"Then you know how hard it is," I say. "You also know it can be done."

"Yeah. Sometimes."

At 6:30 P.M., I'm standing in front of a blackboard, watching a lecture hall fill up. About seventy-five patients, former patients, and their families, partners, and friends—some with several days of sobriety, others with many years—are seated in rows of metal folding chairs in a small bungalow a short stroll from the unit. They represent all types, from businessmen to bikers, homemakers to high school students. They have come to listen to my weekly medical lecture, an in-depth discussion about their disease and its effect on their biology.

The hourlong presentation is aimed at giving them more insight into their disease. Few of them really understand addiction. They don't know the roots of its biology. They don't know why addiction is a disease. If asked why they use, they offer some variation of "I'm fucked up." If asked why they can't stop using, they reply, "I'm fucked up." They cannot see themselves as anything but victims. I believe information is power. The more people understand, the less inclined they will be to blame themselves.

I start by asking, "Who can tell me the difference between abuse and addiction?" That begins a lively discussion. Eventually we conclude that abuse is "the use of any potentially harmful substance with no therapeutic value that affects the brain," and addiction is "the continued use of a substance in spite of consequences." They should give themselves a pat on the back, I tell them: It took the world's brightest scientists decades to figure that one out. We did it in a few minutes.

"Now let me ask a harder question," I say. "Can anyone define *disease*? Before you can say you suffer from a disease, you should know what one is."

This sparks another lively discussion. Though it reveals how little average people know about biology, it is also a tough question. Until recently, experts didn't understand much more than the layman about the secret relationship between drugs, the brain, biology, and disease. Think about it: For decades, drug abusers and alcoholics were thought of as people with low self-control. Even scientists and doctors thought they could control their problems by exercising more willpower. How many addicts were told to change their friends, move neighborhoods, or take a different way home so they wouldn't pass the liquor store?

It got worse. For years, addicts were thought to be morally deficient people who could be saved if they would simply acknowledge and change their sinful ways. Well, in reality, no matter what they acknowledge, addicts can't just stop. That is addiction—the inability to stop, no matter what. Addicts know every consequence of their addiction: lost jobs, screwed-up relationships, squandered money, betrayed relatives, and so on. But they can't help their behavior.

Eventually, though, studies began to show that addicts suffered from a disease, rather than a lack of self-control. And clinicians working with addicts and alcoholics began to recognize the difficulty addicts had in quitting. After former First Lady Betty Ford went public with her drinking problem in the late 1970s, there was wider familiarity, understanding, and even sympathy for people who checked into the Betty Ford Center, Hazelden, Cedar Hills, and other rehab facilities seeking treatment for alcoholism and drug addiction.

But misperceptions lingered. With the growth in the number of treatment facilities, many came to believe these problems could be cleared up in a mere twenty-eight days. But further study has shown the disease to be much more complex. By the early 1990s, new research allowed addiction to be defined more specifically as a biological disorder with a genetic basis, plus progressive use in the face of adverse consequences, and denial of a problem. More recent findings have focused on the relationship between addiction and the drives in the deepest brain structures that are outside of conscious volitional control.

As I talk about this, though, I can see some eyes in the audience start to glaze over. All that scientific jargon—this is starting to sound like school. So I change tack.

"I'm really talking about three things," I say. "Why you use drugs. Why you get addicted. And how you get better. Let's start with why you use. Any guesses?"

"It feels good," a young Latino teenager in front says.

"It lets me escape," an alcoholic woman with a few years' sobriety says from the middle of the room.

"Because if I'd done what I really wanted to do, I'd be in jail for killing my father," a middle-aged man adds. He gets a knowing laugh.

I allow that all those answers are correct. "A healthy person, whether he realizes it or not, populates his emotional world with soothing or reassuring images that can be called upon in times of distress, need, or aloneness. But the individual who has suffered trauma during his formative years retreats from the world as a result of that abuse." I pause. "Look around the room. Think of the people in treatment with you and those in your AA groups. What do you all have in common?"

"Bic lighters," someone jokes.

"Fucked-up lives," someone else says.

"Be more specific," I say.

"Fucked-up parents," a college-age girl calls out.

"We're just fucked up," a guy says.

"You want to know the common denominator among my patients?" I say, turning serious. "They all had traumatic experiences in early life that caused them to feel helpless, powerless, and in grave danger." I see some people nodding. "This feeling of helplessness creates an inability to process feelings and an aversion to exploring other minds. There's no trust. If you can't trust, you can't connect with anyone. Without the capacity to activate the part of the brain that allows for connection and exploration of other people, an individual loses the main mechanism for discovering who we are and the ability to regulate emotions.

"Think about it," I continue. "For all of us, other people function as self-regulating agents. We learn to identify ourselves when we recognize ourselves in others. We constantly think, 'Oh, that's exactly how I feel.' Or you say, 'I was thinking that exact same thing.' Our experiences of ourselves become internalized as a result of this sort of interaction. We figure out who we are.

"But my patients—many of you—automatically take the emotional posture that the abuse you fell victim to was your fault. Why? Because at least then you avoid feeling the threat of the contents of the mind of your abuser. You don't ask why Daddy hits you or Mommy's passed out on the living room floor. If it's your fault, you're more in control.

"You're sacrificing yourself in order to maintain the illusion of control in a situation that otherwise you'd experience as irrational and unpredictable. Of course, if you're at fault, you're also feeling shame. In addition, your brain kicks into an automatic biological response that becomes a permanent mechanism for dealing with interpersonal stress. This is the action your brain takes to escape these situations from which there's no escape, something called dissociation."

A gray-haired man in mechanic's overalls raises his hand. I have treated him and his son.

"So what are you saying that I'm feeling?" he asks.

"What did I say all my patients have in common?"

"Helplessness," he says.

"What do you feel when you're helpless?" I ask.

"Fear," he says.

"Right. The initial response to threat is fear. How does this happen? Well, chemicals flood into the brain as the flight-or-fight response is initiated. When escape seems hopeless, your brain switches into shut-down mode, releasing a flood of endorphins that provide a soothing numbness as you wait for the inevitable to occur.

"The experience that predominates this reaction is what?"

I call on a young guy seated on the side.

"I don't even get what you're saying," he says. "But I'm guessing that it's the sense that you're somewhere else, gone, shut down."

"Exactly," I say. "Dissociation. You separate and isolate yourself from the world, from feelings, from others. While such a reaction may protect you from the horrifying experience—whatever that turns out to be—the price is a long-term difficulty in integrating emotional experiences. Think back to whatever age you suffered trauma. That's when you shut down. That's when you decided you were to blame. That's when you stopped developing and growing in the part of the brain that regulates emotions. That's when you stopped connecting with others."

"You know what picture I'm getting?" a man in front says. "I see one of those Japanese soldiers coming out of the jungle after hiding for thirty years because he didn't know the war had ended. You don't know anything that's going on. You don't know who to trust or which side you're on. Your instinct would be to turn around and run back into the jungle, where it was safe."

"Kind of," I say. "But let me go on. So what happens? The personality that accompanies you as you mature physically tends to have a hard time in relationships. In fact, the original victimization is often recreated over and over again. It's the same problem repeated, and more problems ensue. You can't trust someone with your tender needs in a genuine relationship. Why? It's too dangerous. It's too likely to expose you to trauma again.

"So your ability to develop brain mechanisms to regulate emotions is impaired, since we tend to build these through intimate connections with others. It's a great big mess that causes you to enter your young life looking for solutions to those feelings of being, as most of you say, fucked up. You aren't able to find any peace until you find drugs or alcohol. Then, suddenly, for the first time, everything seems all right."

I see heads nod.

"Are you with me still?"

I get a chorus of yesses.

"Good. We just talked about the consequences of trauma, which basically set the stage for the addictive process. Let's go to the next point: Why are you addicted? The simple answer is that some people are configured biologically in such a way to respond very positively to substances. That's what gets you using. But what makes you an addict is primarily a change in a tiny region of the brain called the nucleus accumbens.

"This region of your brain has started to mistake the chemical message of survival with the message delivered by drugs. The drive to use becomes confused with the drive to survive. This drive overwhelms the centers of the brain where cognitive reasoning and will reside. This shouldn't be confused with the feel-good part of addiction. These are powerful drives that begin emanating from deep nonverbal drive centers of the brain and demand gratification with the same life-or-death intensity as taking a breath. This is what keeps you using even when it doesn't feel good or work for you anymore.

"Interestingly, a certain percentage of people feel shitty when they're exposed to endorphinlike substances."

"Then they aren't real addicts," a black woman who's been in and out of treatment several times says.

"That's partly true," I say. "I had a patient come in with uncontrollable sobbing from, of all drugs, Vicodin."

"Oh, please," she says, waving me off.

"You're like my addict patients," I say.

"No, I *am* one of your addict patients," she laughs.

"My addict patients feel incredible when they're exposed to opiates or any other chemical that tickles the brain's endogenous morphine system, like alcohol, cocaine, sometimes pot—"

"Heroin," someone chimes.

"Yes. In fact, all drugs of addiction have in common that they stimulate the endorphin system. That's the feel-good part of drugs. So these people configured to respond positively to substance feel great when they're using. So great they keep using to regulate their emotional lives. As time goes by, all drugs of addiction cause depletion of brain chemicals."

"What?" one of my more vocal participants asks.

"The endorphin system alters itself in response to months or years of saturation, and so when the drugs are removed the brain is no longer able to screen out discomfort or pain. This of course happens at a time when the patient is trying to come to terms with the pain of acknowledging the consequences of the disease—destroyed relationships, legal problems, health issues, and so on. Not only is the endorphin system altered; the mood center, serotonin, is also depleted, as is the anxiety-regulating GABA system and the stress chemical cortisol. All are profoundly abnormal from drug use, leaving the patient in an impaired and terribly unpleasant brain state."

"Welcome to my world," a guy yells out.

He gets a big laugh.

"Remember, you've relied on drugs to deal with unpleasant or overwhelming emotions often since adolescence. Those same emotional conditions that started you using have remained unchanged. Not only that, the drugs have blocked you from tackling the usual milestones of development. There's even some evidence that certain of these drugs actually impair the brain's growth. And, finally, many of these drugs of addiction damage the brain, leaving biological impairments that affect mood, anxiety regulation, and memory.

"So you enter sobriety with this incredible set of biological and often psychological and developmental circumstances stacked against you. Throw in the misery of withdrawal, the social shame and stigma associated with the disease, the consequences of your behavior, and on top of everything the fact that you really love to do drugs—well, it's no wonder people relapse."

"Amen," the black woman says, to a mix of laughs and clapping.

"But here's the fascinating—or depressing—part," I continue. "This is not the disease itself. What I've described are merely factors that come to bear on the disease. The disease is a disorder of the drive centers of the brain— specifically the so-called mesolimbic reward center, as I've explained, in the nucleus accumbens. That part of the brain is deep in the reptilian core. It doesn't have language or logic. Just as with lower life forms, it exists merely to increase the drive that activates behavior fostering survival. It's the survival center, and it's gone awry.

"I'll give you an example. Every cocaine addict knows that he or she will never get the same high they got from their first hit off the pipe. In fact, they feel shitter and shittier with each hit, yet they continue to use until they're floridly psychotic, sitting in a dark room by themselves, peeking out through the curtains at the black helicopters they imagine are hovering overhead."

"It was army men for me," a guy in a blue suit says.

"I heard paramilitary spacemen hiding in the bushes," a car mechanic seated nearby adds.

"The point is, you continue to use because the drive centers command you to use. Your brain's rational understanding is overwhelmed. Though you know perfectly well that you won't get high and will end up feeling like shit, you can't stop. You can't stop, no matter how hard you try or how badly you want to. That's addiction.

"There's a lot of new science being done in this area, but basically what we have here is a set of very powerful drives being activated beneath conscious control in a region of the brain that can't be influenced by reason, language, or will. We have a terrible time in this country accepting disorders of will. How often do you hear someone explain their behavior by saying, 'Hey, it's a free country.' But as you well know, you're not free from the grips of the biology of this region of the brain and the effect the disease has on it."

I know this is all still pretty technical material, but I can feel a sense of excitement in the room, a tangible buzz as those listening acquire new or additional understanding about why they really are powerless over their addiction. Why does that create such a reaction? Because the first of the twelve steps in Alcoholics Anonymous is admitting that you are powerless over your disease. Now they can really believe it's true, and we can start discussing how you get better.

"Powerlessness," I say, gazing across the room to emphasize that each one of them has this in common. "What kind of feeling does that evoke in you?"

"Pain," a young man in the back of the room says without hesitation.

I nod, smiling. I know the young man well: Patrick, a patient of mine who's recently turned twenty. He's been doing well in recovery. He's even returned to college.

"I just feel pain," he continued.

"Can I use you as an example?" I ask, aware that he has shared in previous groups with many in the room. He says yes, and I encourage him to fill us in on the details. Raised the only child of an alcoholic father and addicted mother, Patrick was on his own from the time he could walk. His life had little structure. He was neglected by his parents and abused by neighbors. He started smoking pot at the age of ten. Two years later he was on to coke. He was thirteen when his father died. His mother floated in and out, either ignorant of or indifferent to his drug use. By sixteen he was using speed. Still, against seemingly insurmountable odds, he managed to get into a city college. He was a major control freak—anything to avoid the instability of his childhood—and yet he couldn't control his drug use.

"It was like I was running all the time," he says. "Even when I was asleep I was still running."

"Running from what?" I ask.

"The pain."

"A specific pain?"

"No, not really. It's more like a feeling of pain that blankets everything. It's just always there. My whole deal has been avoidance through control."

He had articulated something that's key: the fact that the pain that started with the traumas of his childhood was still ongoing in the present. It still felt raw and fresh. It had happened then, it was happening now, and as far as his brain was concerned it was going to keep happening into the future. He was in what some call the "running" phase of post-traumatic stress disorder.

They have no idea how much I relate personally. But ever since I saw the man with the red crosses in his eyes following my mother's miscarriage, I've felt—no, I've known—that bad things are happening to me. Period. Then, now, and always. Like Patrick, I've tamed those feelings by maintaining control, striving for perfection, rescuing people. I even have a job where bad shit happens every day. It's exhausting.

If I'd had the genetic disposition, I would've made a great addict.

"You can see how as a result of those early traumas you have difficulty trusting and opening up to another person," I say. "If you're a kid, why would you trust ever again? But without that capacity to trust, you can't get an accurate read on your own self. You never learn how to regulate your own feelings."

A hand rises from the middle, and a husky man with bushy sideburns and tattooed arms stands up to speak. "How do you learn?" he asks.

"That's the getting-it part of recovery. You have to be willing—willing to follow directions, willing to trust, willing to form connections, willing to explore feelings. That's the essence of recovery, of the twelve steps," I say. "In recovery, you learn how to regulate your emotions without getting high. This is where you learn connection, the connection you didn't learn when it was interrupted by trauma in childhood. The real work gets done when you sit down with a sponsor and trust that that person will be available without shaming or intruding as you express genuine and tender needs. Then, instead of suffering rejection, you experience relief and gradually a new sense of self. It's only through relationships with others that we develop a sense of who we are and the ability to regulate our emotions."

According to Pinsky, why do most persons become addicted to drugs? Do you know people who are addicts or drug users who do not seem to have these underlying issues? Do the users you know have other issues that they are not dealing with emotionally?

The Fix is an online magazine and Web site dedicated to addiction, recovery, and sober living (http://www.thefix.com). Investigate the site and write a short review of the features you found most useful or interesting.

As a class, watch the TV show *Intervention* or another show that deals with drug use or drug trafficking (*Locked Up Abroad*). Discuss the show or film's treatment of drug use and the emotional and social ramifications of addiction.

Journalist David H. Freedman writes about business and science for Time, The Atlantic, The New York Times, *and* Scientific American, *where this clear-eyed article appeared in 2011.*

HOW TO FIX THE OBESITY CRISIS

BY DAVID H. FREEDMAN

Although science has revealed a lot about metabolic processes that influence our weight, the key to success may lie elsewhere.

Obesity is a national health crisis—that much we know. If current trends continue, it will soon surpass smoking in the U.S. as the biggest single factor in early death, reduced quality of life and added health care costs. A third of adults in the U.S. are obese, according to the Centers for Disease Control and Prevention, and another third are overweight, with Americans getting fatter every year. Obesity is responsible for more than 160,000 "excess" deaths a year, according to a study in the *Journal of the American Medical Association.* The average obese person costs society more than $7,000 a year in lost productivity and added medical treatment, say researchers at George Washington University. Lifetime added medical costs alone for a person 70 pounds or more overweight amount to as much as $30,000, depending on race and gender.

All this lends urgency to the question: Why are extra pounds so difficult to shed and keep off? It doesn't seem as though it should be so hard. The basic formula for weight loss is simple and widely known: consume fewer calories than you expend. And yet if it really were easy, obesity would not be the nation's number-one lifestyle-related health concern. For a species that evolved to consume energy-dense foods in an environment where famine was a constant threat, losing weight and staying trimmer in a modern world of plenty fueled by marketing messages and cheap empty calories is, in fact, terrifically difficult. Almost everybody who tries to diet seems to fail in the

IN BRIEF

Modern epidemic: For millennia, not getting enough food was a widespread problem. Nowadays obesity is a global burden that affects one third of Americans. Another third are overweight.

Obesity is complex: Researchers have developed key insights into its metabolic, genetic and neurological causes. But this work has not amounted to a solution to the public health crisis.

Behavior focus: Using techniques that have proved effective in treating autism, stuttering and alcoholism may be the most valuable for either losing weight or preventing weight gain.

Next steps: Behavior studies show that recording calories, exercise and weight; adopting modest goals; and joining a support group increase the chances of success.

long run—a review in 2007 by the American Psychological Association of 31 diet studies found that as many as two thirds of dieters end up two years later weighing *more* than they did before their diet.

Science has trained its big guns on the problem. The National Institutes of Health has been spending nearly $800 million a year on studies to understand the metabolic, genetic and neurological foundations of obesity. In its proposed plan for obesity research funding in 2011, the NIH lists promising research avenues in this order: animal models highlighting protein functions in specific tissues; complex signaling pathways in the brain and between the brain and other organs; identification of obesity-related gene variants; and epigenetic mechanisms regulating metabolism.

This research has provided important insights into the ways proteins interact in our body to extract and distribute energy from food and produce and store fat; how our brains tell us we are hungry; why some of us seem to have been born more likely to be obese than others; and whether exposure to certain foods and toxic substances might modify and mitigate some of these factors. The work has also given pharmaceutical companies numerous potential targets for drug development. What the research has not done, unfortunately, is make a dent in solving the national epidemic.

Maybe someday biology will provide us with a pill that readjusts our metabolism so we burn more calories or resets our built-in cravings so we prefer broccoli to burgers. But until then, the best approach may simply be to build on reliable behavioral-psychology methods developed over 50 years and proved to work in hundreds of studies. These tried-and-true techniques, which are being refined with new research that should make them more effective with a wider range of individuals, are gaining new attention. As the NIH puts it in its proposed strategic plan for obesity research: "Research findings are yielding new and important insights about social and behavioral factors that influence diet, physical activity, and sedentary behavior."

OBESITY EPIDEMIC

A Growing Problem

Increases in overweight and obesity in the U.S., as measured by the body mass index, presage a growing burden of stroke, heart disease, type II diabetes, some types of cancer and other chronic health problems throughout the 21st century.

Sources: CDC/NCHS, National health and nutrition examination survey (BMI changes); National obesity education initiative (BMI chart)

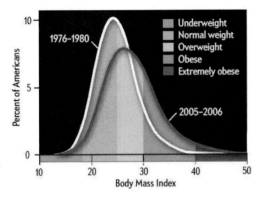

Getting bigger: Just over 34 percent of American adults are obese (orange area under curve)—up from 15 percent in the late 1970s. Thirty-three states have obesity rates over 25 percent (not shown).

Body mass index is a ratio of weight to to the square of height, developed by 19th-century Belgian mathematician and proto-sociologist Adolphe Quetelet. Although BMI does not measure body fat, anyone (except very muscular athletes) with a number over 30 is considered obese.

HOW WE GOT HERE

The desperation of the obese and overweight is reflected in the steady stream of advice pouring daily from sources as disparate as peer-reviewed scientific journals, best-selling books, newspapers and blogs. Our appetite for any diet twist or gimmick that will take the pounds off quickly and for good seems to be as insatiable as our appetite for the rich food that puts the pounds on. We, the public, love to believe in neat fixes, and the media oblige by playing up new scientific findings in headline after headline as if they are solutions.

It doesn't help that the scientific findings on which these headlines are based sometimes appear to conflict. For example, a study in September's *American Journal of Clinical Nutrition* found a link between increased dairy intake and weight loss, although a meta-analysis in the May 2008 *Nutrition Reviews* discovered no such link. A paper in the *Journal of Occupational and Environmental Medicine* in January 2010 postulated a connection between job stress and obesity, but in October a report in the journal *Obesity* concluded there was no such correlation. Part of the problem, too, is that obesity researchers are in some ways akin to the metaphorical blind men groping at different parts of the elephant, their individual study findings addressing only narrow pieces of a complex puzzle.

When the research is taken together, it is clear that the obesity fix cannot be boiled down to eating this or that food type or to taking any other simple action. Many factors contribute to the problem. It is partly environment—the eating habits of your friends, what food is most available in your home and your local stores, how much opportunity you have to move around at work. It is partly biology—there are genetic predispositions for storing fat, for having higher satiety thresholds, even for having more sensitive taste buds. It is partly economics—junk food has become much cheaper than fresh produce. And it is marketing, too—food companies have become masterful at playing on human social nature and our evolutionary "programming" to steer us toward unhealthy but profitable fare. That is why the narrow "eat this" kinds of solutions, like all simple solutions, fail.

When we go on diets and exercise regimens, we rely on willpower to overcome all these pushes to overeat relative to our activity level. And we count on the reward of getting trimmer and fitter to keep us on the wagon. It is rewarding to lose the weight, of course. Unfortunately, time works against us. As the weight comes off, we get hungrier and develop stronger cravings and become more annoyed by the exercise. Meanwhile the weight loss inevitably slows as our metabolism tries to compensate for this deprivation by becoming more parsimonious with calories. Thus, the punishment for sticking to our regimen becomes increasingly severe and constant, and the expected reward recedes into the future. "That gap between the reinforcement of eating and the reinforcement of maybe losing weight months later is a huge challenge," says Sung-Woo Kahng, a neurobehaviorist who studies obesity at the Johns Hopkins University School of Medicine and the Kennedy Krieger Institute.

We would be more likely to stick with the regimen if it remained less punishing and more reliably rewarding. Is there a way to make that happen?

————————ADVANCES IN THE LAB ————————

The Biology of the Lab

The National Institutes of Health has spent nearly $800 million a year on studies to understand the neurological, metabolic and genetic foundations of obesity. In the process, scientists have uncovered complex biochemical pathways and feedback loops that connect the brain and digestive system; a new appreciation for the regulatory functions of fat tissues; subtle hereditary changes that make some groups more prone to obesity than others; and the strong possibility that exposure to certain foods and toxic substances might modify and mitigate some of these factors. Given that it will likely take decades to understand the various causes of obesity, more surprises are no doubt in store.

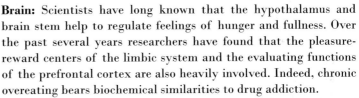

Brain: Scientists have long known that the hypothalamus and brain stem help to regulate feelings of hunger and fullness. Over the past several years researchers have found that the pleasure-reward centers of the limbic system and the evaluating functions of the prefrontal cortex are also heavily involved. Indeed, chronic overeating bears biochemical similarities to drug addiction.

Metabolism: The ability to burn and store energy varies greatly from cell to cell. In 2009 three studies in the *New England Journal of Medicine* demonstrated that at least some women and men continue to benefit well into adulthood from small stores of brown fat, which, unlike white fat, is associated with being lean. Brown fat helps to generate heat and is apparently more closely related to muscle than to white fat, whose primary purpose is to store excess energy.

Genes: Researchers have confirmed variations in 20-odd genes that predispose people to gaining weight easily. But further investigation shows that the effects are modest at best and cannot account for the current obesity epidemic Genes may still play a role, however, through the environment's influence on which ones get turned on or off. So far most such genetic switches for obesity have been identified in mice, although a few likely human candidates are known.

FROM BIOLOGY TO BRAIN

The most successful way to date to lose at least modest amounts of weight and keep it off with diet and exercise employs programs that focus on changing behavior. The behavioral approach, tested over decades, involves making many small, sustainable adjustments in eating and exercise habits that are prompted and encouraged by the people and the rest of the environment around us.

The research in support of behavioral weight-loss approaches extends back more than half a century to Harvard University psychologist B. F. Skinner's development of the science of behavioral analysis. The field is founded on the notion that scientists cannot really know what is going on inside a person's brain—after all, even functional MRIs, the state of the art for peering into the mind, are crude, highly interpretable proxies for cognition and emotion that reduce the detailed firing of billions of neurons in complex circuits to a few blobs of color. But researchers can objectively and reproducibly observe and measure physical behavior and the immediate environment in which the behavior occurs, allowing them to identify links between environment and behavior. That typically includes trying to spot events or situations that may be prompting or triggering certain behaviors and noting what may be rewarding and thus reinforcing of some behaviors or punishing and thus inhibiting of others.

The effectiveness of behavioral interventions has been extensively documented for a wide variety of disorders and problem behaviors. A 2009 meta-analysis in the *Journal of Clinical Child & Adolescent Psychology* concluded that "early intensive behavioral intervention should be an intervention of choice for children with autism." A systematic review sponsored by the U.S. Preventive Services Task Force found that even brief behavioral counseling interventions reduced the number of drinks taken by problem drinkers by 13 to 34 percent for as long as four years. Review studies have found similar behavioral-intervention successes in challenges as diverse as reducing stuttering, increasing athletic performance and improving employee productivity.

To combat obesity, behavioral analysts examine related environmental influences: Which external factors prompt people to overeat or to eat junk food, and which tend to encourage healthful eating? In what situations are the behaviors and comments of others affecting unhealthful eating? What seems to effectively reward eating healthfully over the long term? What reinforces being active? Behavior-focused studies of obesity and diets as early as the

1960s recognized some basic conditions that seemed correlated with a greater chance of losing weight and keeping it off: rigorously measuring and recording calories, exercise and weight; making modest, gradual changes rather than severe ones; eating balanced diets that go easy on fats and sugar rather than dropping major food groups; setting clear, modest goals; focusing on lifelong habits rather than short-term diets; and especially attending groups where dieters could receive encouragement to stick with their efforts and praise for having done so.

If these strategies today sound like well-worn, commonsense advice, it is because they have been popularized for nearly half a century by Weight Watchers. Founded in 1963 to provide support groups for dieters, Weight Watchers added other approaches and advice in keeping with the findings of behavioral studies and used to bill itself as a "behavior-modification" program. "Whatever the details are of how you lose weight, the magic in the sauce is always going to be changing behavior," says nutrition researcher and Weight Watchers chief science officer Karen Miller-Kovach. "Doing that is a learnable skill."

Studies back the behavioral approach to weight loss. A 2003 review commissioned by the U.S. Department of Health and Human Services found that "counseling and behavioral interventions showed small to moderate degrees of weight loss sustained over at least one year"—a year being an eon in the world of weight loss. An analysis of eight popular weight-loss programs published in 2005 in the *Annals of Internal Medicine* found Weight Watchers (at that time in its pre-2010 points-overhaul incarnation) to be the only effective program, enabling a 3 percent maintained body-weight loss for the two years of the study. Meanwhile a 2005 *JAMA* study found that Weight Watchers, along with the Zone diet (which, like Weight Watchers, recommends a balanced diet of protein, carbohydrates and fat), achieved the highest percentage (65 percent) of one-year diet adherence of several popular diets, noting that "adherence level rather than diet type was the key determinant of clinical benefits." A 2010 study in the *Journal of Pediatrics* found that after one year children receiving behavioral therapy maintained a body mass index that was 1.9 to 3.3 lower than children who did not. (BMI is a numerical height-weight relation in which 18.5 is held to be borderline underweight and 25 borderline overweight.) The *Pediatrics* report noted that "more limited evidence suggests that these improvements can be maintained over the 12 months after the end of treatments." A 2010 study in *Obesity* found that continuing members of

Take Off Pounds Sensibly (TOPS), a national, nonprofit behaviorally focused weight-loss organization, maintained a weight loss of 5 to 7 percent of their body weight for the three years of the investigation. The U.K.'s Medical Research Council last year declared that its own long-term study had shown that programs based on behavioral principles are more likely to help people take and keep the weight off than other approaches. (The study was funded by Weight Watchers, but without its participation.)

But Weight Watchers and other mass-market programs tend to fall short when it comes to enlisting a full range of behavioral techniques and customizing them to meet the varied needs of individuals. They cannot routinely provide individual counseling, adapt their advice to specific challenges, assess environmental factors in a member's home, workplace or community, provide much outreach to members who do not come to meetings, or prevent their members from shooting for fast, dramatic, short-term weight loss or from restricting food groups. As a for-profit company, Weight Watchers sometimes even mildly panders to these self-defeating notions in its marketing. "Some people join us to drop 10 pounds for a high school reunion," says Weight Watchers's Miller-Kovach. "They achieve that goal, then stop coming."

To close that gap, a number of researchers have turned their attention in recent years to improving, expanding and tailoring behavioral techniques, with encouraging results. For example, Michael Cameron, head of the graduate behavioral analysis department at Simmons College and a faculty member at Harvard Medical School, is now focusing his research on behavioral weight-loss techniques. He is one year into a four-person study-behavioral analysts generally do very small group or even single-subject studies to more closely tailor the intervention and observe individual effects—in which the subjects meet together with him via online videoconferencing for reinforcement, weigh themselves on scales that transmit results via wireless networks, and have their diets optimized to both reduce caloric density and address individual food preferences. Favorite foods are used as a reward for exercise. So far the subjects have lost between 8 and 20 percent of their body weight.

Matt Normand, a behavioral analyst at the University of the Pacific, has focused on finding ways to more precisely track subjects' calorie intake and expenditure by, for example, collecting receipts for food purchases, providing food checklists to record what is eaten, and enlisting various types of pedometers and other devices for measuring physical activity. He then provides participants with daily detailed accounts of their calorie flow and in one published study showed three of four subjects reduced calorie intake to recommended levels. Richard Fleming, a researcher at the University of Massachusetts Medical School's Shriver Center, has in *Obesity* looked at ways to encourage parents to steer their children to healthier choices. He has found, among other techniques, that showing parents in person what appropriate serving sizes of foods look like on plates is helpful. Another successful Fleming trick: letting children pick out a small treat at a food store-as long as they walk there. "Kids can really respond to that reward for being active," he says.

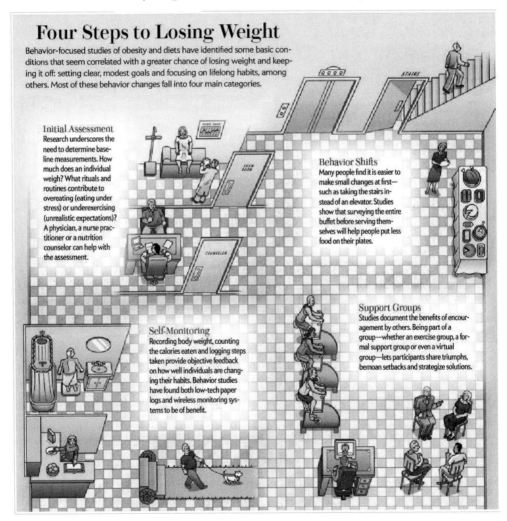

Four Steps to Losing Weight

Behavior-focused studies of obesity and diets have identified some basic conditions that seem correlated with a greater chance of losing weight and keeping it off: setting clear, modest goals and focusing on lifelong habits, among others. Most of these behavior changes fall into four main categories.

Initial Assessment
Research underscores the need to determine baseline measurements. How much does an individual weigh? What rituals and routines contribute to overeating (eating under stress) or underexercising (unrealistic expectations)? A physician, a nurse practitioner or a nutrition counselor can help with the assessment.

Behavior Shifts
Many people find it is easier to make small changes at first—such as taking the stairs instead of an elevator. Studies show that surveying the entire buffet before serving themselves will help people put less food on their plates.

Self-Monitoring
Recording body weight, counting the calories eaten and logging steps taken provide objective feedback on how well individuals are changing their habits. Behavior studies have found both low-tech paper logs and wireless monitoring systems to be of benefit.

Support Groups
Studies document the benefits of encouragement by others. Being part of a group—whether an exercise group, a formal support group or even a virtual group—lets participants share triumphs, bemoan setbacks and strategize solutions.

Why are behavioral interventions effective? Laurette Dubé, a lifestyle psychology and marketing researcher at McGill University's Faculty of Management, notes that our environment is currently one in which ubiquitous, sophisticated marketing efforts prey on our need for sensory gratification as well as our vulnerability to misinformation. In addition, the poor eating and exercise habits we observe in our friends, family and colleagues encourage us to follow suit. In essence, behavioral interventions seek to reconfigure this environment into one in which our needs for information, gratification and social encouragement are tapped to pull us toward healthy food and exercise choices rather than away from them. "When we are getting the right messages in enough ways, we have a better chance of resisting the urge to eat more than we need," Dubé says.

CHANGING POLICY

There is no one-size-fits-all solution, behavioral or otherwise, to the problem of obesity. But although behavioral interventions work best when they are customized to individuals, mass-market behavioral approaches such as Weight Watchers and TOPS are at least fairly effective. Why don't more people lose weight with them? The main reason is that people simply do not sign up for them, often because would-be weight losers are chasing fad diets or supplements or have read that obesity is locked into our genes. Weight Watchers, by far the most popular behavioral weight-loss program, counts only 600,000 meeting-attending members in its ranks in North America. That means that fewer than one out of 100 obese people in the U.S. and about one out of 200 overweight people are part of a formal behavioral-modification program.

Public policy may be changing, however. The U.S. Surgeon General's office and the CDC have both publicly lined up behind behavioral approaches as the main weapon in what is becoming a war on obesity. First Lady Michelle Obama's high-profile Let's Move campaign against childhood obesity consists almost entirely of behavioral weight-loss wisdom—that is, find ways to encourage children to eat less-calorie-dense foods, to become more active, and to enjoy doing it. The recent proposed ban of toys in Happy Meals in San Francisco suggests that more officials may be getting ready to pressure the food industry into easing up on contaminating the environment with what are essentially obesity-supportive marketing tactics. To make it easier and more tempting to buy healthier food in poorer, disproportionately overweight communities, the White House has proposed subsidizing the costs of fruits and vegetables.

Approaching the problem from the other direction, New York City Mayor Michael Bloomberg is among those who have advocated modifying food-assistance programs to restrict the purchase of high-sugar beverages, and last year Washington, D.C., enacted a 6 percent tax on sugary drinks. New York City has also offered vouchers for buying produce at farmers' markets to low-income families and incentives to stores to offer healthier fare.

Some experts are trying to push the government to rewrite zoning and building codes to ensure that neighborhoods and buildings become friendlier to walkers, bikers and stair climbers. A 2009 study by researchers at Louisiana State University Medical School found that a mere 2.8 percent increase in a person's stair usage alone would keep off almost a pound a year. "The correlation between activity levels and healthy weight is one of the best-established ones in all of obesity research," says William M. Hartman, a psychologist and director of the behavioral program of the highly regarded Weight Management Program of the California Pacific Medical Center in San Francisco.

Increasing access to behavior therapy would help, too. Many overweight people might only need online behavioral monitoring, support and progress-sharing tools, which have proved moderately effective in studies. Others may need much more intensive, more personal interventions of the kind Cameron is developing. Given that obesity especially plagues the economically disadvantaged, fees for these programs may have to be heavily subsidized by the government and health care insurers. A weekly session with a behavioral therapist costing $50 would amount to $2,500 a year, or a bit more than a third of the $7,000 per year societal and medical costs of obesity—and the sessions might only be needed for a year or two to establish new, permanent eating and exercise habits, whereas the savings would continue on for a lifetime.

It is too soon to say whether the public will accept government efforts to push it toward healthier choices. In San Francisco, a community known to be especially friendly to public health initiatives, the plan to ban Happy Meals has provoked angry reactions, and Mayor Gavin Newsom vetoed it. Efforts by Let's Move to bring healthier food to school cafeterias have been intensely criticized by some as overly intrusive. Even if these efforts are eventually fully implemented nationwide, there is no way of being sure they will significantly reduce obesity. The current rate of obesity is far beyond any ever seen before on the planet, and thus a large-scale solution will necessarily be an experiment in mass behavior change. But the research suggests that such a grand experiment would be our best shot at fixing obesity and that there is reason to be hopeful it will succeed. Given that more and more scientists, public policy experts and government officials seem eager to get it off the ground, we may well have early findings within this decade.

MORE TO EXPLORE

About Behaviorism. B. F. Skinner. Vintage, 1974. A classic in behavior modification.

You: On a Diet: The Owner's Manual for Waist Management. Michael F. Roizen and Mehmet C. Oz. Free Press, 2006. Good layperson's guide to various aspects of weight management.

Determining the Effectiveness of Take Off Pounds Sensibly (TOPS), a Nationally Available Nonprofit Weight Loss Program. Nia S. Mitchell et al. in *Obesity.* Published online September 23, 2010. wvw.nature. rom/oby/journal/vaop/ncurrent/full/oby2010202a.html The entry portal to the range of NIH research on obesity: obesityresearch.nih.gov.

Collaborate

Freedman asserts that behavioral changes are by far the most reliable and effective means to lose weight, but his article also lists many studies that have discovered correlations between obesity and genetics. As a class, divide into groups and make each group responsible for finding one of the studies to which Freedman refers in his article. Make sure that some groups read behavioral and others genetic studies. After reading your assigned study, do you agree with Freedman that behavioral modification is the best method for losing weight? Report your findings to the class.

Compose

Freedman's article praises Weight Watchers for the company's success in helping people lose weight and fight obesity, but he also mentions that the for-profit company also markets to those who just want to lose a few pounds. Go to Weight Watchers' Web site. Analyze the Web site's design, their tools, and their success stories. What is the overall message being delivered? Who is their audience? What kinds of rhetorical strategies does the Web site use to persuade people to join Weight Watchers? Write up your analysis. Students could also look at Jenny Craig, *The Biggest Loser*, The Zone, and other Web sites and do a compare and contrast essay on two of these Web sites.

Outline Freedman's article and its concerns. While mentioning online tools, the article does not discuss these kinds of virtual support in depth and it does not mention popular reality TV shows, such as *The Biggest Loser*, at all. This article originally was published in *Scientific American*. How does the magazine's potential audience determine the topics that Freedman covers and what he covers in detail?

As a class, watch *The Biggest Loser* or another popular reality TV show that deals with weight loss. Does the show recommend mild to moderate behavioral modification or does it take another approach? Is the show effective in helping people lose weight? If so, how and why? What are the motivating factors? Do these factors line up with Freedman's article? Why is *The Biggest Loser* a popular show?

Nutritionist Marion Nestle, who holds a PhD in molecular biology, is a Professor of Public Health, Nutrition, and Food Studies at New York University. Her best-selling 2006 book What To Eat, *from which this extract comes, won the James Beard Award and was selected by Amazon.com's editors as one of the top ten books on health, mind, and body for that year.*

excerpt from

WHAT TO EAT

By Marion Nestle

Health officials say that in the United States alone bacteria, viruses, and parasites in food cause 76 million cases of illness, 325,000 hospitalizations, and 5,000 deaths, and do so every year. This seems like a huge burden of disease, especially if you are one of the people who gets sick. But the numbers don't seem quite so big if you do the math and add up all of the foods everyone eats on an annual basis. Consider that there are nearly 300 million people who eat multiple foods several times a day 365 days a year—these come to hundreds of trillions of food exposures.

Mind you, nobody in government is really paying close attention to food safety or figuring out which foods cause what illnesses. In the United States food safety oversight is largely shared by two agencies: the Food and Drug Administration (FDA) and the U.S. Department of Agriculture (USDA). The FDA is under siege by Congress, which has given it too much to do and not nearly enough money to do it with. And the USDA is in constant conflict of interest: its primary mission is to promote sales of American agricultural products, and public health is decidedly secondary to these agribusiness interests. Given the lack of real government leadership, the food safety system relies largely on faith that food producers, processors, and handlers do not want to make anyone sick and are doing what they can to prevent illnesses transmitted by food. Food can never be perfectly safe, but it can be safe enough when everyone involved—from farmer to consumer—does the right thing. Mostly everyone does, which is why supermarket produce, no matter where it comes from, rarely causes problems.

Food can never be perfectly safe, but it can be safe enough when everyone involved—from farmer to consumer—does the right thing.

But produce seems especially worrisome because fruits and vegetables are grown in what the FDA charmingly refers to as "non-sterile environments" (translation: in contact with animal manure), and because they are so often eaten raw. Fruits and vegetables are loaded with microbes, but even the ones acquired from feces are mostly harmless. Washing and cooking take care of most microbes on or in food, and any others are usually killed by stomach acid or blocked from doing harm by the immune system. That leaves just the few bad ones—the toxic kinds of *Salmonella* and *E. coli* (especially O157:H7), or hepatitis virus, for example—that make headlines when they harm people who innocently eat them.

Because the government doesn't track food safety very carefully, the Washington, D.C.-based advocacy group Center for Science in the Public Interest (CSPI) steps in to fill one of the gaps by issuing periodic reports about outbreaks—episodes in which more than one person gets sick from eating the same food. By its counts, fresh produce ranks as the number-two cause of outbreaks (but the number-one cause of individual cases of illness), just behind seafood. Between 1990 and 2003, CSPI recorded 554 outbreaks caused by eating produce, an average of 42 per year. These amounted to 12 percent of total outbreaks, but 20 percent of individual cases and more than 28,000 illnesses. Could some of these illnesses have been prevented by better federal regulation? I think so.

If problems arise, fruit and vegetable companies are subject to fines, confiscations, and the like, but the reality is that the safety of produce depends on the honor system.

Fruits and vegetables come under the regulatory umbrella of the FDA, which has never hard enough money or staff to do what it is required to—even before Congress, under pressure from tobacco and drug companies, started slashing its funding and, therefore, its regulatory ability in the 1990s. In 1998, the FDA issued guidelines for the safe handling of produce. These rely on Good Agricultural Practices (GAPs)—methods that food producers can use to protect fruits and vegetables from contamination with microbes coming from water, manure, or sick food handlers. They also rely on Good Manufacturing Practices (GMPs)—methods that food handlers can use to prevent contamination from microbes coming from trucks, storage facilities, equipment, packing materials, or the workers who deal with such things. The GAPs and GMPs, however, are just guidelines. In FDA-speak: "The produce guide is guidance and it is not a regulation." This means that food producers and handlers are not actually required to follow the guidelines. If problems arise, fruit and vegetable companies are subject to fines, confiscations, and the like, but the reality is that the safety of produce depends on the honor system.

Much of the produce sold in American supermarkets comes from developing countries where sanitation conditions are such that you shouldn't even be brushing your teeth with tap water, much less washing your food with it. I learned about the dangers of eating uncooked vegetables in such places when I was in public health school. Fieldwork is a big part of public health training, and part of mine was to study nutrition programs in urban areas of Thailand and Indonesia. Along with weeks of immunizations came firm instructions: do not drink tap water or put ice in drinks; do not eat salads; eat vegetables only if they are cooked and piping hot; and do not eat fruit unless you peel it yourself. Fortunately, it was the height of summer, and I had plenty of exotic tropical fruits to peel—fresh lychees, mangosteens, rambutans, longans, and other marvels I had never tasted before.

The FDA oversees imported produce by inspecting samples—about 2 percent of the total—and rarely is the agency able to dig deeper. In 1999, in one such instance, it tested 1,000 samples of fresh produce imported from 21 countries. About 4 percent of the samples turned out to have fecal microbes, fortunately none toxic. The following year, the FDA did a similar survey of domestic produce, which it usually does not inspect at all. Just 1 percent of the samples were found contaminated with fecal microorganisms, also none toxic. The agency followed up the "violative samples" by sending its agents to visit farms, offering advice about GAPs, and conducting later visits to see if the practices had improved. They had. The low level of contamination is reassuring, as is the attention to problems, but it would be even more reassuring if the FDA had the ability to do more than occasional spot-checks and could act more rapidly. In October 2005, for example, the FDA issued a warning about possible *E. coli* O157:H7 contamination of prepackaged Dole salads a week *after* the "best-if-used-by" dates on the packages. These packages were likely to have already been sold.

Prewashed and precut salads and vegetables go through many hands, and you would expect them to be especially vulnerable to microbial growth, particularly as time gets closer to the "sell by" date—the date voluntarily stamped on most bags to indicate how long the products can be considered "fresh." Processors know this, so they use "modified-atmosphere packaging" and, sometimes, preservatives, to inhibit microbial growth and extend shelf life. But I am less concerned about precut vegetables now than I used to be since I took a side trip to a processing plant after giving a lecture at the Steinbeck Center in Salinas. On the day of my visit, I watched this plant process broccoli and cauliflower heads for use in packages with dips. The freshly picked heads went through repeated washings before machines cleaved them into neat wedges and packed them into plastic containers. The wash water, like all United States public water supplies, is chlorinated to kill microbes, and nobody touches the vegetables once they get on the carrier belt. This process looked just fine to me—as long as the packages are kept cold during shipping.

Even so, I would wash those broccoli wedges again before eating them, especially if they have been sitting on shelves in the produce section getting misted at regular intervals. Some supermarkets keep produce looking fresh by storing it on chilled shelves. The cooling compressors blow a lot of cool air around, and lettuces are particularly prone to drying out if not kept moist. That is why some stores mist the open vegetables so they look dewy at all times. It is best not to look too closely at the misting devices, however. In some of the stores in my neighborhood, the misting gadgets are covered with green algae or encrusted with mold. So wash those lettuces! Washing cannot remove all of the microbes that might be harmful, but it takes care of most of them.

As for that suspicious wax on fruits and vegetables: last winter I bought a box of "candy sweet, easy to peel" clementines from Spain, covered in wax.

> So wash those lettuces! Washing cannot remove all of the microbes that might be harmful, but it takes care of most of them.

The label explained: "coated with food-grade, vegetable, beeswax, and/or shellac-based wax or resin, to maintain freshness." It is common to wax citrus fruits like these—or apples, peppers, cucumbers, and other such fruits and vegetables—to replace the natural waxes that get washed off in processing. One type of wax is carnauba from the leaves of palm trees, which its producers describe as "a superior natural wax emulsion with a high gloss, long shelf life and superior drying characteristics," just exactly what you might want for polishing cars or furniture, its more familiar use. Wax retains the water in fruits and vegetables in the same way that moisturizers do for the skin after bathing. Wax also protects against bruising, prevents the growth of molds, and extends the time the fruits and vegetables last on the shelf without spoiling. Best of all—from the point of view of the supermarket—the high shine from the wax makes produce look fresh and attractive.

But is it safe? I have no problem with the waxes on clementines, avocados, cantaloupes, or pumpkins, because I am not going to eat the skin anyway. But I would rather not have it on apples or green peppers. For one thing, forget about washing it off. It adheres firmly to remaining traces of the natural waxes. For another, I cannot help but think the foods must be old. Why would they need wax if they were fresh?

These concerns are about aesthetics, not safety. Waxes are fats, but such big ones that you cannot easily absorb them; they usually slide right through the digestive tract. One gallon of wax is said to be enough to cover 12,000 pounds of fruit, so any one apple is not going to have much. At some point, food toxicologists tested fruit waxes in rats and beagle dogs, but found no effects on metabolism or cancer risk even when the animals were eating 10 percent of their diet as wax—which you would never do. Waxes are a nuisance, not a health problem. I buy unwaxed fruits and vegetables if I like eating their peels. Otherwise, I try to rinse off whatever I can, and save the worrying for more important times.

SAFETY: ORGANIC VERSUS CONVENTIONAL PRODUCE

The CSPI outbreak reports on produce do not say whether the safety problems were caused by organic or conventionally grown produce. "Conventional" means grown with pesticides; pesticides may kill insects, but they do not kill harmful bacteria or viruses. Because most produce is still conventionally grown you would, on the basis of quantity alone, expect this kind to cause most outbreaks, unless there is some reason why organic methods pose special risks. Critics say they do. They argue that because organic production uses composted manure instead of chemical fertilizers, organic foods are exposed to more potentially dangerous microbes and are riskier. But this argument does not really hold. In order to obtain organic certification, farmers have to follow strict rules about the use of manure to make sure that harmful microbes are destroyed, and they are inspected to make sure they do. Growers of conventional produce do not have to follow such rules.

In order to obtain organic certification, farmers have to follow strict rules about the use of manure to make sure that harmful microbes are destroyed, and they are inspected to make sure they do. Growers of conventional produce do not have to follow such rules.

It would be nice to know more about the comparative safety of organic and conventional produce, but research on this question is minimal. In the first study to directly compare farming practices, University of Minnesota scientists tested for harmless forms of *Salmonella* and *E. coli*, as well as for the deadly *E. coli* O157:H7, on vegetables grown on farms using three methods: conventional, Certified Organic, and supposedly following the organic rules but not certified. All three of the farms used aged or composted manure as fertilizer, but none of the vegetables had any *E. coli* O157:H7, no matter how they were grown. The investigators did find the harmless fecal bacteria on 2 percent of the conventionally grown produce, 4 percent of the Certified Organic, and 11 percent of the noncertified organic. These results require some interpretation. The Certified Organic vegetables seem to have had twice as much contamination as the conventional ones, but the numbers were too small to reach statistical significance—meaning that the difference could have occurred by chance. When you allow for the usual margin of error, the Certified Organic produce was found to be about as safe as conventionally grown produce. The much higher level of contaminants in the noncertified organic vegetables did reach statistical significance, and confirms the notion that Certified Organic farms—which follow organic rules and are inspected to make sure they do—grow safer produce. So could any farm that firmly adhered to organic rules. But without inspection, you have to take what they say on trust. Because conventional food producers are not subject to such rules or inspections, it is difficult to assess the comparative safety of what they grow.

NUTRITIONAL VALUE: ORGANIC VERSUS CONVENTIONAL PRODUCE

So Certified Organic produce appears to be at least as safe as conventional produce. But this says nothing about whether organic production methods make organic fruits and vegetables more nutritious. Here is the deal: if you eat any fruits and vegetables at all, you get nutrients you cannot get as easily from other foods. These foods are loaded with substances that do good things for health. Fruits and vegetables are the main or only sources of vitamin C, folate (the vitamin called folic acid on food labels), and beta-carotene (a precursor of vitamin A), and they provide half the fiber in American diets (the other half comes from grains). They also contain varying combinations of phytonutrients, the chemicals in plants that singly and together protect against disease. These nutrients are all good reasons for eating fruits and vegetables.

If organic foods are grown in better soils, you would expect them to be more nutritious, and you would be right. This is easy to demonstrate for minerals; the mineral content of a plant food depends on how much is in the soil. But differences in the vitamin or phytonutrient content of a food plant are more likely to be due to its genetic strain or to how it is treated after harvest. The postharvest effects on nutrient values especially affect certain vitamins, but I'll defer discussion of the nutritional effects of time, temperature, light, and air for a later discussion of food processing.

Right now, the idea that organic soils yield food that is more nutritious has much appeal, and organic producers would dearly love to prove it. The Organic Trade Association has organized a center to promote research with a "singular focus—the universal benefits of organic production." Consumers, it says, "are looking for scientific justification of their largely intuitive feeling that organic products are safer and more beneficial to human health...[such as] Do organic farming methods have an important effect on the nutritional quality of food?"

If they ask me, I say: Don't go there. I can't think of any reason why organically grown foods would have fewer nutrients than conventionally grown foods, and I have no trouble thinking of several reasons why they might have more, but so what? I doubt the slight increase would be enough to make any measurable difference to health. Just as people differ, carrots or heads of cauliflower differ, and the differences in the nutrient content of one carrot or cauliflower and the next can be substantial.

Consider what you have to do to test for nutritional differences in organic versus conventional carrots. You start with identical carrot seeds and plant some in an organic plot and some in a conventional plot. The plots have to be identical in climate and geography, but will differ in soil quality (because more nutrient-rich soil is one of the underpinnings of organics). You treat the conventional carrots with pesticides but use biological pest control methods for the organic carrots. Once harvested, you perform the same set of nutrient analyses on both samples. Suppose you find differences. You must then ask: Do they mean anything for your health? To find out, you need to feed the carrots to animals or people. But because animals and people eat so many different foods, even a measurable difference in the nutrient content of carrots alone is unlikely to produce a measurable health benefit. Overall, such studies are hard to do, expensive, and difficult to interpret.

Nevertheless, a few intrepid souls have tried the agricultural parts of such studies (the only clinical studies I know about are the ones that demonstrate reassuringly lower levels of pesticides in the bodies of people who eat organics). These show, as expected, that organic foods grown in richer soils have more minerals than conventional foods grown in poorer soils. They also show that organic peaches and pears have somewhat higher levels of vitamin C and E, and organic berries and corn have higher levels of protective antioxidant substances. In general, the studies all point to slightly higher levels of nutrients in organically grown foods, as compared to those that were conventionally grown.

But organic foods, like all foods, are just that: foods. Some will have more of one kind of nutrient, and others will have more of another. Phytochemicals are a case in point. Broccoli is famous for its content of sulforaphane, shown in laboratory studies to protect against cancer. Tomatoes have lycopenes. Onions and garlic have allium compounds. Soybeans have flavonoids. My office file of studies extolling the special nutrient content or health benefits of one or another fruit or vegetable includes work on apples, avocados, broccoli, blueberries, cherries, cranberries, garlic, grapefruit, grapes, onions, pomegranates, raisins, spinach, strawberries, and tomatoes, among others. I conclude from this that *all* fruits and vegetables have something good about them, even though some have more of one good thing and others have more of another. That is why we nutritionists are always telling you to eat a variety of foods. It's the mix that is most beneficial and most protective.

Surely the best reason to eat blueberries is that they are delicious in season.

That all fruits and vegetables have much to offer is also why I don't think it makes much sense to push one over another. Yes, it's great to eat lettuce, but surely not for the reasons given by Wegmans on a shelf label: "High in vitamin A and a good source of folate." I like lettuce, but it is mostly water, and almost all richly colored vegetables—spinach or red peppers, for example—are better sources of folate (folic acid) and of beta-carotene, the vitamin A precursor.

Surely the best reason to eat blueberries is that they are delicious in season. Wegmans, however, undoubtedly sells more of them by displaying them in front of labels saying "A half-cup doubles the antioxidants most people get in a day according to the USDA lab at Tufts University." Other fruits also have antioxidants—and different ones—that may be equally important. Eating fruits and vegetables is a good thing to do for health, and eating a variety of them does even more good.

So: Are fruits and vegetables better if they are organic? Of course they are, but not necessarily for nutritional reasons. In this matter, I defer to Joan Gussow, the former head of the nutrition department at Columbia University, whose thinking about matters of agriculture and health I especially admire. She asks:

> Shouldn't we hope that people will choose organic foods on grounds more reliable than whether they contain a little more carotene or zinc? Isn't the most important story that organic production conserves natural resources, solves rather than creates environmental problems, and reduces the pollution of air, water, soil . . . and food?

So: Are fruits and vegetables better if they are organic? Of course they are, but not necessarily for nutritional reasons.

I like the way she keeps attention focused on these critically important environmental issues. My guess is that researchers will eventually be able to prove organic foods marginally more nutritious than those grown conventionally, and that such findings will make it easier to sell organic foods to a much larger number of people. In the meantime, there are loads of other good reasons to buy organics, and I do.

After reading Nestle's article, do you find that you look at your food a little differently? Are you less or more inclined to wash fruits and vegetables or buy organic or local foods? What claims does she make about the benefits of organic foods? Which studies does she use to support her findings? And what does she say about the nutritional value of organics and conventional produce?

Go to your local grocery store's produce section. Survey the produce that is available. Select two to three different kinds of fruit and vegetables (apples and spinach, for example). Compare the conventional, organic, and locally grown produce. What differences do you notice in price, quality, availability, size, etc.? Buy an organic apple and a conventionally grown apple. Wash both and taste them. Do you notice any difference in taste?

Go to a local farmers' market and survey what is being sold. Strike up conversations with the growers about how they grow and harvest their produce. Ask what measures they take to make sure that their food is safe and where they sell their products, aside from the weekly farmers' market. Write up your interviews and your observations about the farmers' market and the growers' concerns.

Sam Lane, a promising junior at the University of Georgia, was riding his bicycle when a drunken driver knocked him down and left him in a coma. Rushed first to a local neurological unit, and then transferred to a hospital closer to his home in Jackson, Mississippi, Sam lay unconscious for five weeks with a traumatic brain injury. That Sam survived at all amazed those who had witnessed the accident, but even when he awoke, his family, friends, and physicians had no idea whether he would regain any brain function at all or would live the rest of his life unable to communicate with others or to take care of himself. At Mississippi Methodist Rehabilitation Center, Sam gradually came back to life. Every week, for 62 weeks, Katy Houston (mother of Sam's kindergarten, school, and college friend Andrew) brought him a different dessert — the "Treat of the Week" — vowing to "feed [him] back to health." Sam's ongoing recovery demonstrated what his doctors called the astonishing plasticity of young brains; not only did Sam regain the ability to walk, talk, and live independently, he was even able to return to college and complete his English degree. After Sam's graduation, Katy Houston compiled the dessert recipes she had made for Sam into a book, the proceeds from which went towards the rehabilitation center where Sam had received the physical, occupational, and speech therapy he needed after the accident. Each recipe is categorized according to its difficulty level: easy, easy to moderate, moderate, or more difficult. At Sam's suggestion and with the permission of the well-known Athens alternative rock band, R.E.M., the book was titled "Sweetness Follows," after one of their songs. This recipe is labeled "easy."

excerpt from

SWEETNESS FOLLOWS: THE STORY OF SAM AND THE TREAT OF THE WEEK

BY KATY HOUSTON

EASY BLUEBERRY CAKE

1 (2-layer) package butter-recipe cake mix (I prefer Duncan Hines)
8 ounces cream cheese, softened
4 eggs
1/2 cup vegetable oil
1 teaspoon vanilla extract
2 cups blueberries
1/3 cup confectioners' sugar

Preheat the oven to 350 degrees. Beat the cake mix, cream cheese, eggs and oil in a mixing bowl on low speed for 1 minute. Scrape the side of the bowl, then beat on medium speed for 2 to 3 minutes or until smooth and thick. Stir in the vanilla; fold in the blueberries.

Pour the batter into a greased and floured tube pan or bundt pan. Bake for 45 to 50 minutes or until a wooden pick inserted in the center comes out clean. Remove the pan to a wire rack and cool completely. Sift the confectioners' sugar over the cooled cake.

Makes 12 servings.

Explore

Visit the Web site for *Sweetness Follows* (http://sweetnessfollows.com) and listen to the R.E.M. song that gave the book its name (search for it on YouTube or borrow the compact disc *Automatic for the People*, released in 1992, from a library). Do you think that the book is well titled? Write down any words from the lyrics that strike you as particularly appropriate for this story and this book.

Invent

Is there a particular dish or recipe that you associate with healing or well-being within your family or community? Did a parent prepare soup or hot tea when you had a cold? Did a grandparent bake cookies over the holidays? Did a "team parent" bring energy-rich snacks after a tiring sports game? Write an account of one time that you enjoyed a healing or comforting meal, beverage, or food.

Compose

Building on your previous assignment, see whether you can reconstruct the recipe for one of your comfort foods well enough for a group of your classmates to cook it. You may have to experiment with measures and ingredients, and you will certainly have to test your recipe before you share it. Make sure that you include: all necessary ingredients, including information on where to obtain them, if necessary; the time this dish will take to cook or prepare; any special equipment (such as a bundt pan, baking sheet, Dutch oven, or cookie press) that the cook might need; and instructions that are easy to follow.

Collaborate

In small groups, read each others' accounts of memorable and comforting foods and pick one to prepare. How did you enjoy the experiences of shopping, preparing, cooking, and eating together? What were you expecting from this assignment? What aspects of the process took you by surprise? Do you think you will prepare this food again?

Daniel Gilbert, Professor of Psychology at Harvard, writes both nonfiction about his scientific research and short science fiction stories. This excerpt from his 2005 book Stumbling on Happiness *chronicles his discovery that many of us are born with an innate "set-point" for happiness, regardless of our physical health.*

excerpt from

STUMBLING ON HAPPINESS

By Daniel Gilbert

For there is nothing either good or bad, but thinking makes it so.
—Shakespeare, *Hamlet, Prince of Denmark*

PARADISE GLOSSED

Forget yoga. Forget liposuction. And forget those herbal supplements that promise to improve your memory, enhance your mood, reduce your waistline, restore your hairline, prolong your lovemaking, and improve your memory. If you want to be happy and healthy, you should try a new technique that has the power to transform the grumpy, underpaid chump you are now into the deeply fulfilled, enlightened individual you've always hoped to be. If you don't believe me, then just consider the testimony of some folks who've tried it:

"I am so much better off physically, financially, mentally, and in almost every other way." *(JW from Texas)*

"It was a glorious experience." *(MB from Louisiana)*

"I didn't appreciate others nearly as much as I do now." *(CR from California)*

Who are these satisfied customers, and what is the miraculous technique they're all talking about? Jim Wright, former Speaker of the United States House of Representatives, made his remark after committing sixty-nine ethics violations and being forced to resign in disgrace. Moreese Bickham, a former inmate, made his remark upon being released from the Louisiana State Penitentiary where he'd served thirty-seven years for defending himself against the Ku Klux Klansmen who'd shot him. And Christopher Reeve, the dashing star of *Superman*, made his remark after an equestrian accident left him paralyzed from the neck down, unable to breathe without the help of a ventilator. The moral of the story? If you want to be happy, healthy, wealthy, and wise, then skip the vitamin pills and the plastic surgeries and try public humiliation, unjust incarceration, or quadriplegia instead.

Uh-huh. Right. Are we really supposed to believe that people who lose their jobs, their freedom, and their mobility are somehow *improved* by the tragedies that befall them? If that strikes you as a far-fetched possibility, then you are not alone. For at least a century, psychologists have assumed that terrible events—such as having a loved one die or becoming the victim of a violent crime—must have a powerful, devastating, and enduring impact on those who experience them. This assumption has been so deeply embedded in our conventional wisdom that people who *don't* have dire reactions to events such as these are sometimes diagnosed as having a pathological condition known as "absent grief." But recent research suggests that the conventional wisdom is wrong, that the absence of grief is quite normal, and that rather than being the fragile flowers that a century of psychologists have made us out to be, most people are surprisingly resilient in the face of trauma. The loss of a parent or spouse is usually sad and often tragic, and it would be perverse to suggest otherwise. But the fact is that while most bereaved people are quite sad for a while, very few become chronically depressed and most experience relatively low levels of relatively short-lived distress. Although more than half the people in the United States will experience a trauma such as rape, physical assault, or natural disaster in their lifetimes, only a small fraction will ever develop any post-traumatic pathology or require any professional assistance. As one group of researchers noted, "Resilience is often the most commonly observed outcome trajectory following exposure to a potentially traumatic event." Indeed, studies of those who survive major traumas suggest that the vast majority do quite well, and that a significant portion claim that their lives were *enhanced* by the experience. I know, I know. It sounds suspiciously like the title of a country song, but the fact is that most folks do pretty darn good when things go pretty darn bad.

If resilience is all around us, then why are statistics such as these so surprising? Why do most of us find it difficult to believe that *we* could ever consider a lifetime behind bars to be "a glorious experience" or come to see paralysis as "a unique opportunity" that gave "a new direction" to our lives? Why do most of us shake our heads in disbelief when an athlete who has been through several grueling years of chemotherapy tells us that "I wouldn't change anything," or when a musician who has become permanently disabled says, "If I had it to do all over again, I would want it to happen the same way," or when quadriplegics and paraplegics tell us that they are pretty much as happy as everyone else? The claims made by people who have experienced events such as these seem frankly outlandish to those of us who are merely imagining those events—and yet, who are we to argue with the folks who've actually been there?

The fact is that negative events do affect us, but they generally don't affect us as much or for as long as we expect them to. When people are asked to predict how they'll feel if they lose a job or a romantic partner, if their candidate loses an important election or their team loses an important game, if they flub an interview, flunk an exam, or fail a contest, they consistently overestimate how awful they'll feel and how long they'll feel awful. Able-bodied people are willing to pay far more to avoid becoming disabled than disabled people are willing to pay to become able-bodied again because able-bodied people underestimate how happy disabled people are. As one group of researchers noted, "Chronically ill and disabled patients generally rate the value of their lives in a given health state more highly than do hypothetical patients [who are] imagining themselves to be in such states." Indeed, healthy people imagine that eighty-three states of illness would be "worse than death," and yet, people who are actually in those states rarely take their own lives. If negative events don't hit us as hard as we expect them to, then why do we expect them to? If heartbreaks and calamities can be blessings in disguise, then why are their disguises so convincing? The answer is that the human mind tends to *exploit ambiguity*—and if that phrase seems ambiguous to you, then just keep reading and let me exploit it. [. . .]

DISAMBIGUATING OBJECTS

Most stimuli are ambiguous—that is, they can mean more than one thing—and the interesting question is how we *disambiguate* them—that is, how we know which of a stimuli's many meanings to infer on a particular occasion. Research shows that *context, frequency,* and *recency* are especially important in this regard.

Consider *context.* The word *bank* has two meanings in English: "a place where money is kept" and "the land on either side of a river." Yet we never misunderstand sentences such as "The boat ran into the bank" or "The robber ran into the bank" because the words *boat* and *robber* provide a context that tells us which of the two meanings of *bank* we should infer in each case.

Consider *frequency*. Our past encounters with a stimulus provide information about which of its meanings we should embrace. For example, a loan officer is likely to interpret the sentence "Don't run into the bank" as a warning about how to ambulate through his place of business and not as sound advice about the steering of boats because in the course of a typical day the loan officer hears the word *bank* used more frequently in its financial than in its maritime sense.

Consider *recency*. Even a boater is likely to interpret the sentence "Don't run into the bank" as a reference to a financial institution rather than a river's edge if she recently saw an ad for safe-deposit boxes and thus has the financial meaning of *bank* still active in her mind. Indeed, because I've been talking about banks in this paragraph, I am willing to bet that the sentence "He put a check in the box" causes you to generate a mental image of someone placing a piece of paper in a receptacle and not a mental image of someone making a mark on a questionnaire.

Unlike rats and pigeons, then, we respond to meanings—and context, frequency, and recency are three of the factors that determine which meaning we will infer when we encounter an ambiguous stimulus. But there is another factor of equal importance and greater interest. Like rats and pigeons, each of us has desires, wishes, and needs. We are not merely spectators of the world but investors in it, and we often *prefer* that an ambiguous stimulus mean one thing rather than another. Consider, for example, the drawing of a box in figure 18. This object (called the Necker cube after the Swiss crystallographer who discovered it in 1832) is inherently ambiguous, and you can prove this to yourself simply by staring at it for a few seconds. At first, the box appears to be sitting on its side and you have the sense that you're looking out at a box that is *across* from you. The dot is inside the box, at the place where the back panel and the bottom panel meet. But if you stare long enough, the drawing suddenly shifts, the box appears to be standing on its end, and you have the sense that you're looking down on a box that is *below* you. The dot is now perched on the upper right corner of the box. Because this drawing has two equally meaningful interpretations, your brain merrily switches back and forth between them, keeping you mildly entertained until you eventually get dizzy and fall down. But what if one of these meanings were better than the other? That is, what if you *preferred* one of the interpretations of this object? Experiments show that when subjects are rewarded for seeing the box across from them or below them, the orientation for which they were rewarded starts "popping out" more often and their brains "hold on" to that interpretation without switching.[17] In other words, when your brain is at liberty to interpret a stimulus in more than one way, it tends to interpret it the way it *wants* to, which is to say that your preferences influence your interpretations of stimuli in just the same way that context, frequency, and recency do.

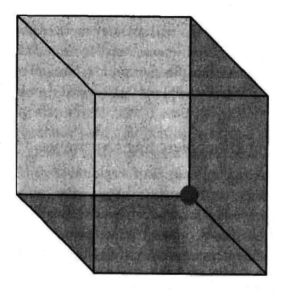

Fig. 18. If you stare at a Necker cube, it will appear to shift its orientation.

This phenomenon is not limited to the interpretation of weird drawings. For example, why is it that you think of yourself as a talented person? (C'mon, give it up. You know you do.) To answer this question, researchers asked some volunteers (definers) to write down their definition of *talented* and then to estimate their talent using that definition as a guide.[18] Next, some other volunteers (nondefiners) were given the definitions that the first group had written down and were asked to estimate their own talent using those definitions as a guide. Interestingly, the definers rated themselves as more talented than the nondefiners did. Because definers were given the liberty to define the word *talented* any way they wished, they defined it *exactly* the way they wished— namely, in terms of some activity at which they just so happened to excel ("I think *talent* usually refers to *exceptional artistic achievement* like, for example, this painting I just finished," or "*Talent* means *an ability you're born with, such as being much stronger than other people. Shall I put you down now?*"). Definers were able to set the standards for talent, and not coincidentally, they were more likely to meet the standards they set. One of the reasons why most of us think of ourselves as talented, friendly, wise, and fair-minded is that these words are the lexical equivalents of a Necker cube, and the human mind naturally exploits each word's ambiguity for its own gratification.

DISAMBIGUATING EXPERIENCE

Of course, the richest sources of exploitable ambiguity are not words, sentences, or shapes but the intricate, variegated, multidimensional *experiences* of which every human life is a collage. If a Necker cube has two possible interpretations and *talent* has fourteen possible interpretations, then *leaving home* or *falling ill* or *getting a job with the U.S. Postal Service* has hundreds or thousands of possible interpretations. The things that *happen* to us—getting married, raising a child, finding a job, resigning from Congress, going to prison, becoming paralyzed—are much more complex than an inky squiggle or a colored cube, and that complexity creates loads of ambiguity that just begs to be exploited. It doesn't have to beg hard. For example, volunteers in one study were told that they would be eating a delicious but unhealthy ice cream sundae (ice cream eaters), and others were told that they would be eating a bitter but healthful plate of fresh kale (kale eaters). Before actually eating these foods, the researchers asked the volunteers to rate the similarity of a number of foods, including ice cream sundaes, kale, and Spam (which everyone considered both unpalatable and unhealthful). The results showed that ice cream eaters thought that Spam was more like kale than it was like ice cream. Why? Because for some odd reason, ice cream eaters were thinking about food in terms of its *taste*—and unlike kale and Spam, ice cream tastes delicious. On the other hand, kale eaters thought that Spam was more like ice cream than it was like kale. Why? Because for some odd reason, kale eaters were thinking about food in terms of its *healthfulness*—and unlike kale, ice cream and Spam are unhealthful. The odd reason isn't really so odd. Just as a Necker cube is both across from you and below you, ice cream is both fattening and tasty, and kale is both healthful and bitter. Your brain and my brain easily jump back and forth between these different ways of thinking about the foods because we are merely reading about them. But if we were preparing to *eat* one of them, our brains would automatically exploit the ambiguity of that food's identity and allow us to think of it in a way that pleased us (delicious dessert or nutritious veggie) rather than a way that did not (fattening dessert or bitter veggie). As soon as our *potential* experience becomes our *actual* experience—as soon as we have a stake in its goodness—our brains get busy looking for ways to think about the experience that will allow us to appreciate it.

Because experiences are inherently ambiguous, finding a "positive view" of an experience is often as simple as finding the "below-you-view" of a Necker cube, and research shows that most people do this well and often. Consumers evaluate kitchen appliances more positively after they buy them, job seekers evaluate jobs more positively after they accept them, and high school students evaluate colleges more positively after they get into them. Racetrack gamblers evaluate their horses more positively when they are leaving the betting window than when they are approaching it, and voters evaluate their candidates more positively when they are exiting the voting booth than when they are entering it. A toaster, a firm, a university, a horse, and a senator are all just fine and dandy, but when they become *our* toaster, firm, university, horse, and senator they are instantly finer and dandier. Studies such as these suggest that people are quite adept at finding a positive way to view things once those things become their own.

COOKING WITH FACTS

In Voltaire's classic novel *Candide*, Dr. Pangloss is a teacher of "metaphysico-theologo-cosmolo-nigology" who believes he lives in the best of all possible worlds.

> "It is clear," he said, "that things cannot be other than the way they are; for as all things have been created for some end, they must necessarily be created for the best end. For instance, noses were made to support spectacles, hence we wear spectacles. Legs, as anyone can see, were made for breeches, and so we wear breeches. Stones were made to be shaped into castles; thus My Lord has a fine castle because the greatest baron in the province ought to have the finest house. And because pigs were made to be eaten, we eat pork all year round. So those who say that everything is well are speaking foolishly; they should say that everything is best."

The research I've described so far seems to suggest that human beings are hopelessly Panglossian; there are more ways to think about experience than there are experiences to think about, and human beings are unusually inventive when it comes to finding the best of all possible ways. And yet, if this is true, then why aren't we all walking around with wide eyes and loopy grins, thanking God for the wonder of hemorrhoids and the miracle of in-laws? Because the mind may be gullible, but it ain't no patsy. The world is *this* way, we wish the world were *that* way, and our experience of the world—how we see it, remember it, and imagine it—is a mixture of stark reality and comforting illusion. We can't spare either. If we were to experience the world exactly as it is, we'd be too depressed to get out of bed in the morning, but if we were to experience the world exactly as we want it to be, we'd be too deluded to find our slippers. We may see the world through rose-colored glasses, but rose-colored glasses are neither opaque nor clear. They can't be opaque because we need to see the world clearly enough to participate in it—to pilot helicopters, harvest corn, diaper babies, and all the other stuff that smart mammals need to do in order to survive and thrive. But they can't be clear because we need their rosy tint to motivate us to *design* the helicopters ("I'm sure this thing will fly"), *plant* the corn ("This year will be a banner crop"), and *tolerate* the babies ("What a bundle of joy!"). We cannot do without reality and we cannot do without illusion. Each serves a purpose, each imposes a limit on the influence of the other, and our experience of the world is the artful compromise that these tough competitors negotiate.

Rather than thinking of people as hopelessly Panglossian, then, we might think of them as having a *psychological immune system* that defends the mind against unhappiness in much the same way that the *physical immune system* defends the body against illness. This metaphor is unusually appropriate. For example, the physical immune system must strike a balance between two competing needs: the need to recognize and destroy foreign invaders such as viruses and bacteria, and the need to recognize and respect the body's own cells. If the physical immune system is hypoactive, it fails to defend the body against micropredators and we are stricken with infections; but if the physical immune system is hyperactive, it mistakenly defends the body against itself and we are stricken with autoimmune disease. A healthy physical immune system must balance its competing needs and find a way to defend us well— but not *too* well.

Analogously, when we face the pain of rejection, loss, misfortune, and failure, the *psychological* immune system must not defend us too well ("I'm perfect and everyone is against me") and must not fail to defend us well enough ("I'm a loser and I ought to be dead"). A *healthy* psychological immune system strikes a balance that allows us to feel good enough to cope with our situation but bad enough to do something about it ("Yeah, that was a lousy performance and I feel crummy about it, but I've got enough confidence to give it a second shot"). We need to be defended—not defenseless or defensive—and thus our minds naturally look for the best view of things while simultaneously insisting that those views stick reasonably closely to the facts. That's why people seek opportunities to think about themselves in positive ways but routinely reject opportunities to think about themselves in *unrealistically* positive ways. For example, college students request new dorm assignments when their current roommates do not think well of them, but they also request new dorm assignments when their current roommates think *too well* of them. No one likes to feel that they are being duped, even when the duping is a pleasure. In order to maintain the delicate balance between reality and illusion, we seek positive views of our experience, but we only allow ourselves to embrace those views when they seem *credible*. So what makes a view seem credible? [. . .]

CHALLENGING FACTS

Whether by choosing information or informants, our ability to cook the facts that we encounter helps us establish views that are both positive and credible. Of course, if you've ever discussed a football game, a political debate, or the six o'clock newscast with someone from the other side of the aisle, you've already discovered that even when people *do* encounter facts that disconfirm their favored conclusions, they have a knack for ignoring them, forgetting them, or seeing them differently than the rest of us do. When Dartmouth and Princeton students see the same football game, both sets of students claim that the facts clearly show that the other school's team was responsible for the unsportsmanlike conduct. When Democrats and Republicans see the same presidential debate on television, both sets of viewers claim that the facts clearly show that their candidate was the winner. When pro-Israeli and pro-Arab viewers see identical samples of Middle East news coverage, both proponents claim that the facts clearly show that the press was biased against their side. Alas, the only thing these facts *clearly* show is that people tend to see what they want to see.

Inevitably, however, there will be times when the unkind facts are just too obvious to set aside. When our team's defensive tackle is caught wearing brass knuckles, or when our candidate confesses to embezzlement on national television, we find it difficult to overlook or forget such facts. How do we manage to maintain a favored conclusion when the brute facts just won't cooperate? Although the word *fact* seems to suggest a sort of unquestionable irrefutability, facts are usually nothing more than conjectures that have met a certain standard of proof. If we set that standard high enough, then nothing can ever be proved, including the "fact" of our own existence. If we set the standard low enough, then all things are true and equally so. Because nihilism and postmodernism are both such unsatisfying philosophies, we tend to set our standard of proof somewhere in the middle. No one can say precisely where that standard should be set, but one thing we do know is that wherever we set it, we must keep it in the same place when we evaluate the facts we favor and the facts we don't. It would be unfair for teachers to give the students they like easier exams than those they dislike, for federal regulators to require that foreign products pass stricter safety tests than domestic products, or for judges to insist that the defense attorney make better arguments than the prosecutor.

And yet, this is just the sort of uneven treatment most of us give to facts that confirm and disconfirm our favored conclusions. In one study, volunteers were asked to evaluate two pieces of scientific research on the effectiveness of capital punishment as a deterrent. They were shown one research study that used the "between-states technique" (which involved comparing the crime rates of states that had capital punishment with the crime rates of states that did not) and one research study that used the "within-states technique" (which involved comparing the crime rates of a single state before and after it instituted or outlawed capital punishment). For half the volunteers, the between-states study concluded that capital punishment was effective and the within-states study concluded it was not. For the other half of the volunteers, these conclusions were reversed. The results showed that volunteers favored whichever technique produced the conclusion that verified their own personal political ideologies. When the within-states technique produced an unfavorable conclusion, volunteers immediately recognized that within-states comparisons are worthless because factors such as employment and income vary over time, and thus crime rates in one decade (the 1980s) can't be compared with crime rates in another decade (the 1990s). But when the between-states technique produced an unfavorable conclusion, volunteers immediately recognized that between-states comparisons are worthless because factors such as employment and income vary with geography, and thus crime rates in one place (Alabama) can't be compared with crime rates in another place (Massachusetts). Clearly, volunteers set the methodological bar higher for studies that disconfirmed their favored conclusions. This same technique allows us to achieve and maintain a positive and credible view of ourselves and our experiences. For example, volunteers in one study were told that they had performed very well or very poorly on a social-sensitivity test and were then asked to assess two scientific reports—one that suggested the test was valid and one that suggested it was not. Volunteers who had performed well on the test believed that the studies in the validating report used sounder scientific methods than did the studies in the invalidating report, but volunteers who performed poorly on the test believed precisely the opposite.

When facts challenge our favored conclusion, we scrutinize them more carefully and subject them to more rigorous analysis. We also require a lot more of them. For example, how much information would you require before you were willing to conclude that someone was intelligent? Would their high school transcripts be enough? Would an IQ test suffice? Would you need to know what their teachers and employers thought of them? Volunteers in one study were asked to evaluate the intelligence of another person, and they required considerable evidence before they were willing to conclude that the person was truly smart. But interestingly, they required much *more* evidence when the person was an unbearable pain in the ass than when the person was funny, kind, and friendly. When we *want* to believe that someone is smart, then a single letter of recommendation may suffice, but when we *don't want* to believe that person is smart, we may demand a thick manila folder full of transcripts, tests, and testimony.

Precisely the same thing happens when we want or don't want to believe something about ourselves. For instance, volunteers in one study were invited to take a medical test that would supposedly tell them whether they did or did not have a dangerous enzyme deficiency that would predispose them to pancreatic disorders. The volunteers placed a drop of their saliva on a strip of ordinary paper that the researchers falsely claimed was a medical test strip. Some volunteers (positive-testers) were told that if the strip turned green in ten to sixty seconds, then they had the enzyme deficiency. Other volunteers (negative-testers) were told that if the strip turned green in ten to sixty seconds, then they *didn't* have the enzyme deficiency. Although the strip was an ordinary piece of paper and hence never turned green, the negative-testers waited much longer than the positive-testers before deciding that the test was complete. In other words, the volunteers gave the test strip plenty of time to prove that they were well but much less time to prove that they were ill. Apparently it doesn't take much to convince us that we are smart and healthy, but it takes a whole lotta facts to convince us of the opposite. We ask whether facts *allow* us to believe our favored conclusions and whether they *compel* us to believe our disfavored conclusions. Not surprisingly, disfavored conclusions have a much tougher time meeting this more rigorous standard of proof.

ONWARD

In July 2004, the City Council of Monza, Italy, took the unusual step of banning goldfish bowls. They reasoned that goldfish should be kept in rectangular aquariums and not in round bowls because "a fish kept in a bowl has a distorted view of reality and suffers because of this." No mention was made of the bland diet, the noisy pump, or the silly plastic castles. No, the problem was that round bowls deform the visual experience of their inhabitants, and goldfish have the fundamental right to see the world as it really is. The good counselors of Monza did not suggest that human beings should enjoy the same right, perhaps because they knew that our distorted views of reality are not so easily dispelled, or perhaps because they understood that we suffer less with them than we would without them. Distorted views of reality are made possible by the fact that experiences are ambiguous—that is, they can be credibly viewed in many ways, some of which are more positive than others. To ensure that our views are credible, our brain accepts what our eye sees. To ensure that our views are positive, our eye looks for what our brain wants. The conspiracy between these two servants allows us to live at the fulcrum of stark reality and comforting illusion. So what does all of this have to do with forecasting our emotional futures? As we are about to see, we may live at the fulcrum of reality and illusion, but most of us don't know our own address.

Most able-bodied persons would imagine that the subjects Gilbert describes—whose health or bodily well-being has deteriorated significantly—would experience a significantly lower quality of life than the traditionally healthy. Yet Gilbert finds that such persons eventually return to the levels of satisfaction and happiness they enjoyed before their injury, debility, or changed circumstances. Did these outcomes surprise you? Where do you think your level of happiness lies? To what extent does your own happiness depend upon your physical health or well-being?

With a group of your classmates, make a list of activities and objects that make you happy or content. Now imagine that you are unable to do two of these activities or to enjoy two of these objects. Can you think of alternatives? Present your findings to the class.

My Left Foot is the autobiography (later made into an Academy-Award-winning film starring Daniel Day-Lewis) about the struggle of author and artist Christy Brown, who was born with cerebral palsy but went on to achieve his aspirations of artistic autonomy and financial independence. Watch this or any other film in the filmography that is concerned with persons who achieve happiness or who fulfill personal goals despite disability or illness. Write a short (150-word) response to the film that you watched.

Search for interviews (online or in print) with other self-defined persons with disabilities or chronic health conditions and analyze their language (for print and online interviews) to identify what makes them happy or joyful. Write a profile of your interviewee.

Kartik Chandaria, a physician for the international charity Doctors Without Borders, helps children fight multi-drug-resistant tuberculosis in Tajikistan. This moving blog post appeared in November 2011. Editor's Note: This chapter has been taken verbatim from Chandaria's blog. Editorial alterations appear within square brackets [thus].

WEATHER AND LANGUAGE LESSONS

By Kartik Chandaria

The potholes that litter the side alleys are bursting at the edges, full of brown water, so it seems easier to step on the recent bed of fallen autumn leaves at the side that leads from the house to the office. The cars veer wide of the large potholes, occasionally jolting into one. The weather has changed and it has rained for the last two weeks, with the temperature dropping to single numbers. The atmosphere is grey and the colour has slowly disappeared from the city, leaving even the grandiose presidential palace looking insignificant. Irony is that for the last 24 hours, while the roads are almost flooded, our water supply was cut off. When it came back on, the electricity switched off, the fuel which heats up the water, and so basically nature has beaten me and the only place to stay warm is the office!

With little to do outside, there is an opportunity to learn the ancient language of Tajik so I may eventually get to know this world and speak to the kids in the hospital. The letters are so foreign to me, that they hurt my eyes and being a slightly impulsive student, the frustration of the poor understanding is even more evident. My teacher is a young Tajik lady who cannot understand why I cannot pronounce the words properly. The language sounds like a mix of [U]rdu and [M]andarin to me, the latter bringing a smile to my attempt at Tajik. The alphabet is the beautiful Cyrillic alphabet which has shape and music to every letter. Well not quite, there are some sounds which are guttural and I have to practice them in front of the mirror to see where the tongue lies! They say the language is poetic and there is a lot of folktale and theatre here but until I have a basic foundation, the nuances of the language are just a dream.

The guards help me a lot here in the office. One guard is Rasul and he is a tall man worthy of a Tajik medal. He offers me bread, an offering that one must never refuse, and patiently teaches me. I like his style: he smile[s] and teaches me with lots of repetitions. The basic greetings are to the gods and health, generally followed by a hand to the heart and a bow of the head (I love it). Any further conversation is a mix between Hindi, Spanish and English in the hope that one of the languages associates with Tajik, and with an innocent smile, I start listening to the words. They slowly start to spring to life, a joy which is difficult to suppress, because slowly, things start to make sense.

The kids in the hospital giggle at any attempt to speak Tajik, so I decide to hold an English class, as a pay-back for giggling. I enter the school/dining room. The low tables are coloured red and the small hand-made wooden seats are the only objects that suggest this might be a small school. The children here are not considered to be infectious to others and are generally quite well.

There are four children who are infectious. They are housed in a separate area, and fall victim to other consequences of this consumptive illness, the separation from normality, from play and learning and helping the others. The two 15 years old girls and two 13 year old girls do not receive any education and spend the cold days in the rooms, mostly sleeping. It is hard to imagine their boredom, but they never complain. This worries me – why are they so accepting of their fate? Is this cultural or the role of poverty that determines the freedom to express one's wishes? Do the children and families receive an informed view of their health and if not, does it matter in this culture? Or should culture be ignored and should MSF serve to enhance the view of the child more? The problem, I feel, is that a western construct of childhood is different to that of another culture and without a good understanding of what Tajik culture is, it is very difficult for me to implement our slightly two dimensional standardized view of how to serve the interests of these children.

I speak to the teacher, a lady of mature years with laughter lines running down her eyes. She has worked as a teacher for 40 years and in the hospital for 4 years. The children love her classes because they can practice their singing and although as yet I have not heard their songs, I look forward to listening to their dulcet (and not so dulcet) tones. There is nothing to draw or write with and the white walls speak of hygiene, but not of stories or messy hand prints and colour. The children, however, are noisy and eager to learn so I ask the teacher if I could teach them the body parts (I feel as a doctor, I know something about body parts). The lesson begins: there is the creek of the small wooden chairs unceremoniously dragged across the floor in two lines and the noise makes me shiver. There are more children than chairs, so those who are able to speak generally have the better seat (the under 2's group themselves on the side and the boys in the back row). I sing "head, shoulders, knees and toes" and there are glazed expression[s]. I repeat "head, shoulders, knees and toes, knees and toes, and eyes and ears and mouth and nose, head, shoulders, knees and toes, knees and toes." There is movement, but the expression is still of confusion. I repeat the song with accompanying gestures, remembering that language is easier to learn through gesture and here we go, we are getting somewhere, and once I get over the image of me looking like a monkey as I place my hand neatly cupped over my head, there is an imitated response. The girls are generally the better at the words but the boys don't do too bad[ly] considering the horror that they are subjected to. We continue for another 10 minutes before the lesson terminates and lunch is served.

I learn through experience not to promise too much to children because the disappointment they show is quite palpable and makes you feel quite sick. Still, I'm sure a few notebooks and a blackboard could be managed, without too much problem and I promise at least to myself that we can buy this. It is the kids in the positive ward that worry me more.

The damp has settled in the bones but after the two weeks, the sun came out for two days. A group of children make a fire out of the nearby fallen twigs and the groups of men and groups of women wander in the streets to celebrate the holiday. Last night, it all changed and the wind returned to Dushanbe. By the morning, there was fresh snow and now there is a foot of thick snow. Earlier than expected, the women are still in their high heel stilettos – a scenario that is always amusing in the slippery surface. I hear a boy shout "mama," when his poor mother slips on the damp snow. I turn around and she smiles hopefully realizing the impracticality that she puts herself in. The snow was dense and lasted for two days before the sun emerged and melted it rapidly, making it fall on unsuspecting foreigners. The pot holes are full again of dirty water. The leaves had fallen prematurely and the hospital grounds have a thick carpet of unwithered leaves, that should have fallen and become crisp from autumn. I returned to the hospital, where the day is beautiful and most of the kids are out. The older ones are at work clearing the fallen leaves in the tarpaulene left over from construction work. And they look healthy today, not cramped away inside the hospital. It also means that I do not have to wear the respirator (mask) as the natural ventilation will rapidly take away the cough particles. The children are relaxed, those that are deemed to be not infectious, but once again, the kids in the positive ward are left to watch what appears to be a normal day outside from within.

Visit the Doctors Without Borders Web site and look for its discussion of "Medical Issues" (http://www.doctorswithoutborders.org/news/issues.cfm?ref=main-menu-ourwork). Pick a public health concern that affects both developing nations and the United States, such as access to medicines, HIV/AIDS treatment, mental health, sexual violence, or immunizations. Or follow the links on Chandaria's blog to learn more about drug-resistant tuberculosis (including its persistence in urban or impoverished areas of the United States). Follow the links to further reading and resources on the Doctors Without Borders site. What did you learn about this issue that you did not know before?

With a group of your classmates, see if you can identify the audience for Chandaria's blog. (If the question puzzles you, look at the comments below particular postings to see if the commenters' experiences give you any clues). Chandaria's blog is one of several by doctors, nurses, and aid workers who write about health care. Now take a look at *Ah Yes, Medical School* (http://ahyesmedschool.blogspot.com), or *A Cartoon Guide to Becoming a Doctor* (http://doccartoon.blogspot.com), written by physicians or medical students, Mediblogopathy (http://mediblogopathy.blogspot.com), *Dora's Nursing* (http://dorasnursing.tumblr.com) or *Head Nurse* (http://head-nurse.blogspot.com), written by nurses, or *Mothers in Medicine* (http://www.mothersinmedicine.com/2009/08/difference.html). Read a range of these blogs and comment upon some of the differences you notice in tone, style, and audience for these writers. Summarize your findings for the class.

This assignment will help you prepare for Major Assignment #4: Service-Learning Social Media Campaign. Think of an audience that you might like to reach in a blog post about public health. List the traits of this audience and then identify rhetorical strategies or content-matter that will help you engage your readers. Now write a short (150–200 word) post.

United States Assistant Surgeon General and Rear Admiral Ali S. Khan holds advanced degrees in both medicine and public health and directs the Office of Public Health Preparedness and Response at the Centers for Disease Control (CDC) in Atlanta, Georgia. His witty blog post from 2011, which used the imagined threat of a zombie apocalypse to teach readers about disaster preparation, quickly went viral and inspired a CDC social media campaign based on zombies.

PREPAREDNESS 101: ZOMBIE APOCALYPSE

By Ali S. Khan

There are all kinds of emergencies out there that we can prepare for. Take a zombie apocalypse for example. That's right, I said z-o-m-b-i-e a-p-o-c-a-l-y-p-s-e. You may laugh now, but when it happens you'll be happy you read this, and hey, maybe you'll even learn a thing or two about how to prepare for a *real* emergency.

A BRIEF HISTORY OF ZOMBIES

We've all seen at least one movie about flesh-eating zombies taking over (my personal favorite is *Resident Evil*), but where do zombies come from and why do they love eating brains so much? The word zombie comes from Haitian and New Orleans voodoo origins. Although its meaning has changed slightly over the years, it refers to a human corpse mysteriously reanimated to serve the undead. Through ancient voodoo and folk-lore traditions, shows like *The Walking Dead* were born.

A couple dressed as zombies—Danny Zucco and Sandy Olson from the movie *Grease* walking in the annual Toronto Zombie Walk.

In movies, shows, and literature, zombies are often depicted as being created by an infectious virus, which is passed on via bites and contact with bodily fluids. Harvard psychiatrist Steven Schlozman wrote a (fictional) medical paper on the zombies presented in *Night of the Living Dead* and refers to the condition as *Ataxic Neurodegenerative Satiety Deficiency Syndrome* caused by an infectious agent. *The Zombie Survival Guide* identifies the cause of zombies as a virus called solanum. Other zombie origins shown in films include radiation from a destroyed NASA Venus probe (as in *Night of the Living Dead*), as well as mutations of existing conditions such as prions, mad-cow disease, measles and rabies.

The rise of zombies in pop culture has given credence to the idea that a zombie apocalypse could happen. In such a scenario zombies would take over entire countries, roaming city streets eating anything living that got in their way. The proliferation of this idea has led many people to wonder "How do I prepare for a zombie apocalypse?"

Well, we're here to answer that question for you, and hopefully share a few tips about preparing for *real* emergencies too!

BETTER SAFE THAN SORRY

So what do you need to do before zombies . . . or hurricanes or pandemics for example, actually happen? First of all, you should have an emergency kit in your house. This includes things like water, food, and other supplies to get you through the first couple of days before you can locate a zombie-free refugee camp (or in the event of a natural disaster, it will buy you some time until you are able to make your way to an evacuation shelter or

Some of the supplies for your emergency kit

utility lines are restored). Below are a few items you should include in your kit, for a full list visit the CDC Emergency page.

Water (1 gallon per person per day)

Food (stock up on non-perishable items that you eat regularly)

Medications (this includes prescription and non-prescription meds)

Tools and Supplies (utility knife, duct tape, battery powered radio, etc.)

Sanitation and Hygiene (household bleach, soap, towels, etc.)

Clothing and Bedding (a change of clothes for each family member and blankets)

Important documents (copies of your driver's license, passport, and birth certificate to name a few)

First Aid supplies (although you're a goner if a zombie bites you, you can use these supplies to treat basic cuts and lacerations that you might get during a tornado or hurricane)

Once you've made your emergency kit, you should sit down with your family and come up with an **emergency plan**. This includes where you would go and who you would call if zombies started appearing outside your door step. You can also implement this plan if there is a flood, earthquake, or other emergency.

Identify the types of emergencies that are possible in your area. Besides a zombie apocalypse, this may include floods, tornadoes, or earthquakes. If you are unsure contact your local Red Cross chapter for more information.

Pick a meeting place for your family to regroup in case zombies invade your home . . . or your town evacuates because of a hurricane. Pick one place right outside your home for sudden emergencies and one place outside of your neighborhood in case you are unable to return home right away.

Family members meeting by their mailbox. You should pick two meeting places, one close to your home and farther away

Identify your emergency contacts. Make a list of local contacts like the police, fire department, and your local zombie response team. Also identify an out-of-state contact that you can call during an emergency to let the rest of your family know you are ok.

Plan your evacuation route. When zombies are hungry they won't stop until they get food (i.e., brains), which means you need to get out of town fast! Plan where you would go and multiple routes you would take ahead of time so that the flesh eaters don't have a chance! This is also helpful when natural disasters strike and you have to take shelter fast.

NEVER FEAR—CDC IS READY

Get a Kit, Make a Plan, Be Prepared

If zombies did start roaming the streets, CDC would conduct an investigation much like any other disease outbreak. CDC would provide technical assistance to cities, states, or international partners dealing with a zombie infestation. This assistance might include consultation, lab testing and analysis, patient management and care, tracking of contacts, and infection control (including isolation and quarantine). It's likely that an investigation of this scenario would seek to accomplish several goals: determine the cause of the illness, the source of the infection/virus/toxin, learn how it is transmitted and how readily it is spread, how to break the cycle of transmission and thus prevent further cases, and how patients can best be treated. Not only would scientists be working to identify the cause and cure of the zombie outbreak, but CDC and other federal agencies would send medical teams and first responders to help those in affected areas (I will be volunteering the young nameless disease detectives for the field work).

To learn more about what CDC does to prepare for and respond to emergencies of all kinds, visit: http://emergency.cdc.gov/cdc/orgs_progs.asp

To learn more about how you can prepare for and stay safe during an emergency visit: http://emergency.cdc.gov/

Join the CDC Zombie Task Force! The CDC Foundation, a non-profit partner of CDC is offering Zombie Task Force t-shirts (click on the picture to find out more). Proceeds go to benefit disaster relief efforts and other important health programs. Get yours before they're gone…

ARE YOU PREPARED? TELL US…

Have you begun preparing for a zombie apocalypse? Or maybe you have been preparing for a more realistic threat like hurricanes or the next flu season? Tell us about what you are doing to prepare! Enter our video contest here: http://prepare.challenge.gov.

Visit the CDC Web site where this blog post originated (http://blogs.cdc.gov/publichealthmatters/2011/05/preparedness-101-zombie-apocalypse) and take a look at the comments that criticize the author for using public money to write a humorous blog post. Later commenters argue that the blog uses humor effectively to teach the public about disaster preparedness. With which perspective do you have more sympathy?

This assignment will help you with Major Assignment #4: Service-Learning Social Media Campaign. The CDC has begun a "Zombie novella" online to help educate the public about disaster preparedness. Pick a natural disaster that might really happen in your region: tornado, hurricane, earthquake, outbreak of a particular disease (such as H1N1 influenza, meningitis, E.coli). Write a chapter of a novella that describes the beginning, middle, or the end of your chosen disaster.

This assignment will help you with Major Assignment #3: Describe a Medical or Therapeutic Procedure or Process. Using the CDC's mock zombie page as a template, write a mock disaster preparation Web page or blog entry for an impossible or improbable disaster such as a vampire attack, a space alien invasion, time-travelling tourists, werewolves, and so on.

Kim Krisberg is a senior editor at The Nation's Health, *the official newspaper of the American Public Health Association, where this down-to-earth article appeared in 2009.*

RU HEALTHY?
PUBLIC HEALTH EFFORTS TAKE ON TEXT MESSAGING

By Kim Krisberg

With a few quick thumb swipes, San Francisco youth literally have health information at their fingertips. They can receive the information anywhere, anytime without having to log into a computer, make a phone call or pick up a pamphlet. For Bay area youth, getting the "411" on sexual health is as easy as hitting "send" on their cell phones.

Thanks to today's texting trend, the youth are getting answers from SexInfo, a public health text messaging service that was launched in 2006. The service received 4,500 sexual health inquiries in just its first 25 weeks of service, with broken condoms, pregnancy and sexually transmitted diseases topping the subject list. The effort came after local health officials spotted rising rates of gonorrhea and chlamydia among black teens in one of the city's low-income neighborhoods, according to Deb Levine, MA, executive director and founder of Internet Sexuality Information Services Inc., which developed SexInfo in partnership with the San Francisco Department of Public Health. While the initial idea was to create a new Web site, both Levine and colleague Jacqueline McCright, MPH, a community-based STD services manager at the public health department, decided it was time to think outside the box. While visiting high schools for inspiration, the new idea walked right in front of their faces: After the school bell rang, students filed out with cell phones in hand. But they weren't talking—they were typing.

"That's when we knew we were on to something," Levine told *The Nation's Health.* While San Francisco's health workers could be considered pioneers in text messaging, public health has been taking advantage of mobile communication devices to improve surveillance and the delivery of health interventions for some time, said Jay Bernhardt, PhD, MPH, director of the National Center for Health Marketing at the Centers for Disease Control and Prevention. But because text messaging is "multidirectional"—in other words, because users can send and receive information in real time—it can be a "real game-changer in public health both domestically and especially globally," said APHA member Bernhardt, who added that CDC took a "big step" last year when it co-sponsored the first Texting4Health conference at Stanford University. Mobile communication platforms, he said, are "the next wave of public health communication and surveillance."

While new communication technologies offer great opportunities for public health, Bernhardt noted, lack of access to tools such as the Internet can be a significant barrier, particularly on the global front. Cell phones, however, are the first interactive communication devices cutting across economic, educational and social divides, he said. In turn, text messaging can be used on a number of health fronts, from delivering information to managing chronic diseases to treatment adherence.

"Today, effective public health requires us to provide our information and interventions to our communities where, when and how they need them," Bernhardt told *The Nation's Health*. "Our communities are using social media and mobile technology as an important part of their lives and if we want to reach them and help them, then we need to communicate with them the way they communicate with each other."

In San Francisco, Levine, McCright and colleagues knew young people were texting each other, but were unsure if youth wanted to receive text messages from their local health department. Fortunately, in focus groups of young black men and women, participants liked the text messaging idea. However, they were insistent that they be the ones initiating the process, Levine said. The resulting SexInfo service allows youth—or anyone interested—to text the word "SexInfo" to a five-digit number to receive a message back with codes telling them to text, for example, "B2 if u think ur pregnant," "D4 to find out about HIV" or "F8 if ur not sure u want to have sex." Participants are then texted back basic health information or referrals for in-person visits. According to a SexInfo study published in the March 2008 issue of APHA's *American Journal of Public Health*, 2,500 of the first 4,500 text inquiries led to access to more information and referrals for testing and screening.

"Things are changing rapidly and we have to do things differently to reach different people," McCright told *The Nation's Health*. "We can't keep doing the same old things and expecting different results. We have to be creative."

Of course, SexInfo's success depends on smart marketing and continually checking in with young people about cell phone trends, Levine said. To spread the word about SexInfo, health workers passed out cards, put up posters, bought billboards, created public service announcements and ran ads on local television and radio shows, according to McCright. The same aggressive marketing is working for the Kaiser Family Foundation's "KnowIt" text messaging campaign, which allows users to find HIV testing sites in their area. First promoted with the help of an ongoing partnership with MTV in the summer of 2007, the service received 15,000 text requests in its first month alone and more than 200,000 text inquiries in 2008, according to Tina Hoff, vice president and director of the foundation's entertainment media partnerships. To use the service, cell phone users send a text message with their ZIP codes to KnowIt and within seconds, receive back a text message with information on nearby HIV testing sites. The service relies on a CDC database of HIV testing sites organized by ZIP codes, and in turn, CDC uses the texting service for its own HIV outreach as well, Hoff said.

"Clearly, it's a format for communicating that (young people) are comfortable with," Hoff said. "One of the nice things about new media technologies is that they're really very accessible, and not exceedingly costly to implement. But for a campaign like ours to work, it's incumbent to have effective promotion strategies. The resource is only as good as the promotions you can do."

Getting the word out is the focus for Lauren Weber, a community health educator with Arizona's Mohave Department of Public Health, whose insights led to the launch of the department's Stop Smoking Over Mobile Phone, or STOMP, program in fall 2008. The youngest member of the department's Tobacco Use Prevention Program, the 23-year-old joined the team in 2007 and began visiting schools to teach students about tobacco use. Weber said she noticed that there was no educational component for students caught on campus with tobacco. When searching online for a tobacco intervention method that would appeal to students, Weber hit upon the company Healthphone Solutions and its text messaging smoking cessation service. Now, Mohave County is the first to use the Healthphone product in the United States.

Today, Mohave County students caught with tobacco can avoid suspension from school by signing up for the smoking text service. The 26-week-program creates a personalized smoking cessation service based on a participant's demographics and quit date. The text messaging service guides users through the preparations for quitting, sends encouraging messages on the quit date, and begins sending multiple texts per day after the quit date. The program is open to anyone interested and about 40 people have taken part so far, said Weber, noting that some participants couple the text messaging program with traditional in-person cessation classes.

"I know I'd rather text than talk," Weber told *The Nation's Health.* "What better way to reach people than to get them on the phones that they're already using."

This assignment will help you prepare Major Assignment #4: Service-Learning Social Media Campaign. Krisberg's article describes the effectiveness of a social media campaign in 2009 that was based on texting. Do you think that texting is still an effective way to reach high-school students and adolescents? Since the article was written, smartphone and tablet apps have come to dominate social digital networks. Imagine that you are an app designer. Could you think of an app to promote sexual health among teens? What features would this app need to have?

With your peers, watch the classic documentary *The Lost Children of Rockdale County.* What are your responses to the children in the film? To their parents? To the filmmakers? What are some interventions that any of these groups could have taken to protect the sexual health of the children before they became infected?

Most school districts offer sexual education, but what they teach varies regionally (http://www.npr.org/templates/story/story.php?storyId=1622610). Find out what kind of education your local school district offers on the subject of sexual health, and at what age students learn about sexual health. Do you think the content and timing of this education is appropriate in your school district?

Irish novelist Anne Enright has won many awards, including the Man Booker Prize in 2007 for her novel The Gathering. *This essay appeared in the* London Review of Books *in 2000 and was reprinted in* Harper's Magazine *in the U.S.; most recently, Enright revised the essay into a chapter for her book,* Making Babies: Stumbling into Motherhood, *which came out in 2012.*

MY MILK: ON BECOMING A MOTHER

BY ANNE ENRIGHT

The milk surprises me. It does not disgust me as much as I thought it would, unless it is not fresh. It is disturbing that a piece of you should decay so quickly. I don't think Freud ever discussed lactation, but the distinction between "good" and "bad" bodily products here is very fine. Women leak so much. Perhaps this is why we clean—which is to say that a man who cleans is always "anal," and a woman who cleans is just a woman.

There certainly is a lot of it, and it gets everywhere, and the laundry is a fright. But what fun to be granted a new bodily function so late in life—as if you woke up one morning and could play the piano. From day to day the child is heavier in your arms: she plumps up from wrist to ankle, she has dimples where her knuckles were, she has fat on her toes. I thought we might trade weight, pound for pound, but she is gaining more than I am losing. I am faced with strange and difficult calculations—the weight of the groceries in a bag versus the weight of her diapers in a bag. Or: my weight, plus a pint of water, minus four ounces of milk, versus her weight, plus four ounces, divided by yesterday. When I was at school, a big-chested friend put her breasts on the scales and figured that they weighed two pounds each. I don't know how she did it, but I still think that she was wrong. Heavier. Much heavier.

It is pleasant when a part of your body makes sense, after many years. A man can fancy your backside, but you still get to sit on it. Breasts, on the other hand, were always just there. Even so, the anxiety of pregnancy is the anxiety of puberty all over again. I feel that I have done this before somehow, that I have passed that exam; I am thirty-seven. I do not believe people when they say these things will be wonderful, that they are "meant." I am suspicious of the gleam in women's eyes, that pack of believers, and listen instead to a friend who breastfed her children until they were fourteen and a half, and who now says, "They're like ticks."

So I feed the child because I should, and resign myself to staying home. I never liked being around nursing women—there was always too much love, too much need in the room. I also suspected it to be sexually gratifying. For whom? Oh, for everyone: for the mother, the child, the father, the father-in-law. Everyone's voice that little bit nervy, as though it weren't happening: everyone taking pleasure in a perv-lite, middle-class sort of way. I thought I sensed a distaste in the midwives, a couple of months ago, who were obliged by hospital and government policy to prod the child and pinch my nipple, though perhaps—let's face it—not quite that hard. It is probably easier for men, who like breasts in general, but I have always found them mildly disgusting, at least up close. Even the word "breast" is difficult.

So let's call it "nursing" and let's be discreet—it's still the best way I know to clear a room. My breast (left or right, whichever is at issue) is not the problem, the "problem" is the noise. Sometimes the child drinks as simply as from a cup, other times she snorts and gulps, half-drowns, sputters and gasps; then she squawks a bit, and starts all over again. This may be an iconized activity made sacred by some and disgusting by others, but it is first and foremost a meal. It is only occasionally serene. It also takes a long time. I do smile at her and coo a bit, but I also read a lot (she will hate books), talk, or type (this, for example). Afterward she throws up. People stare at the whiteness of it, as I did at first. Look. Milk.

"It was the whiteness of the whale that above all things appalled me." The nineteenth century took its breasts very seriously, or so I suspect—I can't really get into a library to check. I am thinking of those references I found particularly exciting or unsettling as a child. The heroes of *King Solomon's Mines*, for example, as they toil up Sheba's left Breast (a mountain), tortured by thirst. The chapter is called "Water! Water!" and comes from a time when you were allowed to be so obvious it hurt. "Heavens, how we did drink!"

These extinct volcanoes are "inexpressibly solemn and overpowering." In the attempt to describe their "extraordinary grandeur and beauty… language seems to fail" him, despite which the narrator staggers on until "as though to veil the majestic sight from our curious eyes, strange mists and clouds gathered and increased around them, till presently we could only trace their pure and gigantic outline swelling ghostlike through the fleecy envelope." In a desperate drama of hunger and satiation our heroes climb through lava and snow up to the hillock of the enormous, freezing nipple. There they find a cave, occupied by a dead man (What?! What?!), and in this cave one of their party also dies: Ventvögel, a "Hottentot" whose "snubnose" had enabled him, when still alive, to sniff out water (we don't want to know).

So far, so infantile. I watch the child's drama at the breast and, when I am not reading, typing, or talking, cheer her along. She wakes with a shout in the middle of the night, and I wonder at her dreams: there is a dead man in a cave, perhaps, somewhere about my person. Oh dear. When did it all get so serious? I turn to Swift for the comedy, as opposed to tragedy, of scale, but Gulliver perched on a Brobdingnagian nipple turns out, on rereading, to be part of a great disgustfest about giant women pissing. None of this seems *true* to me. I have no use for the child's disgust, as she has no use for mine. I am besotted with a being who is, at this stage, just a set of emotions arranged around a gut. Who is just a shitter, who is just a soul.

Are all mothers Manichaeans? This is one of the hundreds of stupid questions that have never been asked about motherhood. What I am interested in is not the drama of being a child but this new drama of being a mother (yes, there are cannibals in my dreams. Yes) about which so little has been written. Can a mother not hold a pen? Or is it just the fact that we are all children when we write?

I venture into Books Upstairs in Dublin, to find a poem by Eavan Boland. The child is in the stroller and I am inordinately, sadly proud of the fact that she is clean. We negotiate the steps, we knock over some books. The child does a spectacular crap in the silence of the shop, in front of the section marked "Philosophy." I say: "Oh, look at all the books. Oh, *look* at all the books," because I believe in talking to her, and I don't know what else to say.

The poem is called "Night Feed" and is beautifully measured and very satisfying: "A silt of milk./The last suck./And now your eyes are open,/Birth-coloured and offended." But the poet chooses a bottle, not a breast, placing the poem in the bland modernity of the suburbs. I grew up in those suburbs. I know what we were running away from. Because the unpalatable fact is, the Ireland of my childhood had the closest thing to a cow-cult outside of India. When I was eleven, I won a Kodak Instamatic camera in "The Milk Competition," a major annual event, when every schoolchild in the country had to write an essay called "The Story of Milk." I can still remember the arrival of the Charolais that was the beginning of Ireland's love affair with Europe. The most exciting thing about economic union, for my farming relatives, was not the government grants but this bug-eyed, nougat-colored breed of bull whose semen could be used in beef or dairy herds—as good, if you will pardon the phrase, for meat as for milk. It was a romantic animal, as hopeful as the moon shot. There were cufflinks made in the shape of the Charolais, and men wore them to mass and to the market. And the romance lingers on. A couple of years ago, a media personality of my acquaintance bought four of them, to match her curtains.

The country was awash with milk. Kitchens and bedrooms were hung with pictures of the Madonna and Child. After the arrival of infant formula in the 1950s, breast-feeding became more of a chosen, middle-class activity, but it was still common in the countryside and was everywhere practiced as a fairly optimistic form of contraception. Still, although it was general all over Ireland, breast-feeding was absolutely hidden. The closest the culture came to an image of actual nursing was in the icon of the Sacred Heart, endlessly offering his male breast, open and glowing, and crowned with thorns.

Actually, you know, breast-feeding hurts. Certainly, at first, it really fucking hurts. On the third night of her life, I was left with a human being the size of a cat and nothing to sustain her with but this *stub*. Madwomen apparently think that their babies are possessed. And they are. They look at you, possessed by their own astonishing selves. You say, where did that come from? You say, where did *you* come from? She is pure need—a need you never knew you had. And all you have to offer is this mute part of your body, that you are told will somehow start "expressing," as though it might start singing "Summertime." You feed your child, it seems, on hope alone. There is nothing to see. You do not believe the milk exists until she throws it back up, and when she does you want to cry. What is not quite yours as it leaves you is definitely yours as it comes back.

So there we were in the hospital dark, me and my white Dracula, her chin running with milk and her eyes black. What I remember is how fully human her gaze was, even though it was so new. She seemed to say that this was a serious business, that we were in it together. New babies have such emotional complexity. I am amazed that "bravery" is one of the feelings she has already experienced, that she should be born so intrepid and easily affronted—that she should be born so much herself.

She is also, at this early stage, almost gender-free. And this is useful. The statistics on how often mothers choose not to breast-feed girl babies are shocking. There are probably a number of reasons for this, but one of them surely is the degree to which our society has sexualized the breast. All in all, sex has ruined breast-feeding. It's a moral business these days—a slightly dirty, slightly wonderful, always unsettling, duty. It has no comic aspects. No one has told the child this: she seems to find it, finally, quite amusing, as indeed do I.

We turn to Sterne for glee, envy, all those ravening eighteenth-century emotions, transmuted by language into delight. Shandy quotes Ambrose Paraeus on the stunting effect of the nursing breast on a child's nose, particularly those "organs of nutrition" that have "firmness and elastic repulsion." These were "the undoing of the child, inasmuch as his nose was so snubb'd, so rebuff'd, so rebated, and so refrigerated thereby, as never to arrive *ad mensuram suam legitimam*." What was needed was a soft, flaccid breast so that, "by sinking into it ... as into so much butter, the nose was comforted, nourish'd, plump'd up, refresh'd, refocillated, and set a growing for ever."

This was still when "breast" was a common, easy word, more often applied to men, in whose tender, or sympathetic, breast emotions arose and secrets were stored. Men placed their hands on their breast, had pistols pointed at it, and were in general so set to a-swelling and a-glowing as to put the girls to shame. There is a distinction between "breast" and "breasts," of course, but it is still charming to think that this seat of honesty and sentiment is the singular of a plural that provoked desire. As if, in modern terms, we got horny watching someone's eyes fill with tears. As, indeed, sometimes we do.

No. The milk surprises me, above all, because it hurts as it is let down, and this foolish pain hits me at quite the wrong times. The reflex is designed to work at the sight, sound, or thought of your baby—which is spooky enough—but the brain doesn't seem to know what a baby *is* exactly and so tries to make you feed anything helpless, or wonderful, or small. So I have let down milk for Russian submariners and German tourists dying on the Concorde. Loneliness and technology get me every time, get my milk every time. Desire, also, stabs me not in the heart but on either side of the heart. But I had expected this. What I had not expected was that there should be some things that do not move me, that move my milk. Or that, sometimes, I only realize I am moved when I feel the pain. I find myself lapsed into a memory I cannot catch, I find myself trying to figure out what it is in the room that is sad or lovely—was it that combination of words, or the look on his face?—what is it that has such a call on my unconscious attention, or my pituitary, or my alveolar cells.

There is a part of me, I have realized, that wants to nurse the stranger on the bus. Or perhaps it wants to nurse the bus itself, or the tree I see through the window of the bus, or the child I once was, paying my fare on the way home from school. This occasional incontinence is terrifying. It makes me want to shout—I am not sure what: either "Take it!" or "Stop!" If the world would stop needing, then my body would come back to me.

I could ask (in a disingenuous fashion) if this is what it is like to be bothered by erections. Is this what it is like to be bothered by tears? Whatever—I think we can safely say that when we are moved, it is some liquid that starts moving, blood, or milk, or salt water. I did not have a very tearful pregnancy, mostly because we don't have a television. Pregnant women cry at ads for toilet tissue: some say it's the hormones, but I think we have undertaken such a great work of imagining that we are prone to wobble on the high wire. Of course, the television has always been a provoker of secondhand tears as well as secondhand desire. Stories, no matter how fake, produce a real biological response in us, and we are used to this. But the questions my nursing body raises are more testing to me. Do we need stories in order to produce emotion, or is an emotion already a story? What is the connection, in other words, between narrative and my alveolar cells?

I suspect, as I search the room for the hunger by the fireplace, or the hunger in her cry, that I have found a place before stories start. Or the precise place where stories start. How else can I explain the shift from language that has happened in my brain? This is why mothers do not write, because motherhood happens in the body as much as in the mind. I thought childbirth was a sort of journey that you could send dispatches home from, but of course it is not—it *is* home. Everywhere else now is "abroad."

A child came out of me. I cannot understand this, or try to explain it. Except to say that my past life has become foreign to me. Except to say that I am prey, for the rest of my life, to every small thing.

Visit the Department of Health and Human Services (DHHS) site on breastfeeding and support (http://www.womenshealth.gov/breastfeeding/why-breastfeeding-is-important). The site ranks the benefits of breastfeeding in this order: it protects infants, benefits mothers, benefits society, and saves lives during emergencies, among other reasons. Read through the reasons that the Surgeon General and the DHHS recommend breastfeeding. Which of these reasons are important to you? Now look at Enright's essay again. Which reasons do you think are important to her?

While most articles about breastfeeding focus on the documented health benefits to mother and child, Enright concentrates instead on the lyrical joy and surprise of developing a new ability or superpower. Have you ever discovered delight in undertaking a task that you began at first for health or medical reasons, such as taking up a sport, learning to cook, shopping at a farmer's market, or practicing meditation? Write a short essay that, like Enright's, celebrates the joy of a bodily skill that many people dismiss as purely medicinal.

Time began publishing in 1923. This controversial image, from a photograph by Martin Schoeller, accompanied an article by Katie Pickert and went viral on the internet even before the print issue hit the newsstands on May 21, 2012.

ARE YOU MOM ENOUGH?

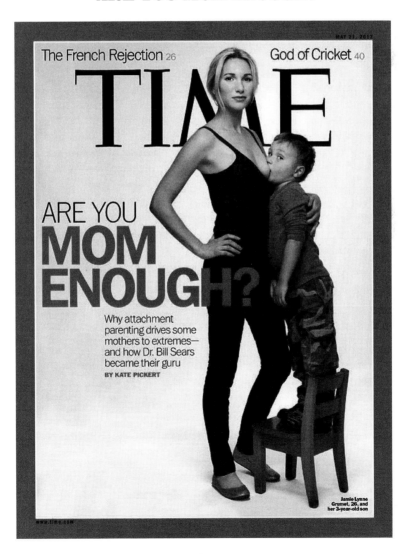

Read the article that accompanied the cover, and read a few of the responses to the cover in online magazines such as *Salon* (http://www.salon.com/2012/05/10/why_times_cover_shocks), *Slate* (http://www.slate.com/articles/news_and_politics/explainer/2012/05/time_magazine_breast_feeding_cover_how_nursing_worked_in_prehistoric_times_.html), or *Jezebel* (http://jezebel.com/5909225/attachment-parenting-freakish-or-feminist). Do the responses have anything in common? Do you agree with any of these writers?

This cover rapidly became an internet meme. With a group of your classmates, look at the images at *Buzzfeed* (http://www.buzzfeed.com/provincialelitist/time-mag-breast-feeding-meme-is-here). You may find some of these images to be obscene, funny, sad, shocking, educational, or all of these things. What are some of the messages that the meme creators are trying to send? Can your group classify the memes and present your findings to the class?

The cover design of *Time* deliberately uses a provocative slogan "Are you Mom Enough?" List some of the effects of accompanying the image with this slogan. What alternatives can you imagine?

There is a long history of presenting breastfeeding mothers in art, especially in Christian art. Take a look at First Things' images of nursing Madonnas (http://www.firstthings.com/blogs/firstthoughts/2012/05/11/the-horror-of-the-times-breastfeeding-cover/#more-42982).
The Washington Post (http://www.washingtonpost.com/blogs/arts-post/post/time-magazine-breast-feeding-cover-its-art-historical-origins-and-what-makes-the-image-so-sensational/2012/05/11/gIQAJtNZIU_blog.html) points out another surprising precedent in fine art. Write a short essay contrasting one of the fine art images and the *Time* magazine cover.

Polemical journalist and mother of three Hanna Rosin stirred up outrage from the American Academy of Pediatrics with the publication of this essay in The Atlantic in 2009.

THE CASE AGAINST BREASTFEEDING

By Hanna Rosin

In certain overachieving circles, breast-feeding is no longer a choice—it's a no-exceptions requirement, the ultimate badge of responsible parenting. Yet the actual health benefits of breast-feeding are surprisingly thin, far thinner than most popular literature indicates. Is breast-feeding right for every family? Or is it this generation's vacuum cleaner—an instrument of misery that mostly just keeps women down?

One afternoon at the playground last summer, shortly after the birth of my third child, I made the mistake of idly musing about breast-feeding to a group of new mothers I'd just met. This time around, I said, I was considering cutting it off after a month or so. At this remark, the air of insta-friendship we had established cooled into an icy politeness, and the mothers shortly wandered away to chase little Emma or Liam onto the slide. Just to be perverse, over the next few weeks I tried this experiment again several more times. The reaction was always the same: circles were redrawn such that I ended up in the class of mom who, in a pinch, might feed her baby mashed-up Chicken McNuggets.

In my playground set, the urban moms in their tight jeans and oversize sunglasses size each other up using a whole range of signifiers: organic content of snacks, sleekness of stroller, ratio of tasteful wooden toys to plastic. But breast-feeding is the real ticket into the club. My mother friends love to exchange stories about subversive ways they used to sneak frozen breast milk through airline security (it's now legal), or about the random brutes on the street who don't approve of breast-feeding in public. When Angelina Jolie wanted to secure her status as America's ur-mother, she posed on the cover of *W* magazine nursing one of her twins. Alt-rocker Pete Wentz recently admitted that he tasted his wife, Ashlee Simpson's, breast milk ("soury" and "weird"), after bragging that they have a lot of sex—both of which must have seemed to him markers of a cool domestic existence.

From the moment a new mother enters the obstetrician's waiting room, she is subjected to the upper-class parents' jingle: "Breast Is Best." Parenting magazines offer "23 Great Nursing Tips," warnings on "Nursing Roadblocks," and advice on how to find your local lactation consultant (note to the childless: yes, this is an actual profession, and it's thriving). Many of the stories are accompanied by suggestions from the ubiquitous parenting guru Dr. William Sears, whose Web site hosts a comprehensive list of the benefits of mother's milk. "Brighter Brains" sits at the top: "I.Q. scores averaging seven to ten points higher!" (Sears knows his audience well.) The list then moves on to the dangers averted, from infancy on up: fewer ear infections, allergies, stomach illnesses; lower rates of obesity, diabetes, heart disease. Then it adds, for good measure, stool with a "buttermilk-like odor" and "nicer skin"—benefits, in short, "more far-reaching than researchers have even dared to imagine."

In 2005, *Babytalk* magazine won a National Magazine Award for an article called "You *Can* Breastfeed." Given the prestige of the award, I had hoped the article might provide some respite from the relentlessly cheerful tip culture of the parenting magazines, and fill mothers in on the real problems with nursing. Indeed, the article opens with a promisingly realistic vignette, featuring a theoretical "You" cracking under the strain of having to breast-feed around the clock, suffering "crying jags" and cursing at your husband. But fear not, You. The root of the problem is not the sudden realization that your ideal of an equal marriage, with two parents happily taking turns working and raising children, now seems like a farce. It turns out to be quite simple: You just haven't quite figured out how to fit "Part A into Part B." Try the "C-hold" with your baby and some "rapid arm movement," the story suggests. Even Dr. Sears pitches in: "Think 'fish lips,'" he offers.

In the days after my first child was born, I welcomed such practical advice. I remember the midwife coming to my hospital bed and shifting my arm here, and the baby's head there, and then everything falling into place. But after three children and 28 months of breast-feeding (and counting), the insistent cheerleading has begun to grate. Buttermilk-like odor? Now Dr. Sears is selling me too hard. I may have put in fewer parenting years than he has, but I do have *some* perspective. And when I look around my daughter's second-grade class, I can't seem to pick out the unfortunate ones: "Oh, poor little Sophie, whose mother couldn't breast-feed. What dim eyes she has. What a sickly pallor. And already sprouting acne!"

I dutifully breast-fed each of my first two children for the full year that the American Academy of Pediatrics recommends. I have experienced what the *Babytalk* story calls breast-feeding-induced "maternal nirvana." This time around, *nirvana* did not describe my state of mind; I was launching a new Web site and I had two other children to care for, and a husband I would occasionally like to talk to. Being stuck at home breast-feeding as he walked out the door for work just made me unreasonably furious, at him and everyone else.

In Betty Friedan's day, feminists felt shackled to domesticity by the unreasonably high bar for housework, the endless dusting and shopping and pushing the Hoover around—a vacuum cleaner being the obligatory prop for the "happy housewife heroine," as Friedan sardonically called her. When I looked at the picture on the cover of Sears's *Breastfeeding Book*—a lady lying down, gently smiling at her baby and *still in her robe*, although the sun is well up—the scales fell from my eyes: it was not the vacuum that was keeping me and my 21st-century sisters down, but another sucking sound.

Still, despite my stint as the postpartum playground crank, I could not bring myself to stop breast-feeding—too many years of Sears's conditioning, too many playground spies. So I was left feeling trapped, like many women before me, in the middle-class mother's prison of vague discontent: surly but too privileged for pity, breast-feeding with one hand while answering the cell phone with the other, and barking at my older kids to get their own organic, 100 percent juice—the modern, multitasking mother's version of Friedan's "problem that has no name."

And in this prison I would have stayed, if not for a chance sighting. One day, while nursing my baby in my pediatrician's office, I noticed a 2001 issue of the *Journal of the American Medical Association* open to an article about breast-feeding: "Conclusions: There are inconsistent associations among breastfeeding, its duration, and the risk of being overweight in young children." Inconsistent? There I was, sitting half-naked in public for the tenth time that day, the hundredth time that month, the millionth time in my life—and the associations were *inconsistent*? The seed was planted. That night, I did what any sleep-deprived, slightly paranoid mother of a newborn would do. I called my doctor friend for her password to an online medical library, and then sat up and read dozens of studies examining breast-feeding's association with allergies, obesity, leukemia, mother-infant bonding, intelligence, and all the Dr. Sears highlights.

After a couple of hours, the basic pattern became obvious: the medical literature looks nothing like the popular literature. It shows that breast-feeding is probably, maybe, a *little* better; but it is far from the stampede of evidence that Sears describes. More like tiny, unsure baby steps: two forward, two back, with much meandering and bumping into walls. A couple of studies will show fewer allergies, and then the next one will turn up no difference. Same with mother-infant bonding, I.Q., leukemia, cholesterol, diabetes. Even where consensus is mounting, the meta studies—reviews of existing studies—consistently complain about biases, missing evidence, and other major flaws in study design. "The studies do not demonstrate a universal phenomenon, in which one method is superior to another in all instances," concluded one of the first, and still one of the broadest, meta studies, in a 1984 issue of *Pediatrics*, "and they do not support making a mother feel that she is doing psychological harm to her child if she is unable or unwilling to breastfeed." Twenty-five years later, the picture hasn't changed all that much. So how is it that every mother I know has become a breast-feeding fascist?

Like many babies of my generation, I was never breast-fed. My parents were working-class Israelis, living in Tel Aviv in the '70s and aspiring to be modern. In the U.S., people were already souring on formula and passing out NO NESTLÉ buttons, but in Israel, Nestlé formula was the latest thing. My mother had already ditched her fussy Turkish coffee for Nescafé (just mix with water), and her younger sister would soon be addicted to NesQuik. Transforming soft, sandy grains from solid to magic liquid must have seemed like the forward thing to do. Plus, my mom believed her pediatrician when he said that it was important to precisely measure a baby's food intake and stick to a schedule. (To this day she pesters me about whether I'm *sure* my breast-fed babies are getting enough to eat; the parenting magazines would classify her as "unsupportive" and warn me to stay away.)

Formula grew out of a late-19th-century effort to combat atrocious rates of infant mortality by turning infant feeding into a controlled science. Pediatrics was then a newly minted profession, and for the next century, the men who dominated it would constantly try to get mothers to welcome "enlightenment from the laboratory," writes Ann Hulbert in *Raising America*. But now and again, mothers would fight back. In the U.S., the rebellion against formula began in the late '50s, when a group of moms from the Chicago suburbs got together to form a breast-feeding support group they called La Leche League. They were Catholic mothers, influenced by the Christian Family Movement, who spoke of breast-feeding as "God's plan for mothers and babies." Their role model was the biblical Eve ("Her baby came. The milk came. She nursed her baby," they wrote in their first, pamphlet edition of *The Womanly Art of Breastfeeding*, published in 1958).

They took their league's name, La Leche, from a shrine to the Madonna near Jacksonville, Florida, called Nuestra Señora de La Leche y Buen Parto, which loosely translates into "Our Lady of Happy Delivery and Plentiful Milk." A more forthright name was deemed inappropriate: "You didn't mention *breast* in print unless you were talking about Jean Harlow," said co-founder Edwina Froehlich. In their photos, the women of La Leche wear practical pumps and high-neck housewife dresses, buttoned to the top. They saw themselves as a group of women who were "kind of thinking crazy," said co-founder Mary Ann Cahill. "Everything we did was radical."

La Leche League mothers rebelled against the notion of mother as lab assistant, mixing formula for the specimen under her care. Instead, they aimed to "bring mother and baby together again." An illustration in the second edition shows a woman named Eve—looking not unlike Jean Harlow—exposed to the waist and caressing her baby, with no doctor hovering nearby. Over time the group adopted a feminist edge. A 1972 publication rallies mothers to have "confidence in themselves and their sisters rather than passively following the advice of licensed professionals." As one woman wrote in another league publication, "Yes, I want to be liberated! I want to be free! I want to be free to be a woman!"

In 1971, the Boston Women's Health Book Collective published *Our Bodies, Ourselves*, launching a branch of feminism known as the women's-health movement. The authors were more groovy types than the La Leche League moms; they wore slouchy jeans, clogs, and bandanas holding back waist-length hair. But the two movements had something in common; *Our Bodies* also grew out of "frustration and anger" with a medical establishment that was "condescending, paternalistic, judgmental and non-informative." Teaching women about their own bodies would make them "more self-confident, more autonomous, stronger," the authors wrote. Breasts were not things for men to whistle and wink at; they were made for women to feed their babies in a way that was "sensual and fulfilling." The book also noted, in passing, that breast-feeding could "strengthen the infant's resistance to infection and disease"—an early hint of what would soon become the national obsession with breast milk as liquid vaccine.

Pediatricians have been scrutinizing breast milk since the late 1800s. But the public didn't pay much attention until an international scandal in the '70s over "killer baby bottles." Studies in South America and Africa showed that babies who were fed formula instead of breast milk were more likely to die. The mothers, it turned out, were using contaminated water or rationing formula because it was so expensive. Still, in the U.S., the whole episode turned breast-feeding advocates and formula makers into Crips and Bloods, and introduced the take-no-prisoners turf war between them that continues to this day.

Some of the magical thinking about breast-feeding stems from a common misconception. Even many doctors believe that breast milk is full of maternal antibodies that get absorbed into the baby's bloodstream, says Sydney Spiesel, a clinical professor of pediatrics at Yale University's School of Medicine. That is how it works for most mammals. But in humans, the process is more pedestrian, and less powerful. A human baby is born with antibodies already in place, having absorbed them from the placenta. Breast milk dumps another layer of antibodies, primarily secretory IgA, directly into the baby's gastrointestinal tract. As the baby is nursing, these extra antibodies provide some added protection against infection, but they never get into the blood.

Since the identification of sIgA, in 1961, labs have hunted for other marvels. Could the oligosaccharides in milk prevent diarrhea? Do the fatty acids boost brain development? The past few decades have turned up many promising leads, hypotheses, and theories, all suggestive and nifty but never confirmed in the lab. Instead, most of the claims about breast-feeding's benefits lean on research conducted outside the lab: comparing one group of infants being breast-fed against another being breast-fed less, or not at all. Thousands of such studies have been published, linking breast-feeding with healthier, happier, smarter children. But they all share one glaring flaw.

An ideal study would randomly divide a group of mothers, tell one half to breast-feed and the other not to, and then measure the outcomes. But researchers cannot ethically tell mothers what to feed their babies. Instead they have to settle for "observational" studies. These simply look for differences in two populations, one breast-fed and one not. The problem is, breast-fed infants are typically brought up in very different families from those raised on the bottle. In the U.S., breast-feeding is on the rise—69 percent of mothers initiate the practice at the hospital, and 17 percent nurse exclusively for at least six months. But the numbers are much higher among women who are white, older, and educated; a woman who attended college, for instance, is roughly twice as likely to nurse for six months. Researchers try to factor out all these "confounding variables" that might affect the babies' health and development. But they still can't know if they've missed some critical factor. "Studies about the benefits of breast-feeding are extremely difficult and complex because of who breast-feeds and who doesn't," says Michael Kramer, a highly respected researcher at McGill University. "There have been claims that it prevents everything—cancer, diabetes. A reasonable person would be cautious about every new amazing discovery."

The study about obesity I saw in my pediatrician's office that morning is a good example of the complexity of breast-feeding research—and of the pitfalls it contains. Some studies have found a link between nursing and slimmer kids, but they haven't proved that one causes the other. This study surveyed 2,685 children between the ages of 3 and 5. After adjusting for race, parental education, maternal smoking, and other factors—all of which are thought to affect a child's risk of obesity—the study found little correlation between breast-feeding and weight. Instead, the strongest predictor of the child's weight was the mother's. Whether obese mothers nursed or used formula, their children were more likely to be heavy. The breast-feeding advocates' dream— that something in the milk somehow reprograms appetite—is still a long shot.

In the past decade, researchers have come up with ever more elaborate ways to tease out the truth. One 2005 paper focused on 523 sibling pairs who were fed differently, and its results put a big question mark over all the previous research. The economists Eirik Evenhouse and Siobhan Reilly compared rates of diabetes, asthma, and allergies; childhood weight; various measures of mother-child bonding; and levels of intelligence. Almost all the differences turned out to be statistically insignificant. For the most part, the "long-term effects of breast feeding have been overstated," they wrote.

Nearly all the researchers I talked to pointed me to a series of studies designed by Kramer, published starting in 2001. Kramer followed 17,000 infants born in Belarus throughout their childhoods. He came up with a clever way to randomize his study, at least somewhat, without doing anything unethical. He took mothers who had already started nursing, and then subjected half of them to an intervention strongly encouraging them to nurse exclusively for several months. The intervention worked: many women nursed longer as a result. And extended breast-feeding did reduce the risk of a gastrointestinal infection by 40 percent. This result seems to be consistent with the protection that sIgA provides; in real life, it adds up to about four out of 100 babies having one less incident of diarrhea or vomiting. Kramer also noted some reduction in infant rashes. Otherwise, his studies found very few significant differences: none, for instance, in weight, blood pressure, ear infections, or allergies—some of the most commonly cited benefits in the breast-feeding literature.

Both the Kramer study and the sibling study did turn up one interesting finding: a bump in "cognitive ability" among breast-fed children. But intelligence is tricky to measure, because it's subjective and affected by so many factors. Other recent studies, particularly those that have factored out the mother's IQ, have found no difference at all between breast-fed and formula-fed babies. In Kramer's study, the mean scores varied widely and mysteriously from clinic to clinic. What's more, the connection he found "could be banal," he told me—simply the result of "breast-feeding mothers' interacting more with their babies, rather than of anything in the milk."

The IQ studies run into the central problem of breast-feeding research: it is impossible to separate a mother's decision to breast-feed—and everything that goes along with it—from the breast-feeding itself. Even sibling studies can't get around this problem. With her first child, for instance, a mother may be extra cautious, keeping the neighbor's germy brats away and slapping the nurse who gives out the free formula sample. By her third child, she may no longer breast-feed—giving researchers the sibling comparison that they crave—but many other things may have changed as well. Maybe she is now using day care, exposing the baby to more illnesses. Surely she is not noticing that kid No.2 has the baby's pacifier in his mouth, or that the cat is sleeping in the crib (trust me on this one). She is also not staring lovingly into the baby's eyes all day, singing songs, reading book after infant book, because she has to make sure that the other two kids are not drowning each other in the tub. On paper, the three siblings are equivalent, but their experiences are not.

What does all the evidence add up to? We have clear indications that breast-feeding helps prevent an extra incident of gastrointestinal illness in some kids—an unpleasant few days of diarrhea or vomiting, but rarely life-threatening in developed countries. We have murky correlations with a whole bunch of long-term conditions. The evidence on IQs is intriguing but not all that compelling, and at best suggests a small advantage, perhaps five points; an individual kid's IQ score can vary that much from test to test or day to day. If a child is disadvantaged in other ways, this bump might make a difference. But for the kids in my playground set, the ones whose mothers obsess about breast-feeding, it gets lost in a wash of Baby Einstein videos, piano lessons, and the rest. And in any case, if a breast-feeding mother is miserable, or stressed out, or alienated by nursing, as many women are, if her marriage is under stress and breast-feeding is making things worse, surely that can have a greater effect on a kid's future success than a few IQ points.

So overall, yes, breast is probably best. But not so much better that formula deserves the label of "public health menace," alongside smoking. Given what we know so far, it seems reasonable to put breast-feeding's health benefits on the plus side of the ledger and other things—modesty, independence, career, sanity—on the minus side, and then tally them up and make a decision. But in this risk-averse age of parenting, that's not how it's done.

In the early '90s, a group of researchers got together to revise the American Academy of Pediatrics' policy statement on breast-feeding. They were of the generation that had fought the formula wars, and had lived through the days when maternity wards automatically gave women hormone shots to stop the flow of breast milk. The academy had long encouraged mothers to make "every effort" to nurse their newborns, but the researchers felt the medical evidence justified a stronger statement. Released in 1997, the new policy recommended exclusive breast-feeding for six months, followed by six more months of partial breast-feeding, supplemented with other foods. The National Organization for Women complained that this would tax working mothers, but to no avail. "The fact that the major pediatric group in the country was taking a definitive stance made all the difference," recalls Lawrence Gartner, a pediatrician and neonatologist at the University of Chicago, and the head of the committee that made the change. "After that, every major organization turned the corner, and the popular media changed radically."

In 2004, the Department of Health and Human Services launched the National Breastfeeding Awareness Campaign. The ads came out just after my second child was born, and were so odious that they nearly caused me to wean him on the spot. One television ad shows two hugely pregnant women in a logrolling contest, with an audience egging them on. "You wouldn't take risks before your baby is born," reads the caption. "Why start after?" The screen then flashes: "Breastfeed exclusively for 6 months." A second spot shows a pregnant woman—this time African American—riding a mechanical bull in a bar while trying to hold on to her huge belly. She falls off the bull and the crowd moans.

To convey the idea that failing to breast-feed is harmful to a baby's health, the print ads show ordinary objects arranged to look like breasts: two dandelions (respiratory illness), two scoops of ice cream with cherries on top (obesity), two otoscopes (ear infections). Plans were made to do another ad showing rubber nipples on top of insulin syringes (suggesting that bottle-feeding causes diabetes), but then someone thought better of it. The whole campaign is so knowing, so dripping with sexual innuendo and condescension, that it brings to mind nothing so much as an episode of *Mad Men*, where Don Draper and the boys break out the whiskey at day's end to toast another victory over the enemy sex.

What's most amazing is how, 50 years after La Leche League's founding, "enlightenment from the laboratory"—judgmental and absolutist—has triumphed again. The seventh edition of *The Womanly Art*, published in 2004, has ballooned to more than 400 pages, and is filled with photographs in place of the original hand drawings. But what's most noticeable is the shift in attitude. Each edition of the book contains new expert testimony about breast milk as an "arsenal against illness." "The resistance to disease that human milk affords a baby cannot be duplicated in any other way," the authors scold. The experience of reading the 1958 edition is like talking with your bossy but charming neighbor, who has some motherly advice to share. Reading the latest edition is like being trapped in the office of a doctor who's haranguing you about the choices you make.

In her critique of the awareness campaign, Joan Wolf, a women's-studies professor at Texas A&M University, chalks up the overzealous ads to a new ethic of "total motherhood." Mothers these days are expected to "optimize every dimension of children's lives," she writes. Choices are often presented as the mother's selfish desires versus the baby's needs. As an example, Wolf quotes *What to Expect When You're Expecting*, from a section called the "Best-Odds Diet," which I remember quite well: "Every bite counts. You've got only nine months of meals and snacks with which to give your baby the best possible start in life ... Before you close your mouth on a forkful of food, consider, 'Is this the best bite I can give my baby?' If it will benefit your baby, chew away. If it'll only benefit your sweet tooth or appease your appetite put your fork down." To which any self-respecting pregnant woman should respond: "I am carrying 35 extra pounds and my ankles have swelled to the size of a life raft, and now I would like to eat some coconut-cream pie. So you know what you can do with this damned fork."

About seven years ago, I met a woman from Montreal, the sister-in-law of a friend, who was young and healthy and normal in every way, except that she refused to breast-feed her children. She wasn't working at the time. She just felt that breast-feeding would set up an unequal dynamic in her marriage—one in which the mother, who was responsible for the very sustenance of the infant, would naturally become responsible for everything else as well. At the time, I had only one young child, so I thought she was a kooky Canadian—and selfish and irresponsible. But of course now I know she was right. I recalled her with sisterly love a few months ago, at three in the morning, when I was propped up in bed for the second time that night with my new baby (note the *my*). My husband acknowledged the ripple in the nighttime peace with a grunt, and that's about it. And why should he do more? There's no use in both of us being a wreck in the morning. Nonetheless, it's hard not to seethe.

The Bitch in the House, published in 2002, reframed *The Feminine Mystique* for my generation of mothers. We were raised to expect that co-parenting was an attainable goal. But who were we kidding? Even in the best of marriages, the domestic burden shifts, in incremental, mostly unacknowledged ways, onto the woman. Breast-feeding plays a central role in the shift. In my set, no husband tells his wife that it is her womanly duty to stay home and nurse the child. Instead, both parents together weigh the evidence and then make a rational, informed decision that she should do so. Then other, logical decisions follow: she alone fed the child, so she naturally knows better how to comfort the child, so she is the better judge to pick a school for the child and the better nurse when the child is sick, and so on. Recently, my husband and I noticed that we had reached the age at which friends from high school and college now hold positions of serious power. When we went down the list, we had to work hard to find any women. Where had all our female friends strayed? Why had they disappeared during the years they'd had small children?

The debate about breast-feeding takes place without any reference to its actual context in women's lives. Breast-feeding exclusively is not like taking a prenatal vitamin. It is a serious time commitment that pretty much guarantees that you will not work in any meaningful way. Let's say a baby feeds seven times a day and then a couple more times at night. That's nine times for about a half hour each, which adds up to more than half of a working day, every day, for at least six months. This is why, when people say that breast-feeding is "free," I want to hit them with a two-by-four. It's only free if a woman's time is worth nothing.

That brings us to the subject of pumping. Explain to your employer that while you're away from your baby, "you will need to take breaks throughout the day to pump your milk," suggest the materials from the awareness campaign. Demand a "clean, quiet place" to pump, and a place to store the milk. A clean, quiet place. So peaceful, so spa-like. Leave aside the preposterousness of this advice if you are, say, a waitress or a bus driver. Say you are a newspaper reporter, like I used to be, and deadline is approaching. Your choices are (a) leave your story to go down to the dingy nurse's office and relieve yourself; or (b) grow increasingly panicked and sweaty as your body continues on its merry, milk-factory way, even though the plant shouldn't be operating today and the pump is about to explode. And then one day, the inevitable will happen. You will be talking to a male colleague and saying to yourself, "Don't think of the baby. Please don't think of the baby." And then the pump *will* explode, and the stigmata will spread down your shirt as you rush into the ladies' room.

This year alone I had two friends whose babies could not breast-feed for one reason or another, so they mostly had to pump. They were both first-time mothers who had written themselves dreamy birth plans involving hot baths followed by hours of intimate nursing. When that didn't work out, they panicked about their babies' missing out on the milky elixir. One of them sat on my couch the other day hooked up to tubes and suctions and a giant deconstructed bra, looking like some fetish ad, or a footnote from the Josef Mengele years. Looking as far as humanly possible from Eve in her natural, feminine state.

In his study on breast-feeding and cognitive development, Michael Kramer mentions research on the long-term effects of mother rats' licking and grooming their pups. Maybe, he writes, it's "the physical and/or emotional act of breastfeeding" that might lead to benefits. This is the theory he prefers, he told me, because "it would suggest something the formula companies can't reproduce." No offense to Kramer, who seems like a great guy, but this gets under my skin. If the researchers just want us to lick and groom our pups, why don't they say so? We can find our own way to do that. In fact, by insisting that milk is some kind of vaccine, they make it less likely that we'll experience nursing primarily as a loving maternal act—"pleasant and relaxing," in the words of *Our Bodies, Ourselves* and more likely that we'll view it as, well, dispensing medicine.

I continue to breast-feed my new son some of the time—but I don't do it slavishly. When I am out for the day working, or out with friends at night, he can have all the formula he wants, and I won't give it a second thought. I'm not really sure why I don't stop entirely. I know it has nothing to do with the science; I have no grandiose illusions that I'm making him lean and healthy and smart with my milk. Nursing is certainly not pure pleasure, either; often I'm tapping my foot impatiently, waiting for him to finish. I do it partly because I can get away with breast-feeding part-time. I work at home and don't punch a clock, which is not the situation of most women. Had I been more closely tied to a workplace, I would have breast-fed during my maternity leave and then given him formula exclusively, with no guilt.

My best guess is something I can't quite articulate. Breast-feeding does not belong in the realm of facts and hard numbers; it is much too intimate and elemental. It contains all of my awe about motherhood, and also my ambivalence. Right now, even part-time, it's a strain. But I also know that this is probably my last chance to feel warm baby skin up against mine, and one day I will miss it.

This assignment will help you with Major Assignment #5: The Persuasive Research Paper. Rosin's position conflicts with that of the American Academy of Pediatrics (http://www2.aap.org/breastfeeding/PolicyOnBreastfeeding.html) and the World Health Organization (http://www.who.int/features/factfiles/breastfeeding/en/index.html). Read the position statements on breastfeeding of both these organizations. Who is Rosin's audience, and who is the audience for the position statements of the AAP and the WHO? Do you trust Rosin's journalism over the body of research cited by the major medical organizations, or are you skeptical? What do you think Rosin's motives are in writing this essay?

Break into pairs, and pick a single health benefit accrued to breastfeeding, for either mother or infant (such as reduced risk of breast cancer for the mother, lower incidence of post-partum depression in the mother, reduced risk of obesity for the infant, or higher intelligence for the infant). One of you will look for evidence to support this health claim for breastfeeding, and the other will look for evidence to undermine it. Present your findings to your class. Which benefits had widespread credence, and which were more tendentious? Were the sources affirming health benefits different in kind, tone, or scale from those denying them?

Rosin writes very critically about some members of her peer group, some of whom she claims as friends. How would you feel if one of your friends published an article, blog post, or status update that criticized your health choices? Have you ever been tempted to do so yourself? Are there gentler ways to critique the health and life of a friend? As writers, do we have to distance ourselves from our subjects?

A perspective necessarily missing from Rosin's discussion of breastfeeding is that of her youngest child, whom she admits she is still planning to continue nursing despite her ambivalence. Do you know now, as an adult, whether you were breast- or bottle-fed? Would it make a difference to your feelings about your body, your mother, or your family, if you found out that you were fed one way or another during your infancy? Write down your response.

Science writer Dan Hurley has written about the multi-million-dollar vitamin and supplement industry in his book Natural Causes: Death, Lies, and Politics in America's Vitamin and Herbal Supplement Industry. *This thoughtful essay appeared in* The New York Times Magazine *in 2011.*

A DRUG FOR DOWN SYNDROME

By Dan Hurley

Early in the evening of June 25, 1995, hours after the birth of his first and only child, the course of Dr. Alberto Costa's life and work took an abrupt turn. Still recovering from a traumatic delivery that required an emergency Caesarean section, Costa's wife, Daisy, lay in bed, groggy from sedation. Into their dimly lighted room at Methodist Hospital in Houston walked the clinical geneticist. He took Costa aside to deliver some unfortunate news. The baby girl, he said, appeared to have Down syndrome, the most common genetic cause of cognitive disabilities, or what used to be called "mental retardation."

Costa, himself a physician and neuroscientist, had only a basic knowledge of Down syndrome. Yet there in the hospital room, he debated the diagnosis with the geneticist. The baby's heart did not have any of the defects often associated with Down syndrome, he argued, and her head circumference was normal. She just didn't look like a typical Down syndrome baby. And after all, it would take a couple weeks before a definitive examination would show whether she had been born with three copies of all or most of the genes on the 21st chromosome, instead of the usual two.

Costa had dreamed that a child of his might grow up to become a mathematician. He had even prevailed upon Daisy to name their daughter Tyche, after the Greek goddess of fortune or chance, and in honor of the Renaissance astronomer Tycho Brahe. Now he asked the geneticist what the chances were that Tyche (pronounced Tishy) really had Down syndrome.

"In my experience," he said, "close to a hundred percent."

Costa and his wife had been trying to have a baby for a couple of years. Daisy's first pregnancy ended in a miscarriage, which they knew can occur because of a genetic disorder in the fetus. When Daisy became pregnant a second time, Costa insisted they get a chorionic villus sampling, an invasive prenatal genetic test. But the procedure caused a miscarriage. (The test showed that the fetus was genetically normal.) Costa vowed that if there was a third pregnancy—this one—they would conduct no prenatal tests.

Now, with Tyche bundled peacefully in a bassinet at the foot of Daisy's bed, and Daisy asleep, Costa sat up through most of the night crying. He had gone into the research side of medicine in part to avoid scenes like this—parents devastated by a diagnosis. But by morning, he found himself doing what any father of a newborn might: hovering by the crib, holding his daughter's hand and marveling at her beauty.

"From that day, we bonded immediately," he told me during one of our many talks over the last year. "All I could think is, She's my baby, she's a lovely girl and what can I do to help her? Obviously I was a physician and a neuroscientist who studies the brain. Here was this new life in front of me and holding my finger and looking straight in my eyes. How could I not think in terms of helping that kid?"

With no experience in the study of Down syndrome, Costa took a short walk the next day to a library affiliated with Baylor College of Medicine, where he worked as a research associate in neuroscience. Reading the latest studies, he learned that the prognosis was not nearly as dire as it was once considered. Life expectancies had grown, education reforms had produced marked gains in functioning and—of particular interest to Costa—a mouse model of the disorder had recently been developed, opening the door to experimentation. He soon made a decision: he would devote himself to the study of Down syndrome.

In 2006, using mice with the equivalent of Down syndrome, Costa published one of the first studies ever to show that a drug could normalize the growth and survival of new brain cells in the hippocampus, a structure deep within the brain that is essential for memory and spatial navigation. In people with Down syndrome, the slower pace of neuron growth in the hippocampus is suspected to play a key role in cognitive deficits. Follow-up studies by other researchers reached conflicting results as to whether the drug Costa had tested, the antidepressant Prozac, could produce practical gains on learning tests to match its ability to boost brain-cell growth. Undeterred, Costa moved on to another treatment strategy. In 2007 he published a study that showed that giving mice with Down syndrome the Alzheimer's drug memantine could improve their memory.

Now Costa has taken the next step: he is completing the first randomized clinical trial ever to take a drug that worked in mice with Down and apply it to humans with the disease, a milestone in the history of Down-syndrome research.

"This was a disorder for which it was believed there was no hope, no treatment, and people thought, Why waste your time?" says Craig C. Garner, a professor of psychiatry and behavioral sciences and co-director of the Center for Research and Treatment of Down Syndrome at Stanford University. "The last 10 years have seen a revolution in neuroscience, so that we now realize that the brain is amazingly plastic, very flexible, and systems can be repaired."

But the effects of that revolution on Down research may yet be cut short. A competing set of scientists are on the cusp of achieving an entirely different kind of medical response to Down syndrome: rather than treat it, they promise to prevent it. They have developed noninvasive, prenatal blood tests which would allow for routine testing for Down syndrome in the first trimester of a pregnancy, raising the specter that many more parents would terminate an affected pregnancy. Some predict that one of the new tests could be available to the public within the year.

Costa, like others working on drug treatments, fears that the imminent approval of those tests might undercut support for treatment research, and even raises the possibility that children like Tyche will be among the last of a generation to be born with Down syndrome.

"It's like we're in a race against the people who are promoting those early screening methods," Costa, who is 48, told me. "These tests are going to be quite accessible. At that point, one would expect a precipitous drop in the rate of birth of children with Down syndrome. If we're not quick enough to offer alternatives, this field might collapse."

So recently was the genetic cause of Down syndrome established that just this past March, Costa actually met the widow of the French scientist, Jérôme Lejeune, who made the discovery in 1959. The scene of their meeting was a Paris conference, named in honor of Lejeune, where neuroscientists from around the world discussed progress into treatments for Down and related diseases. Such a conference would have been inconceivable when Costa entered the field 15 years ago.

"If you think about most genetic diseases, they're usually caused by one gene, and in fact one mutation at one amino acid," says Roger Reeves, a professor at the Institute for Genetic Medicine at the Johns Hopkins University School of Medicine. "But with Down syndrome, you have an extra copy of all 500 or so genes on Chromosome 21." In the first two decades after Lejeune's discovery, the very idea of grappling with those hundreds of triplicated genes scared off scientists from any serious effort to find a treatment for what they were soon calling "trisomy 21." It just seemed impossibly complex. "The turning point," Reeves says, "came when Muriel Davisson made her mouse."

Davisson, now semiretired from Jackson Laboratory in Bar Harbor, Me., spent the 1980s developing a mouse, known as Ts65Dn, that had many of the traits associated with Down syndrome, including, incredibly, the distinctive facial characteristics associated with the disease and the same slightly uncoordinated gait.

Five years after publishing news of her mouse, Davisson received an e-mail from a young neuroscientist named Alberto Costa. Her work, he told her, opened the door for him to conduct meaningful new drug research.

"It was an epiphany, that, oh, this is a field where I can apply a lot that I've learned," Costa says. "Science is usually unforgiving with people who try to change career paths, but it was a risk I was willing to take." Having earned his Ph.D. studying the electrical and chemical basis of communication between brain cells, "I figured, O.K., if there is something that can be done in this field, it's going to be done at that level of neuronal electrophysiology." After months of reading the latest studies, Costa knew he needed Davisson's mice.

"He twisted my arm till I took him into my lab," Davisson says with a laugh. "I didn't have funding. He wrote a grant to get the funding. He is very enthusiastic." She also found out that he was a "perfectionist, and not very tolerant of people who aren't perfectionists. He doesn't do experiments without being sure he's doing them right. When he makes a finding, you know that it's real."

Using Davisson's mice, Costa's 2006 study with Prozac produced cellular changes in the brain. In 2007, Craig Garner at Stanford took the next step, reporting behavioral improvements in Ts65Dn mice after weeks of drug treatment. (Earlier this year, a company he co-founded to pursue that strategy received funding from a venture-capital firm.) Four months later, Costa published his memantine study, showing that a single injection of the drug produced behavioral benefits within minutes, enabling Down-equivalent mice to learn as well as standard mice.

Memantine works, Costa hypothesizes, not by boosting the growth of brain cells but by normalizing how existing cells use the neurotransmitter glutamate. Because people with Down syndrome have three copies of all or most of the genes on Chromosome 21 instead of just two, they have about 50 percent more of any proteins encoded in that chromosome. One result, Costa has shown, is that the NMDA receptors of Ts65Dn mice are "hyperactive"—they overreact to stimuli. By responding to too many things, they learn too little; the signal is lost amid the noise. But giving memantine to quiet the noisy NMDA receptors, Costa has found, makes the brain cells react almost normally.

Other drugs that work on different systems in the brain have also shown benefits in the Ts65Dn mouse. In 2009, Dr. William C. Mobley, chairman of neurosciences at the University of California, San Diego, and one of the most active and visible researchers in the field, co-wrote a study showing that a combination of drugs designed to raise norepinephrine levels in the brain normalized the mice's learning abilities. Most recently, last year the Nobel laureate Paul Greengard of Rockefeller University showed that memory and learning could be normalized in Ts65Dn mice by lowering levels of beta amyloid, the protein goop that has long been known to clog the brains of people with Alzheimer's disease.

"There's been a sea change in our ability to understand and treat Down syndrome," Mobley says. "There's just been an explosion of information. As recently as the year 2000, no drug company would possibly have thought about developing therapies for Down syndrome. I am now in contact with no less than four companies that are pursuing treatments."

Costa's current memantine study began by testing memory and spatial learning in 40 young adults with Down syndrome. Daily, for 16 weeks, half received memantine pills, the other half a placebo. This fall, Costa will present preliminary results at a scientific meeting in Illinois on whether taking the drug made those with Down, in a word, smarter.

A half-hour from his office and laboratory at the University of Colorado-Denver School of Medicine, where he is an associate professor of medicine and neuroscience, Costa pulled into a parking space in front of his modest two-bedroom apartment. The figure of a girl in green dashed toward the car—and then vanished.

"Tyche," Costa called to his daughter, "where'd you go?"

We both stepped out to look for her. I found her standing in front of another car, a Subaru Forester, waiting to get in. Dressed in a lime-colored shirt and skirt, the bangs of her mahogany hair framed by a hair band, Tyche stood just 4 feet 6 inches tall, with a round face, broad nose and heavy-lidded eyes.

Seeing my puzzled look, Costa explained that they also owned the Subaru—which he usually drove with Tyche. He led her to the Toyota we'd arrived in, where she sat down in the back seat. As Costa drove us to his office, I asked what she thought of her father's work.

"He's the greatest scientist," she said, in a slurred, high-pitched voice. Then she added with a laugh, "And he builds evil machines."

"That's from watching too many cartoons," Costa said. "Her favorite is 'Phineas and Ferb.' Of course, there's an evil scientist in it who builds all kinds of machines."

"Like the Smell-inator," added Tyche, who turned 16 in June.

Back at Costa's office, Tyche demonstrated to me what people with Down can be capable of even without medication. (Because she's not an adult, Tyche is ineligible to participate in her father's study.) On the whiteboard at the front of the room, Costa wrote out an algebra problem for her to solve: $8x^2 - 7 = 505$.

"She's one of only two people with Down syndrome who I've ever known to be capable of doing algebra," Costa said. "Normally we give her a problem before she goes to bed." As she solved the equation, taking six steps to conclude that X equals 8, he said, "It's basically instead of a bedtime story." This past Christmas, he proudly noted, he gave her the Rosetta Stone language program for learning Portuguese, and by March she had finished with Level 1 and begun Level 2.

It turns out that with vigorous education and support, many people with Down do far better than once thought possible. Medical care of heart and other physical ailments associated with the disorder have likewise achieved significant benefits, doubling the average lifespan from 25 to 49, in just the 14 years between 1983 and 1997.

Still, with an I.Q. that is typically around 50 points lower than average—with some far lower and others, like Tyche, reaching higher—something more than education alone would be necessary to enable the majority of people with Down syndrome to live independently. Costa said he hopes that memantine might be that something, raising I.Q. noticeably, even if modestly. For him, the goal is to help people with Down syndrome achieve autonomy. "At some point, you want your children to have their own life," he said. "It's about independence."

Costa was raised in Brazil, the son of a marine officer and a seamstress. When he was 14, his parents divorced. His father sent little support, and he and his two siblings lived with their mother in poverty. Perhaps inevitably for someone who had to struggle to rise above his circumstances, he comes across as intense and consumed by his work; he hasn't taken a vacation since Tyche was 3. But he is also devoted to his daughter and wife, spending most of every weekend with them.

"She's a great kid," he said. "She has a very strong personality. In many ways she has features of a regular teenager. She doesn't like me to get into her bedroom. She loves pop music and vampires." Her relatively high functioning, he told me, is important to him. "If Tyche were really severely affected, I don't know if I would have had the energy to go on with this business." Then again, he admits to having paternal feelings toward all 40 young adults in his study, whose cognitive abilities vary widely. "At the end of the day," he said, "their parents know someone really cares for their kid. It's not an academic experience for me. It's my life."

In January, and again in March, a spate of news reports described new studies of the noninvasive blood tests that would allow pregnant women to check for Down syndrome without the risks and discomfort associated with chorionic villus sampling and amniocentesis. Few of the articles, however, took note of the profound unease many medical ethicists, including some who are ardently pro-choice, feel about the tests and how they might lead to a dramatic reduction in the Down syndrome population.

"Even people who are traditionally against abortion are sometimes willing to condone it when the abortion is of a fetus with a disabling trait," says Erik Parens, a bioethicist at the Hastings Center in Garrison, N.Y. "But it's important to recognize that there is a huge range of genetic disorders. In their own way, a lot of kids with Down syndrome flourish, and so do their families."

Advocates of the new tests insist that parents will be given news of an affected pregnancy by a trained geneticist who will present the information fairly and fully. Critics, including Costa and many other parents of children with Down syndrome, say that such dispassionate approaches rarely happen in practice, with many obstetricians and genetic counselors providing unduly negative or misleading information.

But Stephen Quake, a professor of bioengineering and applied physics at Stanford and a developer of one of the new tests, says: "It's a gross oversimplification to assume that these tests are going to lead to the wholesale elimination of Down-syndrome births. My wife's cousin has Down syndrome. We just celebrated his 21st birthday. He's a wonderful person. It's not an obvious step that you would terminate an affected pregnancy."

But Costa points to a falloff in the financing of Down-syndrome research since the prenatal tests have been in development. Although it's difficult to compare the numbers, money from the National Institutes of Health dropped to $16 million in 2007 from $23 million in 2003, before creeping back up to $22 million in 2011. That's far less than the $68 million slated for cystic fibrosis, which affects an estimated 30,000 people in the United States, at most one-tenth of the 300,000 to 400,000 people who have Down.

"The geneticists expect Down syndrome to disappear," Costa says, "so why fund treatments?"

Alan Guttmacher, director of the National Institute of Child Health and Human Development, denies that this is the calculus used by his organization. Yet he offered no clear answer when I asked him why about $3,000 in research dollars is spent by N.I.H. for every person with cystic fibrosis, compared with less than $100 for every person with Down.

"The number affected is a fair metric to use," Guttmacher said. But, he pointed out, most of N.I.H.'s funding decisions are based on the strength of proposals coming from researchers. Advocacy groups for disorders like AIDS, autism and breast cancer have certainly played a role in their gaining increased funding, he said. And perhaps, he speculated, Down suffers from an image problem. "Part of it is that Down syndrome has been around for so long," he said.

Representative Cathy McMorris-Rodgers, Republican of Washington, who co-founded the Congressional Down Syndrome Caucus soon after her 4-year-old son, Cole, was born with the disorder, has had little success in having money appropriated for Down research.

"I find myself wondering how N.I.H. really sets their priorities," she told me. "I'm quite concerned that so many of the researchers in the Down-syndrome field have difficulty getting funded." She continued, "My fear is that for some, they believe that it's been taken care of through prenatal diagnosis."

Even Costa has struggled to secure financing. He lives with Tyche and Daisy in a rented apartment, having never felt he had enough job security to buy a home. At his laboratory, some of his most expensive and sophisticated equipment for studying Down syndrome remains in storage, literally gathering dust for want of financing to use it. One source of his research money has been the Anna and John J. Sie Foundation, based nearby in Denver, and run by Michelle Sie Whitten, whose 8-year-old daughter has Down syndrome. Three years ago, the foundation established a research institute at the University of Colorado in Denver, where Costa works.

Plainly, though, he didn't get into Down-syndrome research for the money. "There's a reason why I'm doing what I'm doing," he told me, nodding toward Tyche.

Not all parents of children with Down syndrome embrace Costa's vision of a medical treatment targeting intelligence. In a recent survey conducted in Canada, parents were asked what they would do if there was a "cure" for their child's Down syndrome. A surprising 27 percent said they would definitely not use it, and another 32 percent said they were unsure.

Meanwhile, the major not-for-profit advocacy groups devoted to Down syndrome spend little on research, instead preferring to lobby and offer parental support. Fresh energy has come from two relatively new groups determined to turn the situation around—Research Down Syndrome and the Down Syndrome Research and Treatment Foundation—but even they have so far succeeded in each raising only about $1 million a year, a fraction of the annual research budgets of many other disease-advocacy groups.

Behind the ambivalence toward treatments, some parents say, is a fear that increasing their children's intelligence might change their personalities—their very identities.

"Nobody would be against giving insulin for diabetes," said Michael Bérubé, director of the Institute for the Arts and Humanities at Pennsylvania State University and author of the 1996 book "Life as We Know It," published five years after his second son, Jamie, was born with the disorder. "But Down syndrome isn't diabetes or smallpox or cholera. It's milder and more variable and more complicated. I'd be very leery of messing with the attributes Jamie has. He's pretty fabulous. At the same time, I'm not doctrinaire. If you're talking about a medication that allows people to function in society and hold jobs, how can you be against that?"

The parents I met whose children participated in Costa's study expressed little of Bérubé's ambivalence. Peggy Hinkle told me about changes she saw in her 26-year-old daughter. "When Christina was on the pills, she told me one morning about a dream she had. She gave me five full, complete sentences. Which is a very big deal. Not only that, she left the room and came back later and told me another sentence about the dream. And she started to do Jumble word puzzles in the newspaper. I don't know if she was on the drug or on placebo, but after five weeks there was a change. Boom. That's why we participated: to expand her horizons."

For his part, Costa has no doubts about the work to which he has devoted the last 15 years of his life. "If you have a disorder that's changing the function of an organ, which in this case is the brain, and you use a medication to bring the function of that organ closer to where it was meant to be from millions of years of evolution, that's as fair as treating any other disease," he said. "I don't see it as any different." If his current study is successful, Costa's ultimate goal is to test it in youths, like Tyche, during the crucial early years of development. Costa is quick to point out that he has not offered her memantine outside the study, and he discourages other physicians from doing so until its safety and effectiveness is proved. But from his perspective as both a researcher and a father, he said: "The sooner you start, obviously, the greater would be your hopes. All I know is, the clock is ticking."

Imagine that you are suddenly and solely responsible for a dependent child with special needs. What resources are available in your area to help those in your situation? Write out your daily schedule and now imagine how you would incorporate your new charge into your life. How would you support yourself and your ward? Would you request public assistance, or charitable outreach, or both?

As this article attests, scientists have come a long way in understanding Down Syndrome in the last two decades. Dr. Alberto Costa's drug trials for adults with Down Syndrome were in the beginning phases when Hurley wrote this article. How have Costa's findings progressed since this article was published in 2011? Research updates for Costa's memantine drug trials or another drug or procedure mentioned in the article. Share your findings with the class.

Dr. Alberto Costa, a father of a Down Syndrome child and a neuroscientist who studies the disorder, is concerned that funding for the treatment of Down Syndrome will decrease dramatically if parents have the option to have "non-invasive, prenatal blood tests" for Down Syndrome in the first three months of the pregnancy. As the article reveals, both terminating Down Syndrome fetuses and treating Down Syndrome as a disorder that must be cured are ethical issues of debate, about which you might consider writing for Major Assignment #5. For now, focus on the financial support that Costa's research desperately needs. Imagine you are a member of an advocacy group for Down Syndrome or another underfunded disorder or illness. Write a letter, asking for more funding to be allotted for research, to your local congressperson or to the director of the National Institute of Child Health and Human Development.

With your class, watch the feature film *Gattaca* or the documentary *Google Baby*. Discuss the pros and cons of parents knowing more about their fetuses or about their own genomes.

The son of a Welsh coalminer, the great British statesman Aneurin ("Nye") Bevan is commonly called the author of Great Britain's National Health Service, which has provided free health care for all, regardless of income, since the middle of the twentieth century. The excerpts below come from his speech at the second reading of the National Health Service Bill in the House of Commons on April 30th, 1946.

HOUSE OF COMMONS DEBATES, 30 APRIL 1946

BY ANEURIN BEVAN

NATIONAL HEALTH SERVICE BILL

The Minister of Health (Mr. Aneurin Bevan): In the last two years there has been such a clamor from sectional interests in the field of national health that we are in danger of forgetting why these proposals are brought forward at all. It is, therefore, very welcome to me . . . that consideration should now be given . . . to the requirements of the British people as a whole. The scheme which anyone must draw up dealing with national health must necessarily be conditioned and limited by the evils it is intended to remove. . . .

The first reason why a health scheme of this sort is necessary at all is because it has been the firm conclusion of all parties that money ought not to be permitted to stand in the way of obtaining an efficient health service. Although it is true that the national health insurance system provides a general practitioner service and caters for something like 21 million of the population, the rest of the population have to pay whenever they desire the services of a doctor. It is cardinal to a proper health organization that a person ought not to be financially deterred from seeking medical assistance at the earliest possible stage. It is one of the evils of having to buy medical advice that, in addition to the natural anxiety that may arise because people do not like to hear unpleasant things about themselves, and therefore tend to postpone consultation as long as possible, there is the financial anxiety caused by having to pay doctors' bills. Therefore, the first evil that we must deal with is that which exists as a consequence of the fact that the whole thing is the wrong way round. A person ought to be able to receive medical and hospital help without being involved in financial anxiety.

In the second place, the national health insurance scheme does not provide for the self-employed, nor, of course, for the families of dependants. It depends on insurance qualification, and no matter how ill you are, if you cease to be insured you cease to have free doctoring. Furthermore, it gives no backing to the doctor in the form of specialist services. The doctor has to provide himself, he has to use his own discretion and his own personal connections, in order to obtain hospital treatment for his patients and in order to get them specialists, and in very many cases, of course— in an overwhelming number of cases—the services of a specialist are not available to poor people.

Not only is this the case, but our hospital organization has grown up with no plan, with no system; it is unevenly distributed over the country and indeed it is one of the tragedies of the situation, that very often the best hospital facilities are available where they are least needed. In the older industrial districts of Great Britain hospital facilities are inadequate. Many of the hospitals are too small—very much too small. About 70 percent. have less than 100 beds, and over 30 percent. have less than 30. No one can possibly pretend that hospitals so small can provide general hospital treatment. There is a tendency in some quarters to defend the very small hospital on the ground of its localism and intimacy, and for other rather imponderable reasons of that sort, but everybody knows today that if a hospital is to be efficient it must provide a number of specialized services. Although I am not myself a devotee of bigness for bigness sake, I would rather be kept alive in the efficient if cold altruism of a large hospital than expire in a gush of warm sympathy in a small one.

In addition to these defects, the health of the people of Britain is not properly looked after in one or two other respects. The condition of the teeth of the people of Britain is a national reproach. As a consequence of dental treatment having to be bought, it has not been demanded on a scale to stimulate the creation of sufficient dentists, and in consequence there is a woeful shortage of dentists[...] at the present time. Furthermore, about 25 percent. of the people of Great Britain can obtain their spectacles and get their eyes tested and seen to by means of the assistance given by the approved societies, but the general mass of the people have not such facilities.[1] Another of the evils from which

1 Approved societies: charitable organizations set up to help the poor

this country suffers is the fact that sufficient attention has not been given to deafness, and hardly any attention has been given so far to the provision of cheap hearing aids and their proper maintenance. [...]

One added disability from which our health system suffers is the isolation of mental health from the rest of the health services. Although the present Bill does not rewrite the Lunacy Acts—we shall have to come to that later on—nevertheless, it does, for the first time, bring mental health into the general system of health services. It ought to be possible, and this should be one of the objectives of any civilized health service, for a person who feels mental distress, or who fears that he is liable to become unbalanced in any way to go to a general hospital to get advice and assistance, so that the condition may not develop into a more serious stage. All these disabilities our health system suffers from at the present time, and one of the first merits of this Bill is that it provides a universal health service without any insurance qualifications of any sort. It is available to the whole population, and not only is it available to the whole population freely, but it is intended, through the health service, to generalize the best health advice and treatment. It is intended that there shall be no limitation on the kind of assistance given—the general practitioner service, the specialist, the hospitals, eye treatment, spectacles, dental treatment, hearing facilities, all these are to be made available free.

There will be some limitations for a while, because we are short of many things. We have not enough dentists and it will therefore be necessary for us, in the meantime, to give priority treatment to certain classes—expectant and nursing mothers, children, school children in particular and later on we hope adolescents. Finally we trust that we shall be able to build up a dental service for the whole population. We are short of nurses and we are short, of course, of hospital accommodation, and so it will be some time before the Bill can fructify fully in effective universal service. Nevertheless, it is the object of the Bill, and of the scheme, to provide this as soon as possible, and to provide it universally.

Specialists will be available not only at institutions but for domiciliary visits when needed. Hon. Members in all parts of the House know from their own experience that very many people have suffered unnecessarily because the family has not had the financial resources to call in skilled people.[2] The specialist services, therefore, will not only be available at the hospitals, but will

2 Honorable Member: the customary term used to address a member of the British Parliament

be at the back of the general practitioner should he need them. The practical difficulties of carrying out all these principles and services are very great. When I approached this problem, I made up my mind that I was not going to permit any sectional or vested interests to stand in the way of providing this very valuable service for the British people.

There are, of course, three main instruments through which it is intended that the Health Bill should be worked. There are the hospitals; there are the general practitioners; and there are the health centers. The hospitals are in many ways the vertebrae of the health system, and I first examined what to do with the hospitals. The voluntary hospitals of Great Britain have done invaluable work. When hospitals could not be provided by any other means, they came along. The voluntary hospital system of this country has a long history of devotion and sacrifice behind it, and it would be a most frivolously minded man who would denigrate in any way the immense services the voluntary hospitals have rendered to this country. But they have been established often by the caprice of private charity. They bear no relationship to each other. Two hospitals close together often try to provide the same specialist services unnecessarily, while other areas have not that kind of specialist service at all. They are, as I said earlier, badly distributed throughout the country. It is unfortunate that often endowments are left to finance hospitals in those parts of the country where the well-to-do live while, in very many other of our industrial and rural districts there is inadequate hospital accommodation. These voluntary hospitals are, very many of them, far too small and, therefore, to leave them as independent units is quite impracticable.

Furthermore—I want to be quite frank with the House—I believe it is repugnant to a civilized community for hospitals to have to rely upon private charity. I believe we ought to have left hospital flag days behind.[3] I have always felt a shudder of repulsion when I have seen nurses and sisters who ought to be at their work, and students who ought to be at their work, going about the streets collecting money for the hospitals. I do not believe there is an hon. Member of this House who approves that system. It is repugnant, and we must leave it behind—entirely. But the implications of doing this are very considerable.

I have been forming some estimates of what might happen to voluntary hospital finance when the all-in insurance contributions to be paid by the

3 Charity drives in which paper "flags" were sold to raise money for the care of indigent patients.

people of Great Britain, when the Bill is passed and becomes an Act, and they are entitled to free hospital services. The estimates I have go to show that between 80 percent. and 90 percent. of the revenues of the voluntary hospitals in these circumstances will be provided by public funds, by national or rate funds.[4] [...] In the mining districts, in the textile districts, in the districts where there are heavy industries it is the industrial population who pay the weekly contributions for the maintenance of the hospitals. When I was a miner I used to find that situation, when I was on the hospital committee. We had an annual meeting and a cordial vote of thanks was moved and passed with great enthusiasm to the managing director of the colliery company for his generosity towards the hospital; and when I looked at the balance sheet, I saw that 97½ percent. of the revenues were provided by the miners' own contributions; but nobody passed a vote of thanks to the miners. [...]

But, of course, it is a misuse of language to call these "voluntary hospitals." They are not maintained by legally enforced contributions; but, mainly, the workers pay for them because they know they will need the hospitals, and they are afraid of what they would have to pay if they did not provide them. So it is, I say, an impossible situation for the State to find something like 90 percent. of the revenues of these hospitals and still to call them "voluntary." So I decided, for this and other reasons, that the voluntary hospitals most be taken over.

I knew very well when I decided this that it would give rise to very considerable resentment in many quarters, but, quite frankly, I am not concerned about the voluntary hospitals' authorities: I am concerned with the people whom the hospitals are supposed to serve. Every investigation which has been made into this problem has established that the proper hospital unit has to comprise about 1,000 beds—not in the same building but, nevertheless, the general and specialist hospital services can be provided only in a group of that size. This means that a number of hospitals have to be pooled, linked together, in order to provide a unit of that sort. This cannot be done effectively if each hospital is a separate, autonomous body. It is proposed that each of these groups should have a large general hospital, providing general hospital facilities and services, and that there should be a group round it of small feeder hospitals. Many of the cottage hospitals strive to give services that they are not able to give.[5] It very often happens that a cottage hospital harbors ambitions to

4 Voluntary hospitals: private, charity hospitals
5 Cottage hospitals: small, rural hospitals

the hurt of the patients, because they strive to reach a status that they never can reach. In these circumstances, the welfare of the patients is sacrificed to the vaulting ambitions of those in charge of the hospital. If, therefore, these voluntary hospitals are to be grouped in this way, it is necessary that they should submit themselves to proper organization, and that submission, in our experience, is impracticable if the hospitals, all of them, remain under separate management.

Now, this decision to take over the voluntary hospitals meant, that I then had to decide to whom to give them. Who was to be the receiver? So I turned to an examination of the local government hospital system. Many of the local authorities in Great Britain have never been able to exercise their hospital powers. They are too poor. They are too small. Furthermore, the local authorities of Great Britain inherited their hospitals from the Poor Law, and some of them are monstrous buildings, a cross between a workhouse and a barracks—or a prison. The local authorities are helpless in these matters. They have not been able to afford much money. Some local authorities are first-class. Some of the best hospitals in this country are local government hospitals. But, when I considered what to do with the voluntary hospitals when they had been taken over, and who was to receive them I had to reject the local government unit, because the local authority area is no more an effective gathering ground for the patients of the hospitals than the voluntary hospitals themselves.[6] My hon. Friend said that some of them are too small, and some of them too large. London is an example of being too small and too large at the same time.

It is quite impossible, therefore, to hand over the voluntary hospitals to the local authorities. Furthermore—and this is an argument of the utmost importance—if it be our contract with the British people, if it be our intention that we should universalize the best, that we shall promise every citizen in this country the same standard of service, how can that be articulated through a rate-borne institution which means that the poor authority will not be able to carry out the same thing at all? It means that once more we shall be faced with all kinds of anomalies, just in those areas where hospital facilities are most needed, and in those very conditions where the mass of the poor people will be unable to find the finance to supply the hospitals. Therefore, for reasons which must be obvious —because the local authorities are too small, because their financial capacities are unevenly distributed—I decided that local authorities

---

6 Local authority: local government, town council

could not be effective hospital administration units. There are, of course, a large number of hospitals in addition to the general hospitals which the local authorities possess. Tuberculosis sanatoria, isolation hospitals, infirmaries of various kinds, rehabilitation, and all kinds of other hospitals are all necessary in a general hospital service. So I decided that the only thing to do was to create an entirely new hospital service, to take over the voluntary hospitals, and to take over the local government hospitals and to organize them as a single hospital service. If we are to carry out our obligation and to provide the people of Great Britain, no matter where they may be, with the same level of service, then the nation itself will have to carry the expenditure, and cannot put it upon the shoulders of any other authority.

A number of investigations have been made into this subject from time to time, and the conclusion has always been reached that the effective hospital unit should be associated with the medical school. If you grouped the hospitals in about 16 to 20 regions around the medical schools, you would then have within those regions the wide range of disease and disability which would provide the basis for your specialized hospital service. Furthermore, by grouping hospitals around the medical schools, we should be providing what is very badly wanted, and that is a means by which the general practitioners are kept in more intimate association with new medical thought and training. One of the disabilities, one of the shortcomings of our existing medical service, is the intellectual isolation of the general practitioners in many parts of the country. The general practitioner, quite often, practices in loneliness and does not come into sufficiently intimate association with his fellow craftsmen and has not the stimulus of that association, and in consequence of that the general practitioners have not got access to new medical knowledge in a proper fashion. By this association of the general practitioner with the medical schools through the regional hospital organization, it will be possible to refresh and replenish the fund of knowledge at the disposal of the general practitioner.

This has always been advised as the best solution of the difficulty. It has this great advantage to which I call the close attention of honorable Members. It means that the bodies carrying out the hospital services of the country are, at the same time, the planners of the hospital service. One of the defects of the other scheme is that the planning authority and executive authority are different. The result is that you get paper planning or bad execution. By making the regional board and regional organization responsible both for the planning and the administration of the plans, we get a better result, and we get from time to time, adaptation of the plans by the persons accumulating the experience in the course of their administration. The other solutions to this problem which I have looked at all mean that you have an advisory body of planners in the background who are not able themselves to accumulate the experience necessary to make good planners. The regional hospital organization is the authority with which the specialized services are to be associated, because, as I have explained, this specialized service can be made available for an area of that size, and cannot be made available over a small area. [...]

When we come to the general practitioners we are, of course, in an entirely different field. The proposal which I have made is that the general practitioner shall not be in direct contract with the Ministry of Health, but in contract with new bodies. There exists in the medical profession a great resistance to coming under the authority of local government—a great resistance, with which I, to some extent, sympathize. There is a feeling in the medical profession that the general practitioner would be liable to come too much under the medical officer of health, who is the administrative doctor. This proposal does not put the doctor under the local authority; it puts the doctor in contract with an entirely new body—the local executive council, coterminous with the local health area, county or county borough. On that executive council, the dentists, doctors and chemists will have half the representation. In fact, the whole scheme provides a greater degree of professional representation for the medical profession than any other scheme I have seen.

I have been criticized in some quarters for doing that. I will give the answer now: I have never believed that the demands of a democracy are necessarily satisfied merely by the opportunity of putting a cross against someone's name every four or five years. I believe that democracy exists in the active participation in administration and policy. Therefore, I believe that it is a wise thing to give the doctors full participation in the administration of their own profession. They must, of course, necessarily be subordinated to lay control— we do not want the opposite danger of syndicalism. Therefore, the communal interests must always be safeguarded in this administration. The doctors will be in contract with an executive body of this sort. One of the advantages of that proposal is that the doctors do not become—as some of them have so wildly stated—civil servants. Indeed, one of the advantages of the scheme is that it does not create an additional civil servant.

It imposes no constitutional disability upon any person whatsoever. Indeed, by taking the hospitals from the local authorities and putting them under the regional boards, large numbers of people will be enfranchised who are now disfranchised from participation in local government. So far from this being a huge bureaucracy with all the doctors little civil servants—the slaves of the Minister of Health, as I have seen it described—instead of that, the doctors are under contract with bodies which are not under the local authority, and which are, at the same time, ever open to their own influence and control.

One of the chief problems that I was up against in considering this scheme was the distribution of the general practitioner service throughout the country. The distribution, at the moment, is most uneven. In South Shields before the war there were 4,100 persons per doctor; in Bath 1,590; in Dartford nearly 3,000 and in Bromley 1,620; in Swindon 3,100; in Hastings under 1,200. That distribution of general practitioners throughout the country is most hurtful to the health of our people. It is entirely unfair, and, therefore, if the health services are to be carried out, there must be brought about a re-distribution of the general practitioners throughout the country. [...]

One of the first consequences of that decision was the abolition of the sale and purchase of practices. If we are to get the doctors where we need them, we cannot possibly allow a new doctor to go in because he has bought somebody's practice. Proper distribution kills by itself the sale and purchase of practices. I know that there is some opposition to this, and I will deal with that opposition. I have always regarded the sale and purchase of medical practices as an evil in itself. It is tantamount to the sale and purchase of patients. Indeed, every argument advanced about the value of the practice is itself an argument against freedom of choice, because the assumption underlying the high value of a practice is that the patient passes from the old doctor to the new. If they did not pass there would be no value in it. I would like, therefore, to point out to the medical profession that every time they argue for high compensation for the loss of the value of their practices, it is an argument against the free choice which they claim. [...]

The doctors claim that the proposals of the Bill amount to direction—not all the doctors say this but some of them do. There is no direction involved at all. When the Measure starts to operate, the doctors in a particular area will be able to enter the public service in that area. A doctor newly coming along would apply to the local executive council for permission to practice in a particular area. His application would then be re-referred to the Medical Practices Committee. The Medical Practices Committee, which is mainly a professional body, would have before it the question of whether there were sufficient general practitioners in that area. If there were enough, the committee would refuse to permit the appointment. No one can really argue that that is direction, because no profession should be allowed to enter the public service in a place where it is not needed. By that method of negative control over a number of years, we hope to bring about over the country a positive redistribution of the general practitioner service. It will not affect 55 the existing situation, because doctors will be able to practice under the new service in the areas to which they belong, but a new doctor, as he comes on, will have to find his practice in a place inadequately served.

I cannot, at the moment, explain to the House what are going to be the rates of remuneration of doctors. [...] I have not been able to get the full report. Therefore, it is not possible to deal with remuneration. However, it is possible to deal with some of the principles underlying the remuneration of general practitioners. Some of my hon. Friends on this side of the House are in favor of a full salaried service. I am not. I do not believe that the medical profession is ripe for it, and I cannot dispense with the principle that the payment of a doctor must in some degree be a reward for zeal, and there must be some degree of punishment for lack of it. Therefore, it is proposed that capitation should remain the main source from which a doctor will obtain his remuneration. But it is proposed that there shall be a basic salary and that for a number of very cogent reasons. One is that a young doctor entering practice for the first time needs to be kept alive while he is building up his lists. The present system by which a young man gets a load of debt around his neck in order to practice is an altogether evil one. The basic salary will take care of that.

Furthermore, the basic salary has the additional advantage of being something to which I can attach an increased amount to get doctors to go into unattractive areas. It may also—and here our position is not quite so definite—be the means of attaching additional remuneration for special courses and special acquirements. The basic salary, however, must not be too large otherwise it is a disguised form of capitation. Therefore, the main source at the moment through which a general practitioner will obtain his remuneration will be capitation. I have also made—and I quite frankly admit it to the House—a further concession which I know will be repugnant in some quarters. The doctor, the general practitioner and the specialist, will be able to obtain fees, but not from anyone who is on any of their own lists, nor will a doctor be able to obtain fees from persons on the lists of his partner, nor from those he has worked with in group practice, but I think it is impracticable to prevent him having any fees at all. To do so would be to create a black market. There ought to be nothing to prevent anyone having advice from another doctor other than his own. Hon. Members know what happens in this field sometimes. An individual hears that a particular doctor in some place is good at this, that or the other thing, and wants to go along for a consultation. He gets a consultation and pays a fee for it. If the other doctor is better than his own all he will need to do is to transfer to him and he gets him free. It would be unreasonable to keep the patient paying fees to a doctor whose services can be got free. So the amount of fee payment on the part of the general population will be quite small. Indeed, I confess at once if the amount of fee paying is great, the system will break down, because the whole purpose of this scheme is to provide free treatment with no fee paying at all. The same principle applies to the hospitals.

If an individual wishes to consult [a specialist], there is no reason why he should be stopped. As I have said, the fact that a person can transfer from one doctor to another ought to keep fee paying within reasonable proportions.

The same principle applies to the hospitals. Specialists in hospitals will be allowed to have fee-paying patients. I know this is criticized and I sympathize with some of the reasons for the criticism, but we are driven inevitably to this fact, that unless we permit some fee-paying patients in the public hospitals, there will be a rash of nursing homes all over the country. If people wish to pay for additional amenities, or something to which they attach value, like privacy in a single ward, we ought to aim at providing such facilities for everyone who wants them. But while we have inadequate hospital facilities, and while rebuilding is postponed it inevitably happens that some people will want to buy something more than the general health service is providing. If we do not permit fees in hospitals, we will lose many specialists from the public hospitals for they will go to nursing homes. I believe that nursing homes ought to be discouraged. They cannot provide general hospital facilities, and we want to keep our specialists attached to our hospitals and not send them into nursing homes. Behind this there is a principle of some importance. If the State owned a theatre it would not charge the same prices for the different seats....It is not entirely analogous, but it is an illustration. For example, in the dental service the same principle will prevail. The State will provide a certain standard of dentistry free, but if a person wants to have his teeth filled with gold, the State will not provide that.

The third instrument to which the health services are to be articulated is the health center, to which we attach very great importance indeed. It has been described in some places as an experimental idea, but we want it to be more than that, because to the extent that general practitioners can operate through health centers in their own practice, to that extent will be raised the general standard of the medical profession as a whole. Furthermore, the general practitioner cannot afford the apparatus necessary for a proper diagnosis in his own surgery. This will be available at the health center. The health center may well be the maternity and child welfare clinic of the local authority also. The provision of the health center is, therefore, imposed as a duty on the local authority. There has been criticism that this creates a trichotomy in the services. It is not a trichotomy at all. If you have complete unification it would bring you back to paper planning. You cannot get all services through the regional authority, because there are many immediate and personal services which the local authority can carry out better than anybody else. So, it is proposed to leave those personal services to the local authority, and some will be carried out at the health center. The center will vary; there will be large centres at which there will be dental clinics, maternity and child welfare services, and general practitioners' consultative facilities, and there will also be smaller center—surgeries where practitioners can see their patients. [. . .]

Some have said that the preventive services should be under the same authority as the curative services. I wonder whether Members who advance that criticism really envisage the situation which will arise. What are the preventive services? Housing, water, sewerage, river pollution prevention, food inspection —are all these to be under a regional board? If so, a regional board of that sort would want the Albert Hall in which to meet. This, again, is paper planning. It is unification for unification's sake. There must be a frontier at which the local joins the national health service. You can fix it here or there, but it must be fixed somewhere. It is said that there is some contradiction in the health scheme because some services are left to the local authority and the rest to the national scheme. Well, day is joined to night by twilight, but nobody has suggested that it is a contradiction in nature. The argument that this is a contradiction in health services is purely pedantic, and has no relation to the facts.

It is also suggested that because maternity and child welfare services come under the local authority, and gynecological services come under the regional board, that will make for confusion. Why should it? Continuity between one and the other is maintained by the user. The hospital is there to be used. If there are difficulties in connection with birth, the gynecologist at the hospital center can look after them. All that happens is that the midwife will be in charge—the mother will be examined properly, as she ought to be examined—then, if difficulties are anticipated, she can have her child in hospital, where she can be properly looked after by the gynecologist. When she recovers, and is a perfectly normal person, she can go to the maternity and child welfare center for post-natal treatment. There is no confusion there. The confusion is in the minds of those who are criticizing the proposal on the ground that there is a trichotomy in the services, between the local authority, the regional board and the health center. [...] The two Amendments on the Order Paper rather astonish me. The hon. Member for Denbigh (Sir H. Morris-Jones) informs me, in his Amendment, that I have not sufficiently consulted the medical profession.... I have met the medical profession, the dental profession, the pharmacists, nurses and midwives, voluntary hospitals, local authorities, eye services, medical aid services, herbalists, insurance committees, and various other organizations. I have had 20 conferences. The consultations have been very wide. In addition, my officials have had 13 conferences, so that altogether there have been 33 conferences with the different branches of the profession about the proposals. Can anybody argue that that is not adequate consultation? Of course, the real criticism is that I have not conducted negotiations. I am astonished that such a charge should lie in the mouth of any Member of the House. If there is one thing that will spell the death of the House of Commons it is for a Minister to negotiate Bills before they are presented to the House. I had no negotiations, because once you negotiate with outside bodies two things happen. They are made aware of the nature of the proposals before the House of Commons itself; and furthermore, the Minister puts himself into an impossible position, because, if he has agreed things with somebody outside he is bound to resist Amendments from Members in the House. Otherwise he does not play fair with them. I protested against this myself when I was a Private Member. I protested bitterly, and I am not prepared, strange though it may seem, to do something as a Minister which as a Private Member I thought was wrong. So there has not been negotiation, and there will not be negotiation, in this matter. The House of Commons is supreme, and the House of Commons must assert its supremacy, and not allow itself to be dictated to by anybody, no matter how powerful and how strong he may be.

The opposition to the Bill is not as strong as it was thought it would be. On the contrary, there is very considerable support for this Measure among the doctors themselves. I myself have been rather aggrieved by some of the statements which have been made. They have misrepresented the proposals to a very large extent, but as these proposals become known to the medical profession, they will appreciate them, because nothing should please a good doctor more than to realize that, in future, neither he nor his patient will have any financial anxiety arising out of illness.

The leaders of the Opposition have on the Order Paper an Amendment which expresses indignation at the extent to which we are interfering with charitable foundations. The Amendment states that the Bill gravely menaces all charitable foundations by diverting to purposes other than those intended by the donors the trust funds of the voluntary hospitals. I must say that when I read that Amendment I was amused. [...] Do hon. Members opposite suggest that the intelligent planning of the modern world must be prevented by the endowments of the dead? Are we to consider the dead more than the living? Are the patients of our hospitals to be sacrificed to a consideration of that sort? [...]

We are not interfering with the teaching hospitals' endowments. Academic medical education will be more free in the future than it has been in the past. Furthermore, something like £32 million belonging to the voluntary hospitals as a whole is not going to be taken from them. On the contrary, we are going to use it, and a very valuable thing it will be; we are going to use it as a shock absorber between the Treasury, the central Government, and the hospital administration. They will be given it as free money which they can spend over and above the funds provided by the State. [...]

I should have thought it ought to have been a pride to hon. Members in all parts of the House that Great Britain is able to embark upon an ambitious scheme of this proportion. When it is carried out, it will place this country in the forefront of all countries of the world in medical services. I myself, if I may say a personal word, take very great pride and great pleasure in being able to introduce a Bill of this comprehensiveness and value. I believe it will lift the shadow from millions of homes. It will keep very many people alive who might otherwise be dead. It will relieve suffering. It will produce higher standards for the medical profession. It will be a great contribution towards the wellbeing of the common people of Great Britain. For that reason, and for the other reasons I have mentioned, I hope hon. Members will give the Bill a Second Reading.

Read Franklin Delano Roosevelt's speech on healthcare (http://newdeal.feri.org/speeches/1935b.htm), and watch and listen to Ronald Reagan's warning against "socialized medicine" (http://www.youtube.com/watch?v=AYrlDlrLDSQ). Bevan, Roosevelt, and Reagan represent very different points on the continuum between single-payer, universal, government-sponsored health care and capitalized, restricted, employer-sponsored medical treatment. What rhetorical strategies do they nonetheless share? Do they have any common ground?

With a group of classmates, each select a role from the following: small-business staff member in a business with five or fewer employees; recent college graduate, aged 23, with employed parents; full-time, benefited state or federal employee; single, self-employed parent; unbenefited part-time worker at a large retail store. Now imagine that each of you has a chronic disease such as diabetes or asthma. How would you go about finding affordable health insurance or health care? (Here's a hint to start you off: you can search current salaries in databases such as Salary Wizard and compare health care policies at http://finder.healthcare.gov).

Now imagine a change in your situation: if you were one of the employed persons in the exercise above, imagine that you have lost your job; if you were the self-employed person, imagine that your disease has incapacitated you so that you are unable to follow your previous profession. Could you find affordable health insurance or health care under these changed circumstances?

This assignment will help you prepare for Major Assignment #5: The Persuasive Research Paper. Where do you stand on the health care continuum? Is the good health of individual citizens a public good that benefits all of society, a private benefit that workers should earn, or a divinely conferred privilege that some forfeit through their behavior or beliefs? Write a position paper that acknowledges the complexities of the situation, namely: the difficulties that many persons encounter in finding health insurance, the problems of financing health care, and the need for personal responsibility. What solutions do you think are possible, desirable, or imperative?

Denise Kersten Wills was described as a freelance writer and editor based in Washington, D.C. in Yoga Journal, *where this essay came out in 2012.*

HEALING LIFE'S TRAUMAS

BY DENISE KERSTEN WILLS

New studies show that people suffering from post-traumatic stress disorder can find real relief with yoga.

When Sara talks about the benefits of practicing yoga, the 56-year-old from Boston uses the same terms as other yogis: being grounded and present, gaining an awareness of her body and its strength, feeling calm and in control of her thoughts. But as a victim of physical and sexual abuse who suffers from post-traumatic stress disorder (PTSD), Sara experiences these things a little differently.

For Sara—who asked that her real name not be used—being grounded literally means feeling her feet on the floor; being present means knowing where she is and what's going on around her. These are things she can't feel when she's suddenly jerked into the past, reliving episodes of her ex-husband's violence, like the night he chased her through the house and pushed through every door she hid behind.

"It can be very difficult to stay in your own body when you're getting flashbacks," she says. "The lighting changes, and you feel like you're not even in the room." Sara's flashbacks come with little warning and can be triggered by anything that reminds her of the abuse.

This painful reliving of events is a common symptom of PTSD, a chronic anxiety disorder that can develop after someone is involved in a traumatic event, whether it's a sexual or physical assault, a war, a natural disaster, or even a car accident. Existing treatments—which include group and individual therapy and drugs such as Prozac—work only for some patients.

Yoga can make a big difference, recent research suggests. In a study published last year in the *Annals of the New York Academy of Sciences*, a prominent PTSD expert found that a group of female patients who completed eight hatha yoga classes showed significantly more improvement in symptoms—including the frequency of intrusive thoughts and the severity of jangled nerves—than a similar group that had eight sessions of group therapy. The study also reported that yoga can improve heart-rate variability, a key indicator of a person's ability to calm herself.

"This is a really promising area that we need to examine," says Rachel Yehuda, a professor of psychiatry at the Mount Sinai School of Medicine and the PTSD program director at the James J. Peters Veterans Affairs Medical Center in the Bronx. Soldiers returning from Iraq have high rates of PTSD and other mental health problems; one study reported the total at one in five. Veterans from other wars continue to suffer from PTSD—at times worsened by news from Iraq that reminds them of their own experiences.

The study's most striking findings were patients' own descriptions of how their lives changed, says the author, Bessel van der Kolk, a professor of psychiatry at the Boston University School of Medicine and medical director of the Trauma Center, a clinic and training facility in Brookline, Massachusetts. Van der Kolk, who has studied trauma since the 1970s, is considered a pioneer in the field.

"I've realized that I'm a very strong person," says Sara, who continues to practice yoga. She says the slow but steady progress she's made helps her face her ex-husband in court each time he violates a restraining order. By filing charges for every offense, she hopes to send the message that he can no longer be part of her life. "[Yoga] reminds me that if I just keep plodding along, I can get there," she says. "I can face it in little chunks and say, "I can work with this piece.""

MIND/BODY CONNECTION

Van der Kolk first became interested in yoga several years ago, after he concluded that therapists treating psychological trauma need to work with the body as well as the mind. "The memory of the trauma is imprinted on the human organism," he says. "I don't think you can overcome it unless you learn to have a friendly relationship with your body."

To learn more about yoga, van der Kolk decided to try it himself. He chose hatha yoga because the style is widely available, got hooked on it, and became convinced it could help his patients. "The big question became: How can you help people confront their internal sensations?" he says. "Yoga is one way you can do that."

Van der Kolk found yoga a safe and gentle means of becoming reacquainted with the body. "Yoga reestablishes the sense of time," he says. "You notice how things change and flow inside your body." Learning relaxation and breathing techniques helps PTSD patients calm themselves down when they sense that a flashback or panic attack is coming. And yoga's emphasis on self-acceptance is important for victims of sexual assault, many of whom hate their bodies.

Already, the military has begun to investigate yoga's therapeutic potential. In a preliminary study at Walter Reed Army Medical Center in Washington, D.C., nine active-duty soldiers with PTSD were able to sleep better and felt less depressed after 12 weeks of Yoga Nidra (also known as yogic sleep, a practice that elicits deep relaxation). "They felt more comfortable with situations that they couldn't control, and as a result, they felt more control over their lives," says Richard Miller, who is serving as a consultant to the Walter Reed researchers. Miller is a Sebastopol, California-based clinical psychologist, yoga teacher, and cofounder of the International Association of Yoga Therapy. A larger Yoga Nidra study, of 100 active-duty soldiers, is slated to start in late 2007 or early 2008. Still another, at the Atlanta Veterans Affairs Medical Center, will look at a combination of meditation, hatha yoga, and other techniques with veterans recently returned from Iraq.

SOLDIERS' STORIES

Some former soldiers have already discovered yoga's calming effects. Tom Boyle, who served in Vietnam and now works as a counselor at the Vets Center in Worcester, Massachusetts, began practicing two years ago after a patient told him that yoga had helped control his symptoms. Boyle has since worked with a group of former soldiers—including some who served in Iraq—who take classes specifically for veterans with PTSD at Central Mass Yoga Institute in nearby West Boylston.

"Our military training conditioned us for an aggressive response to threat," Boyle explains. "You have to have anger in order to carry out your mission. To be able to relax and surrender yourself to the poses dissipates the anger." The men in his group also report fewer problems sleeping, and one has been able to stop taking antidepressant drugs.

Such promising anecdotes underscore the need for more research, says Richard Brown, an associate professor of clinical psychiatry at Columbia University. Brown teaches trauma survivors Sudarshan Kriya, a yoga and meditation practice created by the Indian spiritual master Sri Sri Ravi Shankar. Brown, who plans to publish his own findings, says many questions remain, including how to prepare patients for yoga, which symptoms respond best, and how to integrate yoga with standard treatment.

Hoping to explore these questions, van der Kolk has applied for funding from the National Institutes of Health. In the meantime, he's working with Dave Emerson, director of the Trauma Center's yoga program, to develop a protocol that will incorporate what they've learned about teaching yoga to PTSD patients. For example, the studio needs to be out of public view, and instructors shouldn't touch students without asking permission.

Some trauma survivors initially find yoga threatening. "The yoga study had the highest dropout rate of any study I've ever done," van der Kolk says. "It was more scary for many traumatized women to discover their bodies than to take a pill."

The first time Emerson led a group of women from the Trauma Center into Happy Baby Pose, asking them to lie on their backs, bend their knees with shins perpendicular to the floor, and hold their feet, two of the women left. One never came back. Anne, a 50-year-old participant who endured sexual abuse starting in early childhood, can't fathom why the pose is called Happy Baby. When she first tried it, her legs shook uncontrollably. "To me," says Anne (not her real name), "that's a baby waiting to be hurt." She prefers Balasana (Child's Pose), which makes her feel sheltered and safe.

Such powerful responses to Happy Baby led van der Kolk and Emerson to question whether the pose was worth attempting. They decided to continue teaching it very gently, encouraging students not to try it if it made them uncomfortable. "The goal became making them feel safe in Happy Baby

Pose," says van der Kolk. "The women who stuck with it had extraordinary changes."

For Anne, who was recently able to go calmly into the pose, yoga's effect has been profound. "There is no way to describe what it has done for me," she says. More than 20 years of therapy had helped her continue to function in daily life and end self-destructive behaviors. "But I didn't think I would find peace of mind," she says, "and now I think I will."

TREATMENT FOR TRAUMA

Despite its association with combat veterans, post-traumatic stress disorder (PTSD) is actually more common in women than men. In the United States, 10 percent of women and 5 percent of men have the disorder at some point in their lives, according to the National Center for PTSD.

Psychiatrists, psychologists, and clinical social workers can diagnose and treat the condition. To find a mental health professional, ask your doctor for recommendations or check the Anxiety Disorders Association of America's Web site (www.adaa.org).

It's too soon to say whether yoga should replace traditional therapy as a treatment for PTSD, says trauma expert Bessel van der Kolk, a professor of psychiatry at Boston University School of Medicine. But he recommends it as a complementary practice. "Unless you befriend your body," he says, "you cannot become well."

Try different types of yoga until you find one that suits you, and tell instructors before class if you're uncomfortable being touched. Don't feel that you need to explain your trauma history. "Yoga is not about talking about your trauma," says van der Kolk. "It's about you and your relationship to your own body."

People practice different kinds of yoga, depending on the results they want to achieve. Research ashtanga yoga, bikram yoga, integral yoga, and hatha yoga online (start with Wikipedia, Britannica Online, and a Google search) or read up on several of the different kinds of yoga that *Yoga Journal* discusses: http://www.yogajournal.com/lifestyle/2984. What kind(s) of yoga does Wills's article seem to be advising for people with PTSD? Broad's "How Yoga Can Wreck Your Body" takes a very different approach to discussing yoga. What kinds of yoga do Broad and his respondents warn against?

According to the article, Dr. Bessel van der Kolk believes that practicing yoga can help patients with PTSD in ways that traditional therapy and medications cannot. He sees the connection between the mind and the body as integral to a patient's health. But it seems that doctors must be as cautious in asking patients to hold certain poses, such as the Happy Baby pose, as they ought to be when asking certain questions in more traditional types of psychotherapy. Do the mind's insecurities also inform our bodies' trauma and/or limitations? Should therapists be trained in how to practice and teach yoga to their patients, much as they are trained to treat their patients with cognitive behavioral therapy and medications?

In examining Broad's article and Wills's essay, what commonalities do you see between the two authors' claims for how yoga can help heal the body and the mind? Do the benefits outweigh the costs? Should sports fitness clubs have more information available on the risks of yoga (as well as other fitness classes)? Write an essay for a fitness club's monthly newsletter or pamphlet in which you defend the practice of yoga or warn people against taking yoga classes.

Science journalist William J. Broad published The Science of Yoga: Risks and Rewards *in 2012. This essay from* The New York Times Magazine *in the same year excerpts and adapts portions of the book.*

HOW YOGA CAN WRECK YOUR BODY

By William J. Broad

On a cold Saturday in early 2009, Glenn Black, a yoga teacher of nearly four decades, whose devoted clientele includes a number of celebrities and prominent gurus, was giving a master class at Sankalpah Yoga in Manhattan. Black is, in many ways, a classic yogi: he studied in Pune, India, at the institute founded by the legendary B. K. S. Iyengar, and spent years in solitude and meditation. He now lives in Rhinebeck, N.Y., and often teaches at the nearby Omega Institute, a New Age emporium spread over nearly 200 acres of woods and gardens. He is known for his rigor and his down-to-earth style. But this was not why I sought him out: Black, I'd been told, was the person to speak with if you wanted to know not about the virtues of yoga but rather about the damage it could do. Many of his regular clients came to him for bodywork or rehabilitation following yoga injuries. This was the situation I found myself in. In my 30s, I had somehow managed to rupture a disk in my lower back and found I could prevent bouts of pain with a selection of yoga postures and abdominal exercises. Then, in 2007, while doing the extended-side-angle pose, a posture hailed as a cure for many diseases, my back gave way. With it went my belief, naïve in retrospect, that yoga was a source only of healing and never harm.

At Sankalpah Yoga, the room was packed; roughly half the students were said to be teachers themselves. Black walked around the room, joking and talking. "Is this yoga?" he asked as we sweated through a pose that seemed to demand superhuman endurance. "It is if you're paying attention." His approach was almost free-form: he made us hold poses for a long time but taught no inversions and few classical postures. Throughout the class, he urged us to pay attention to the thresholds of pain. "I make it as hard as possible," he told the group. "It's up to you to make it easy on yourself." He drove his point home with a cautionary tale. In India, he recalled, a yogi came to study at Iyengar's school and threw himself into a spinal twist. Black said he watched in disbelief as three of the man's ribs gave way—pop, pop, pop.

After class, I asked Black about his approach to teaching yoga—the emphasis on holding only a few simple poses, the absence of common inversions like headstands and shoulder stands. He gave me the kind of answer you'd expect from any yoga teacher: that awareness is more important than rushing through a series of postures just to say you'd done them. But then he said something more radical. Black has come to believe that "the vast majority of people" should give up yoga altogether. It's simply too likely to cause harm.

Not just students but celebrated teachers too, Black said, injure themselves in droves because most have underlying physical weaknesses or problems that make serious injury all but inevitable. Instead of doing yoga, "they need to be doing a specific range of motions for articulation, for organ condition," he said, to strengthen weak parts of the body. "Yoga is for people in good physical condition. Or it can be used therapeutically. It's controversial to say, but it really shouldn't be used for a general class."

Black seemingly reconciles the dangers of yoga with his own teaching of it by working hard at knowing when a student "shouldn't do something—the shoulder stand, the headstand or putting any weight on the cervical vertebrae." Though he studied with Shmuel Tatz, a legendary Manhattan-based physical therapist who devised a method of massage and alignment for actors and dancers, he acknowledges that he has no formal training for determining which poses are good for a student and which may be problematic. What he does have, he says, is "a ton of experience."

"To come to New York and do a class with people who have many problems and say, 'O.K., we're going to do this sequence of poses today'—it just doesn't work."

According to Black, a number of factors have converged to heighten the risk of practicing yoga. The biggest is the demographic shift in those who study it.

Indian practitioners of yoga typically squatted and sat cross-legged in daily life, and yoga poses, or asanas, were an outgrowth of these postures. Now urbanites who sit in chairs all day walk into a studio a couple of times a week and strain to twist themselves into ever-more-difficult postures despite their lack of flexibility and other physical problems. Many come to yoga as a gentle alternative to vigorous sports or for rehabilitation for injuries. But yoga's exploding popularity—the number of Americans doing yoga has risen from about 4 million in 2001 to what some estimate to be as many as 20 million in 2011—means that there is now an abundance of studios where many teachers lack the deeper training necessary to recognize when students are headed toward injury. "Today many schools of yoga are just about pushing people," Black said. "You can't believe what's going on—teachers jumping on people, pushing and pulling and saying, 'You should be able to do this by now.' It has to do with their egos."

When yoga teachers come to him for bodywork after suffering major traumas, Black tells them, "Don't do yoga."

"They look at me like I'm crazy," he goes on to say. "And I know if they continue, they won't be able to take it." I asked him about the worst injuries he'd seen. He spoke of well-known yoga teachers doing such basic poses as downward-facing dog, in which the body forms an inverted V, so strenuously that they tore Achilles tendons. "It's ego," he said. "The whole point of yoga is to get rid of ego." He said he had seen some "pretty gruesome hips." "One of the biggest teachers in America had zero movement in her hip joints," Black told me. "The sockets had become so degenerated that she had to have hip replacements." I asked if she still taught. "Oh, yeah," Black replied. "There are other yoga teachers that have such bad backs they have to lie down to teach. I'd be so embarrassed."

Among devotees, from gurus to acolytes forever carrying their rolled-up mats, yoga is described as a nearly miraculous agent of renewal and healing. They celebrate its abilities to calm, cure, energize and strengthen. And much of this appears to be true: yoga can lower your blood pressure, make chemicals that act as antidepressants, even improve your sex life. But the yoga community long remained silent about its potential to inflict blinding pain. Jagannath G. Gune, who helped revive yoga for the modern era, made no allusion to injuries in his journal Yoga Mimansa or his 1931 book *Asanas*. Indra Devi avoided the issue in her 1953 best seller *Forever Young, Forever Healthy*, as did B. K. S.

Iyengar in his seminal *Light on Yoga*, published in 1965. Reassurances about yoga's safety also make regular appearances in the how-to books of such yogis as Swami Sivananda, K. Pattabhi Jois and Bikram Choudhury. "Real yoga is as safe as mother's milk," declared Swami Gitananda, a guru who made 10 world tours and founded ashrams on several continents.

But a growing body of medical evidence supports Black's contention that, for many people, a number of commonly taught yoga poses are inherently risky. The first reports of yoga injuries appeared decades ago, published in some of the world's most respected journals—among them, *Neurology*, *The British Medical Journal* and *The Journal of the American Medical Association*. The problems ranged from relatively mild injuries to permanent disabilities. In one case, a male college student, after more than a year of doing yoga, decided to intensify his practice. He would sit upright on his heels in a kneeling position known as vajrasana for hours a day, chanting for world peace. Soon he was experiencing difficulty walking, running and climbing stairs.

Doctors traced the problem to an unresponsive nerve, a peripheral branch of the sciatic, which runs from the lower spine through the buttocks and down the legs. Sitting in vajrasana deprived the branch that runs below the knee of oxygen, deadening the nerve. Once the student gave up the pose, he improved rapidly. Clinicians recorded a number of similar cases and the condition even got its own name: "yoga foot drop."

More troubling reports followed. In 1972 a prominent Oxford neurophysiologist, W. Ritchie Russell, published an article in *The British Medical Journal* arguing that, while rare, some yoga postures threatened to cause strokes even in relatively young, healthy people. Russell found that brain injuries arose not only from direct trauma to the head but also from quick movements or excessive extensions of the neck, such as occur in whiplash—or certain yoga poses. Normally, the neck can stretch backward 75 degrees, forward 40 degrees and sideways 45 degrees, and it can rotate on its axis about 50 degrees. Yoga practitioners typically move the vertebrae much farther. An intermediate student can easily turn his or her neck 90 degrees—nearly twice the normal rotation.

Hyperflexion of the neck was encouraged by experienced practitioners. Iyengar emphasized that in cobra pose, the head should arch "as far back as possible" and insisted that in the shoulder stand, in which the chin is tucked deep in the chest, the trunk and head forming a right angle, "the body should be in one straight line, perpendicular to the floor." He called the pose, said to stimulate the thyroid, "one of the greatest boons conferred on humanity by our ancient sages."

Extreme motions of the head and neck, Russell warned, could wound the vertebral arteries, producing clots, swelling and constriction, and eventually wreak havoc in the brain. The basilar artery, which arises from the union of the two vertebral arteries and forms a wide conduit at the base of the brain, was of particular concern. It feeds such structures as the pons (which plays a role in respiration), the cerebellum (which coordinates the muscles), the occipital lobe of the outer brain (which turns eye impulses into images) and the thalamus (which relays sensory messages to the outer brain). Reductions in blood flow to the basilar artery are known to produce a variety of strokes. These rarely affect language and conscious thinking (often said to be located in the frontal cortex) but can severely damage the body's core machinery and sometimes be fatal. The majority of patients suffering such a stroke do recover most functions. But in some cases headaches, imbalance, dizziness and difficulty in making fine movements persist for years.

Russell also worried that when strokes hit yoga practitioners, doctors might fail to trace their cause. The cerebral damage, he wrote, "may be delayed, perhaps to appear during the night following, and this delay of some hours distracts attention from the earlier precipitating factor."

In 1973, a year after Russell's paper was published, Willibald Nagler, a renowned authority on spinal rehabilitation at Cornell University Medical College, published a paper on a strange case. A healthy woman of 28 suffered a stroke while doing a yoga position known as the wheel or upward bow, in which the practitioner lies on her back, then lifts her body into a semicircular arc, balancing on hands and feet. An intermediate stage often involves raising the trunk and resting the crown of the head on the floor. While balanced on her head, her neck bent far backward, the woman "suddenly felt a severe throbbing headache." She had difficulty getting up, and when helped into a standing position, was unable to walk without assistance. The woman was rushed to the hospital. She had no sensation on the right side of her body; her left arm and leg responded poorly to her commands. Her eyes kept glancing involuntarily to the left. And the left side of her face showed a contracted pupil, a drooping upper eyelid and a rising lower lid—a cluster of symptoms known as Horner's syndrome. Nagler reported that the woman also had a tendency to fall to the left.

Her doctors found that the woman's left vertebral artery, which runs between the first two cervical vertebrae, had narrowed considerably and that the arteries feeding her cerebellum had undergone severe displacement. Given the lack of advanced imaging technologies at the time, an exploratory operation was conducted to get a clearer sense of her injuries. The surgeons who opened her skull found that the left hemisphere of her cerebellum suffered a major failure of blood supply that resulted in much dead tissue and that the site was seeped in secondary hemorrhages.

The patient began an intensive program of rehabilitation. Two years later, she was able to walk, Nagler reported, "with [a] broad-based gait." But her left arm continued to wander and her left eye continued to show Horner's syndrome. Nagler concluded that such injuries appeared to be rare but served as a warning about the hazards of "forceful hyperextension of the neck." He urged caution in recommending such postures, particularly to individuals of middle age.

The experience of Nagler's patient was not an isolated incident. A few years later, a 25-year-old man was rushed to Northwestern Memorial Hospital, in Chicago, complaining of blurred vision, difficulty swallowing and controlling the left side of his body. Steven H. Hanus, a medical student at the time, became interested in the case and worked with the chairman of the neurology department to determine the cause (he later published the results with several colleagues). The patient had been in excellent health, practicing yoga every morning for a year and a half. His routine included spinal twists in which he rotated his head far to the left and far to the right. Then he would do a shoulder stand with his neck "maximally flexed against the bare floor," just as Iyengar had instructed, remaining in the inversion for about five minutes. A series of bruises ran down the man's lower neck, which, the team wrote in *The Archives of Neurology*, "resulted from repeated contact with the hard floor surface on which he did yoga exercises." These were a sign of neck trauma. Diagnostic tests revealed blockages of the left vertebral artery between the c2 and c3 vertebrae; the blood vessel there had suffered "total or nearly complete occlusion"—in other words, no blood could get through to the brain.

Two months after his attack, and after much physical therapy, the man was able to walk with a cane. But, the team reported, he "continued to have pronounced difficulty performing fine movements with his left hand." Hanus and his colleagues concluded that the young man's condition represented a new kind of danger. Healthy individuals could seriously damage their vertebral arteries, they warned, "by neck movements that exceed physiological tolerance." Yoga, they stressed, "should be considered as a possible precipitating event." In its report, the Northwestern team cited not only Nagler's account of his female patient but also Russell's early warning. Concern about yoga's safety began to ripple through the medical establishment.

These cases may seem exceedingly rare, but surveys by the Consumer Product Safety Commission showed that the number of emergency-room admissions related to yoga, after years of slow increases, was rising quickly. They went from 13 in 2000 to 20 in 2001. Then they more than doubled to 46 in 2002. These surveys rely on sampling rather than exhaustive reporting—they reveal trends rather than totals—but the spike was nonetheless statistically significant. Only a fraction of the injured visit hospital emergency rooms. Many of those suffering from less serious yoga injuries go to family doctors, chiropractors and various kinds of therapists.

Around this time, stories of yoga-induced injuries began to appear in the media. The Times reported that health professionals found that the penetrating heat of Bikram yoga, for example, could raise the risk of overstretching, muscle damage and torn cartilage. One specialist noted that ligaments—the tough bands of fiber that connect bones or cartilage at a joint—failed to regain their shape once stretched out, raising the risk of strains, sprains and dislocations.

In 2009, a New York City team based at Columbia University's College of Physicians and Surgeons published an ambitious worldwide survey of yoga teachers, therapists and doctors. The answers to the survey's central question— What were the most serious yoga-related injuries (disabling and/or of long duration) they had seen?—revealed that the largest number of injuries (231) centered on the lower back. The other main sites were, in declining order of prevalence: the shoulder (219), the knee (174) and the neck (110). Then came stroke. The respondents noted four cases in which yoga's extreme bending and contortions resulted in some degree of brain damage. The numbers weren't alarming but the acknowledgment of risk—nearly four decades after Russell first issued his warning—pointed to a decided shift in the perception of the dangers yoga posed.

In recent years, reformers in the yoga community have begun to address the issue of yoga-induced damage. In a 2003 article in *Yoga Journal*, Carol Krucoff—a yoga instructor and therapist who works at the Integrative Medicine center at Duke University in North Carolina—revealed her own struggles. She told of being filmed one day for national television and after being urged to do more, lifting one foot, grabbing her big toe and stretching her leg into the extended-hand-to-big-toe pose. As her leg straightened, she felt a sickening pop in her hamstring. The next day, she could barely walk. Krucoff needed physical therapy and a year of recovery before she could fully extend her leg again. The editor of *Yoga Journal*, Kaitlin Quistgaard, described reinjuring a torn rotator cuff in a yoga class. "I've experienced how yoga can heal," she wrote. "But I've also experienced how yoga can hurt—and I've heard the same from plenty of other yogis."

One of the most vocal reformers is Roger Cole, an Iyengar teacher with degrees in psychology from Stanford and the University of California, San Francisco. Cole has written extensively for *Yoga Journal* and speaks on yoga safety to the American College of Sports Medicine. In one column, Cole discussed the practice of reducing neck bending in a shoulder stand by lifting the shoulders on a stack of folded blankets and letting the head fall below it. The modification eases the angle between the head and the torso, from 90 degrees to perhaps 110 degrees. Cole ticked off the dangers of doing an unmodified shoulder stand: muscle strains, overstretched ligaments and cervical-disk injuries.

But modifications are not always the solution. Timothy McCall, a physician who is the medical editor of *Yoga Journal*, called the headstand too dangerous for general yoga classes. His warning was based partly on his own experience. He found that doing the headstand led to thoracic outlet syndrome, a condition that arises from the compression of nerves passing from the neck into the arms, causing tingling in his right hand as well as sporadic numbness. McCall stopped doing the pose, and his symptoms went away. Later, he noted that the inversion could produce other injuries, including degenerative arthritis of the cervical spine and retinal tears (a result of the increased eye pressure caused by the pose). "Unfortunately," McCall concluded, "the negative effects of headstand can be insidious."

Almost a year after I first met Glenn Black at his master class in Manhattan, I received an e-mail from him telling me that he had undergone spinal surgery. "It was a success," he wrote. "Recovery is slow and painful. Call if you like."

The injury, Black said, had its origins in four decades of extreme backbends and twists. He had developed spinal stenosis—a serious condition in which the openings between vertebrae begin to narrow, compressing spinal nerves and causing excruciating pain. Black said that he felt the tenderness start 20 years ago when he was coming out of such poses as the plow and the shoulder stand. Two years ago, the pain became extreme. One surgeon said that without treatment, he would eventually be unable to walk. The surgery took five hours, fusing together several lumbar vertebrae. He would eventually be fine but was under surgeon's orders to reduce strain on his lower back. His range of motion would never be the same.

Black is one of the most careful yoga practitioners I know. When I first spoke to him, he said he had never injured himself doing yoga or, as far as he knew, been responsible for harming any of his students. I asked him if his recent injury could have been congenital or related to aging. No, he said. It was yoga. "You have to get a different perspective to see if what you're doing is going to eventually be bad for you."

Black recently took that message to a conference at the Omega Institute, his feelings on the subject deepened by his recent operation. But his warnings seemed to fall on deaf ears. "I was a little more emphatic than usual," he recalled. "My message was that 'Asana is not a panacea or a cure-all. In fact, if you do it with ego or obsession, you'll end up causing problems.' A lot of people don't like to hear that."

Broad observes, "the number of Americans doing yoga has risen from about 4 million in 2001 to what some estimate to be as many as 20 million in 2011." Why have so many people taken up yoga? When you think of yoga, what do you see as its health benefits? Do Glenn Black's anecdotes about injuries change your view of yoga and its benefits? Should people stop doing certain kinds of yoga or revise their understanding of our bodies' limitations in flexibility?

Read these two short articles on step aerobics: http://www.livestrong. com/article/372811-hip-pain-during-step-aerobics/ and http://www. aapsm.org/ct1198.html or do a google search on "step aerobics history" and "step aerobics injuries." When step aerobics were introduced in the late 1980s, these classes became the newest fitness craze, but as you can determine from the articles or your search, step aerobics can lead to serious injuries. What are the differences between aerobics and yoga? What does each promise? What are the commonalities between the two? Is yoga a fad, like step aerobics, that might help some but injure others, or a series of exercises that anyone may try to restore calm and balance?

Much of Broad's evidence in this article is anecdotal, as is Denise Wills' in "Healing Life's Traumas." Broad's book, *The Science of Yoga*, however, delves deeper into the empirical evidence for yoga's risks and benefits. Select a chapter from *The Science of Yoga* and contrast the evidence Broad uses in his book to the anecdotes he highlights in his article or to Wills' article. Which approach do you find more effective? Which version is more likely to lead to changes in policy at the national level (for example, the accreditation of yoga teachers), and which is more likely to lead to changes in the reader's personal behavior?

Science journalist Shannon Brownlee published her first book, Overtreated: Why Too Much Medicine is Making Us Sicker and Poorer, *from which we have taken this excerpt, in 2007.*

excerpt from

OVERTREATED: WHY TOO MUCH MEDICINE IS MAKING US SICKER AND POORER

BY SHANNON BROWNLEE

THE MOST DANGEROUS PLACE

On a chilly Tuesday evening in February 2001, eighteen-month-old Josie King arrived at the pediatric intensive care unit of Johns Hopkins Medicine with second-degree burns covering 60 percent of her small body. The accident had happened in a flash. Earlier that evening, the King family was gathered around the fire after dinner, when Josie crept upstairs behind one of her three older siblings, toddled to a bathroom, and turned on the scalding hot water. Josie had already scrambled out of the bath by the time her mother, Sorrel, heard her screams and raced up the stairs after her. [...]

Though Josie was seriously burned, Sorrel and Tony King had no doubts their daughter would fully recover at Johns Hopkins, which they knew by reputation was one of the best hospitals in the country, if not the world. Even before moving to Baltimore a year earlier—when Tony, a trader for Wachovia Securities, was transferred there from Richmond, Virginia—they had heard of Johns Hopkins. A wry, no-nonsense thirty-four-year-old, Sorrel King found comfort in the calm competence of the team of doctors caring for Josie. There was Milissa McKee, a pediatric surgical fellow, who provided much of Josie's day-to-day doctoring, always under the supervision of Charles Paidas, the director of pediatric trauma at the hospital and a world-renowned pediatric trauma surgeon. An entire team of pain specialists, anesthesiologists, and nurses kept Josie comfortable with methadone, a powerful narcotic, and other painkillers. Half a dozen intensive care nurses rotated through the unit over the course of a day. Amal Murarka was Josie's pediatric intensive care specialist. A warm, handsome thirty-two-year-old who was just at the beginning of his career, Murarka stopped in to check on Josie regularly and became one of her mother's favorites.

The gravest dangers facing Josie, like any patient with extensive burns, were infection and dehydration. Without the first two protective layers of skin, burn victims are acutely vulnerable to bacteria trying to get in and the water in their bodies leaking out. Infants and toddlers lose water through their damaged skin more quickly than older children and adults, because the surface of their bodies is larger in comparison to their bodies' volume. To keep her hydrated, Josie's doctors needed to give her intravenous fluids, but with so much of her skin burned, they had trouble finding a place to put an IV line. Two days after she arrived at the hospital, she was sent to the operating room, where she was given a "central line," a tube inserted just under the collarbone into the large central vein leading directly to her heart. She underwent repeated skin grafts, and her caregivers took pains to keep her wounds as sterile as possible.

Within two weeks, the toddler was well enough to be moved from intensive care to a "step-down unit," a sort of halfway house for patients who are ready to leave the ICU but not quite well enough for the regular wards. Sorrel King, who had spent much of the time at her daughter's side, confided to Paidas that she was worried about the move. None of the nurses were familiar, she told him. Was Josie really ready? Paidas assured King that her daughter was practically healed. Yet within a day of the move to the step-down unit, Josie began vomiting and having bouts of diarrhea. She spiked intermittent fevers, a signal to her doctors that she had a systemic infection. Paidas suspected the source was her central line, a common portal for bacteria unless it is kept scrupulously clean. Tests came back negative, but he decided to remove the central line anyway and treat Josie with oral antibiotics.

As Josie's vomiting and diarrhea tapered off over the next two days, King noticed that her daughter seemed perpetually thirsty. The child whimpered or screamed as she reached for a cup or soda can if anyone nearby was drinking. The nurses instructed King not to give Josie anything by mouth; they were carefully monitoring her intake of fluids and did not want her to drink anything that went unrecorded. On February 18, the night before her discharge, Josie seemed listless to her mother, who noticed she sucked furiously on her washcloth while she was being bathed. By the time King tucked her daughter into bed, the child was unable to raise her head. King summoned a nurse, asking her to page a doctor.

The nurse checked Josie's vital signs—her temperature, blood pressure, and heart rate—and reassured King her daughter was fine. King said again that her daughter seemed thirsty and asked that another nurse be called. When the second nurse confirmed that all was well, King went home, reluctantly, to see Tony before he left the next morning on a business trip to California. She woke twice in the middle of the night and called the hospital, only to be told not to worry.

King arrived at the hospital at five thirty the next morning. After one look at Josie, she ran into the hall. "Get in here now," she said to McKee, the surgical fellow who performed many of Josie's skin grafts. "I need a team in here now, now, now."

McKee found a lethargic and pale child, her eyes dilated and sunken in their sockets. The doctors and nurses gathered around the bed, wondering aloud if perhaps Josie was reacting to the methadone. This theory seemed to be confirmed when she perked up after an injection of Narcan, a drug that reverses the effects of narcotics. King told McKee her daughter was thirsty and asked a nurse to bring her something to drink. Josie gulped down a liter of juice, the equivalent of more than four cups.

McKee paged Paidas. After consulting with McKee about Josie's response to the Narcan, he wrote in the girl's chart that she was not to be given any more pain medication unless he was consulted. Then he left for surgery. About an hour later, Josie got another shot of Narcan. She seemed more alert to King, looking around the room and watching a Scooby-Doo cartoon on television. Still worried, King asked McKee to be ready to return at a moment's notice.

Just before lunch, a pediatric anesthesiologist from the pain team stopped in. Worried that Josie might suffer withdrawal symptoms without another dose of methadone, the doctor paged Paidas to get his permission to reinstate the drug. He was still in surgery, so the pain doctor consulted with another member of the pediatric surgical team before ordering a lower dose of methadone. At one in the afternoon, a nurse on duty entered Josie's room with a syringe of the drug.

Knowing only that Paidas had ordered a halt to the methadone, King questioned the nurse, who told her there was a new order in Josie's record. King asked her to double-check. After confirming the change, the nurse gave Josie the medicine. Within minutes, Josie's eyes rolled back in her head, and her body went slack.

Murarka, the young intensive care specialist who had watched closely over Josie's recovery in the pediatric ICU, heard the code for cardiac arrest over the loudspeaker. When he rushed into her room, he did not recognize the patient at first, or her mother, standing horrified in a corner. Nurses and doctors crowded around the little girl, pumping her chest, trying to find a vein for an IV needle, slipping a breathing tube down her trachea. Murarka drew close enough to realize it was Josie. Later he would recall thinking to himself, "This is not happening. I can't believe this child is going to die right here."

A MILLION PATIENTS

A string of errors—oversights and a crucial miscommunication—led to Josie King's death in what may seem the least likely place for such a thing to occur. In a prestigious medical center, under the care of rigorously trained specialists and experienced, caring nurses, the toddler became profoundly dehydrated, so dehydrated that a small dose of methadone pushed her over the edge into cardiac arrest. There was no overt or gross negligence, no disregard for a little girl's well-being. [...] Certainly her parents never once considered the possibility that her life was in jeopardy either from her burns or from being hospitalized. Yet she died as a result of treatment intended to prevent her from being scarred for life. [...]

For the most part, patients are cared for by people who are competent and dedicated—who want nothing more than to do their very best to heal. Yet in a hospital, the most innocent of mistakes can, and with astonishing frequency does, result in dire peril. [...]In addition to human error, patients risk hospital-borne infection and complications from treatment—even when the treatment is correctly administered. The more often a patient is hospitalized and the longer the stay, the greater the chance of something going wrong. More invasive procedures—injections, IVs, central lines, surgeries—equal more potential dangers.

This is not to say that hospitals must or should be avoided, or treatment refused. Overall, the benefits of modern medicine far outweigh the risks. [...] Yet that care, the most advanced care available, failed because of the opportunities it presented for something—or a cascade of somethings—to go wrong.

Such opportunities for disaster become even more worrisome when considered in light of the research compiled by the Dartmouth group and others. Unlike little Josie, many patients enter the hospital not because they need to be there, and are given tests and treatments not because they are necessary, but because of other factors—reasons that stem from the culture and economics of medicine as it is practiced in the United States. [...]

In 2003, the *Annals of Internal Medicine* published a landmark pair of papers, the results of the study led by Dartmouth's Elliott Fisher that showed for the first time the potential for harm inherent in unnecessary medical care. An internist and one of the first researchers to join Jack Wennberg at Dartmouth back in the 1980s, Fisher and his colleagues had a seemingly simple objective for their massive study, which analyzed the medical care received by nearly one million Medicare beneficiaries. They wanted to determine whether or not regions of the country that spend more on health care provide better care.

[...] Are hospitals that use the most Medicare dollars producing better outcomes? And are they any better at delivering the treatments that are considered the most effective—a prescription for heart attack patients to take an aspirin a day, for instance, and flu shots? Are they making sure their female patients get regular Pap smears, and do they take steps to ensure that surgical patients don't contract infections? [...]

If you wanted to create the perfect study that would show how spending affects patient outcomes, you would first find lots and lots of people with the same diagnosis and roughly the same risk of dying from their disease. You would then tell several hospitals how much each could spend on its patients with that particular diagnosis. Then you would randomly assign your patients to the various hospitals. Finally, you would look at how the patients fared over time.

Of course, researchers can't very well go around telling patients where to get their medical care and hospitals how much they get to spend, so Fisher and his team did the next best thing. First, they categorized the nation's 306 hospital referral regions into five groups, or quintiles, according to how much the regions had spent in the past, on average, on Medicare recipients in the last six months of life. (Just to give an idea of the huge range of spending, the highest-spending regions devoted $14,644 worth of care to the average Medicare patient compared with $9,074 on average for patients in the lowest-spending regions.)

Next, the team combed through millions of Medicare records in order to find three groups, or cohorts, of patients who were equally sick at the time of diagnosis. The patients they chose all had one of three conditions: 159,393 patients had had an acute myocardial infarction, or heart attack; 195,429 had colorectal cancer; and 614,503 had a fractured hip. The researchers had to dig deep into the medical records of their Medicare patients to extract information not only about how much was spent on their care but also about any "comorbidities," other conditions they had that might influence their outcomes. The team looked at what procedures and tests patients underwent; which drugs they took; and whether or not their health was improved by any of it. They even looked at socioeconomic status, which can independently affect health outcomes.

The research team then followed the patients, through their medical records, over the course of several years. They could see if the members of their cohorts in high-spending regions were more likely to receive high-quality care than those in low-spending regions—and were more likely to recover from their illnesses as a result. Two years—and hundreds of hours of number crunching—later, the study's findings surprised even Fisher.[...] Fisher and his team looked at several dozen different things that could be done for patients, from office visits to brain CTs to having a feeding tube inserted. They looked at how many days patients spent in an ICU; how often they were given a pulmonary function test, a measure of lung capacity and strength; and how many times they underwent an intubation.

True to form, hospitals that historically spent the most money on Medicare recipients in the last six months of life also spent the most on Fisher's cohorts over the course of several years—and gave them lots of tests and procedures. Remember, all of these patients were basically identical in terms of how sick they were and what they needed to get better. Yet patients received 60 percent more care in the highest-spending regions than in the lower-spending regions. [...]

But it was the outcomes of the researchers' three cohorts that proved to be the most startling finding. Fisher and his colleagues discovered that patients who went to hospitals that spent the most—and did the most—were 2 to 6 percent more likely to die than patients who went to hospitals that spent the least.

The upshot of this finding is inescapable. More care may not only be useless (and expensive), it may also be downright dangerous. "The most reasonable explanation for the higher mortality rate," says Fisher, "is that the additional medicine patients are getting in the high-cost regions is leading to harm." When doctors give unnecessary treatment, patients are exposed to all the risks—but not the benefits—of medicine, risks that include hospital-borne infections, the complications and side effects that can come with any treatment, and medical errors like the ones that led to Josie King's death. Hospitals, says Fisher, "can be dangerous places." [...]

BAD DOCTORS

In 1999, the prestigious Institute of Medicine published *To Err Is Human*, a report that documented the scope and outcome of medical error in American hospitals. The report stunned even health care professionals. The institute estimated that medical errors kill between forty-four thousand and ninety-eight thousand Americans each year. Some 4 percent of the thirty-three million people who are hospitalized annually, about 1.3 million patients, suffer from a complication—or in medical argot, an "adverse event"—that leads to a longer stay in the hospital, disability, or death. [...] Some critics of the two large studies that formed the basis for the Institute of Medicine's report argue that the number of adverse events may be inflated. Yet even using the Institute's lower, more-conservative estimate makes preventable hospital error the eighth leading cause of death annually, ahead of motor vehicle accidents (43,458), breast cancer (42,297), and AIDS (16,516).

Drug errors are the most common mistakes of all, and on average at least one occurs for every patient admitted to the hospital. No lasting harm is done most of the time, yet even so, according to a 1995 study, two out of every one hundred patients admitted to hospitals were hurt when they received the wrong drug, the wrong dose of the right drug, or two drugs that interacted badly. [...]

It's tempting to lay all medical error at the feet of bad doctors, but that can't be the whole story, as Harvard surgeon Atul Gawande points out, for the simple reason that good doctors make mistakes too. Studies of specific types of medical error suggest that it is not just a small subset of doctors who commit them, a rotten few who are responsible for all the problems. Rather, every physician is destined to make at least one horrible mistake in the course of a career—and most will carry the memory and shame of it for the rest of their lives.

It isn't just doctors who err. Virtually every person who has direct responsibility for the care of sick people falls down on the job sometimes, and the more people involved in an individual patient's care—and the most procedures the patient undergoes—the more likely it is that somebody in the medical supply chain is going to blow it.

Just think for a moment about the sheer number of people who have a hand in whether a patient lives or dies. There are the orderlies who must deliver blood samples to the lab on time and the pathologists who must correctly identify infectious agents so doctors can prescribe the right antibiotic. Pharmacists have to provide the right drug at the right dose to the right patient. Somebody has to scrub down every bacteria-harboring nook of an operating room, thoroughly sterilize equipment and linens, stock supply closets, fill soap dispensers, and maintain heart monitors and ventilators. Every single person must do his or her job right every single time or risk the well-being of patients.

When you think about how many people touch a patient, either directly or indirectly, and how many tasks they must perform with precision in order to keep patients safe, it's hard not to wonder how patients ever leave a hospital intact. The sense that hospitals are dangerous places is only intensified by studies of near misses. This research suggests that the errors that get recorded represent only a fraction of the number that actually occur. One ICU that tracked near misses reported 1.7 errors per day per patient, about 30 percent of which could have been serious or fatal. [...]

In his book *Human Error*, British psychologist James Reason argues that complex systems that depend upon everybody doing everything right all the time are inevitably filled with what he calls "latent errors," accidents just waiting to happen. Not surprisingly, latent errors abound in medicine. Workloads for doctors and nurses can be staggering; communication between multiple caregivers can be hit or miss; and in teaching hospitals, young, inexperienced doctors provide the lion's share of the day-to-day care of patients, and they do it on minimal sleep. (Doctors have a saying: Never get admitted to a teaching hospital in July, because that's when all the new interns arrive fresh from medical school.)

Yet despite the abundance of latent errors in complex systems, a single misstep rarely results in disaster. Rather, adverse medical events generally evolve over time, according to Reason's logic, largely because human beings possess the capacity to change course when they realize things are going terribly wrong. [...]

It's when multiple, often small, errors are missed that catastrophes blossom. In his remarkably candid book *Complications*, Atul Gawande tells the story of botching an emergency tracheotomy, a surgical procedure that involves cutting a hole in a patient's neck just below the larynx in order to insert a breathing tube when the patient's trachea is obstructed. As a young surgical resident, Gawande was ill prepared in every possible way for the procedure. He had previously performed only one emergency "trach" (pronounced "trake") in his life—on a goat. He failed to get out the equipment he needed—the lighting, suction tubing, sterile instruments—the moment he first suspected the patient's airway was shutting down. He waited too long to call a more-experienced doctor. Finally, as panic threatened to take hold, he cut into her neck in the wrong direction, causing so much bleeding that he could not see well enough to complete the job. Luckily, the patient survived, because another doctor was finally able to slip a breathing tube past her vocal cords. Gawande describes his feelings after the event as a "burning ulcer." He writes, "This was not guilt: guilt is what you feel when you have done something wrong. What I felt was shame: I was what was wrong."

THINGS THAT HAPPEN IN HOSPITALS

The chances that multiple errors will snowball into full-blown disasters have grown in recent decades, for the simple reason that medical treatment has grown more complex. Just think about the sheer number of things doctors can do for patients today that they couldn't do a generation ago. Here's an example. Thirty-five years ago, a sixty-year-old man who was carried into an emergency room in the midst of a heart attack might have gotten morphine, to ease his pain, and lidocaine (a drug that has recently been shown to cause more harm than good in stable heart attack patients). Physicians could have administered an electrical shock to his heart if it had stopped, or if he had gone into fibrillation, an abnormal rhythm of the heart. Beyond that, there was little else his doctors could have done but hope he survived. Today, that same patient would be treated according to a complex algorithm, depending upon what kind of myocardial infarction, or MI, he was having and how serious it was. He would probably get clot-busting thrombolytics. He might receive drugs called glycoprotein inhibitors, nicknamed "super-aspirins," to help prevent further clots from forming; beta-blockers to restore an even heartbeat; and maybe angioplasty and a stent to hold open the blocked artery.

All that new technology has helped cut the death rate from heart attacks by nearly two thirds for men in their fifties and sixties—a spectacular medical achievement. But it has also created a paradox: The same new drugs and treatments that have decreased a man's chances of dying from his acute MI have also increased the number of latent errors that are possible and the potential for complications. A physician gives an injection of heparin without first performing a rectal exam, to make sure the patient isn't bleeding in his gut, and the blood thinner causes the patient to hemorrhage. Thrombolytics, the very drugs that can bust the clot in his coronary arteries, can also cause catastrophic bleeding in the brain. The man could suffer an allergic reaction to a drug. Maybe the beta-blocker causes his blood pressure to drop precipitously and he "bottoms out," a side effect of the drug that can aggravate the damage to his heart and even cause sudden cardiac arrest. The cardiologist could accidentally perforate an artery while she's threading a catheter into the man's heart.

On balance, of course, the new treatments are obviously well worth such risks. Far more heart patients' lives are saved than lost by new technology, and nobody in his right mind would want to go back to the days when all doctors could do was give a heart attack patient a painkiller and hope for the best. Yet physicians and nurses know that a certain number of their patients are going to be killed not by their heart attacks but by the treatment that is supposed to save them. [...]

Even aspirin can be lethal. If you've already had an acute MI, taking an aspirin a day can reduce the odds of dying from a second one by more than 15 percent, a bigger risk reduction than any single treatment or surgery a doctor can prescribe for heart disease. But taking aspirin daily when you aren't likely to have a heart attack might not be such a good idea, since aspirin can trigger hemorrhaging in the brain, stomach, and intestines.

At least the trade-offs for aspirin are well defined. Given clear information about the risks and potential benefits of this drug, patients and their doctors can choose whether they are willing to trade short-term safety for possible long-term gain. Most of the time, however, the scales of medicine aren't so easy to read. [...] When a little girl is burned over 60 percent of her body and needs fluids, nobody stops to ponder the risk of infection while putting in a central line. [...]

CONTROLLED CHAOS

Here, then, is an explanation for Fisher's discovery that Medicare patients with the same well-defined medical conditions, the same chances of survival, and even the same socioeconomic status are more likely to die in parts of the country where Medicare spends the most. Spending more means doing more, and doing more increases the chances of errors being committed and of patients being hit with a complication. The corollary to this stark fact is that the more days a patient spends in the hospital, and the more complex treatment he receives, the greater the odds he'll suffer an adverse event. [...]

"Look at the extra stuff that's done more often in the high-cost regions," Fisher says. "Most of it is relatively minor procedures and imaging and diagnostic tests." Most major surgeries, on the other hand, hardly vary at all between regions. Surgery for colon cancer, for instance, is relatively constant, as is hernia repair. For cataract removal, the rate is only slightly higher in hospitals in high-spending regions compared with low-spending ones.

For many other procedures, however, the differences are striking. Fisher runs a finger down the list and stops at a procedure called a laryngoscopy. "That's for looking down your throat to see why you're hoarse," he says. "It's done three and a half times more often in high-cost regions. [...] The thing that's really startling is that the differences we see are all explained by these decisions around discretionary treatment, things that don't fall into the category of absolutely necessary, important medicine." [...]

"Discretionary" means these procedures and tests are employed at the doctor's discretion. [...] Even when their patients are equally ill and equally likely to survive—as Fisher showed of the three cohorts in his gigantic study—the doctors at one hospital are far more likely to decide to perform a laryngoscopy or a pulmonary function test than the doctors at another. [...]

Young physicians don't just learn to perform procedures by example; they also absorb lessons about when it's appropriate to use a particular test or treatment. Residents learn from attending physicians, who learned when they themselves were residents, when to put in a vena cava filter, which patients need a central line, and how to treat postsurgical abdominal pain. [...]

Young doctors learn to be more or less aggressive in their treatment during their internships and residencies, but they don't stop absorbing the cultural messages around them the minute they finish their training and enter practice. Physicians who work in the same hospital share knowledge and opinions whenever they are thrown together, discussing cases over coffee or standing in front of the nurses' station—and shaping, in the process, a kind of groupthink about how best to handle different conditions. One surgeon wants all of his patients to receive a vena cava filter. Another physician disagrees, arguing the device should only be used in patients who can't be given heparin to prevent clots. Since there's often little evidence to support one approach over another, this give-and-take can drive the collective clinical decisions made by doctors at a particular hospital.

But while cultural transmission of practice styles certainly plays a central role, it isn't the whole explanation for why the care in high-spending regions is more intense—and expensive—than in low-spending regions. Another key factor, says Fisher, is the high number of specialists in the highest-spending regions. [...]

What Fisher is saying is that the care that patients are likely to get results from the interplay between culturally transmitted practice styles, which evolve at individual hospitals, and the availability of different kinds of doctors. The more specialists around for any given physician to call in for a consult, the more likely it is that a specialist will be called in. [...]

At first, the idea that more specialists can make for worse medical care seems thoroughly wrongheaded. [...] Specialists have detailed knowledge that at times can be critical in making a correct diagnosis, and they acquire skills, by dint of years of practice, that make them far more qualified to perform certain procedures. You wouldn't want a gastroenterologist operating on your knee.

At the same time, anyone who has witnessed the whir of activity in a busy hospital can see how more specialists can lead to more confusion. Here's an example of how the confusion starts. A physician sees a patient, prescribes a drug, and then records the order in the patient's chart—sometimes illegibly. The next specialist comes along, misreads the previous doctor's hieroglyphics, and proceeds to give the patient another drug that causes a bad reaction with the first. [...] Busy specialists don't always consult one another directly, even by phone, and it's almost unheard of for all the doctors involved in a single patient's care to gather together in one room and actually discuss how best to treat him.

And so each specialist focuses on the part of the body he or she knows best.[...]

That leaves only two people in the entire hospital who may know what's happening to the whole patient. If you come in for surgery, one of those two people might be your surgeon, except for the fact that surgeons are often far too busy to keep tabs on what all the other specialists are doing to their patients. If you're lucky, your primary care physician takes time off from his office schedule to make regular visits to the hospital and check up on you. [...] But most of the time, the only person in a position to be aware of everything that is happening during a hospital stay is you, the patient—and often you're too sick to pay attention. Even family members can't be expected to stand watch twenty-four hours a day, much less keep track of the complexities of modern medical treatment. [...]

In his slim and eloquent volume *Escape Fire: Lessons for the Future of Health Care*, Donald Berwick illustrates just how absurd it is to expect patients or their families to monitor their own care when they're in a hospital—even when a family member is a physician. A Massachusetts pediatrician, Berwick is now president and CEO of the Institute for Healthcare Improvement, a group that advises hospitals on how to reduce error and improve quality. Berwick was radicalized, as he puts it, in 1999, when his wife, Ann, was hospitalized six separate times for a mysterious and debilitating spinal cord disorder.

Over the course of several months, Ann Berwick spent a total of sixty days at three different hospitals, including one of the most prestigious hospitals in the country. [...] Berwick was stunned nonetheless by the lack of coordination he witnessed. During one admission, he writes, "The neurologist told us in the morning, 'By no means should you be getting anticholinergic agents'; and a medication with profound anticholinergic activity was given that afternoon. The attending neurologist during another admission told us by phone that a crucial and potentially toxic drug should be started immediately. He said, 'Time is of the essence.' That was on Thursday morning at 10:00 am. The first dose was given 60 hours later— Saturday night, at 10:00 pm. Nothing I could do, nothing I did, nothing I could think of made any difference. It nearly drove me mad." [...]

THE WHOLE PATIENT

[...] What Berwick saw firsthand is sometimes called the "network effect," the barely controlled chaos of multiple caretakers in an environment where there is little coordination of care. A former head of Kaiser Permanente dubbed it the "adhoc-cracy" of medicine. Whatever you call it, health care doesn't work well when there is no single individual, in particular no generalist, who's in charge of coordinating a patient's care. This persistent and widespread lack of coordination may help explain the "undertreatment"—the failure to deliver needed care—that Fisher and his colleagues recorded in the highest-spending regions. The group found that high-spending regions weren't delivering better care, or even needed care, just more of it.

This may be Fisher's most stunning finding of all. If you are a patient who happens to live in a region where hospitals have lots of resources and lots of specialists, you are more likely to be *undertreated*—that is, your hospital may fail to deliver care that's known to be effective for your particular condition. In the highest-spending regions, for instance, about 75 percent of heart attack patients were sent home from the hospital with orders to take a baby aspirin a day—the single most effective drug for reducing a patient's risk of suffering a second event. In the lowest-spending regions, by contrast, more than 83 percent of heart attack patients went home with their baby aspirin. Major teaching hospitals, which are considered the crème de la crème of American medicine, were only a little better than most, and on only a few quality measures. Hospitals that spent more and were overtreating patients with certain kinds of care were simultaneously undertreating them.

[...] The bottom line is this: Whether you are rushed to the hospital or you walk in the door, your chances of getting all the treatment that is recommended for any given condition are about the same as flipping a coin. Nobody can quite explain why so much necessary treatment simply falls through the cracks— and why it happens more often, as Fisher found, at hospitals that are delivering the most intensive treatment. It may be the result of the network effect, a case of confusion that leads health care providers to repeatedly drop the ball. Or maybe physicians and hospitals don't make sure their patients get what they really need because they aren't specifically paid for it.

That's the idea behind Medicare's new reimbursement system, called "pay for performance," which offers small bonuses to hospitals for sweating the small stuff, like ensuring that heart attack patients get their aspirin and giving every Medicare recipient who walks through their doors a flu vaccine. This approach assumes that hospitals (and the physicians and nurses who work in them) fail to do what's right because there's no money in it, and that paying them will get them to focus on reducing undertreatment. This assumption could well be true, though the pay-for-performance initiative is too new to produce results that would tell us one way or another.

What is known is that regions that have fewer specialists in relation to the population—and more primary care physicians—have better overall health, a result that has turned up time and time again in various studies. [...] While Americans worship the specialist for his knowledge and technical expertise, the most important doctor for ensuring good health may be the underappreciated primary care physician.

What all of this says is that somebody needs to keep watch over the whole patient, not just his various parts. [...] Hospitals and physicians are not rewarded for keeping patients safe or coordinating their care. Doctors aren't paid to keep decent records and hospitals aren't reimbursed for retaining the right mix of specialists and primary care physicians. Both physicians and hospitals are paid, by and large, to do more, and distortions in what gets reimbursed most richly have ensured that the simplest, most effective care often falls through the cracks in favor of more-invasive, complicated treatment—care that involves more doctors than necessary and that may put patients at unnecessary risk.

In Josie King's case, it's difficult to pinpoint exactly what went wrong and when. First there was the infection that her doctor initially suspected had entered through her central line. Central line infections are so common in hospitals that they are not even considered to be errors in the strictest sense, or the result of negligence—though they should be—but simply a complication of care, a potentially lethal adverse event. About 250,000 patients a year suffer a central line infection, and as many as 60,000 die from it. (This hazard declines dramatically when hospitals institute well-defined protocols for keeping the insertion of central lines fastidiously clean.) Josie's infection did not kill her directly; it led to vomiting and diarrhea, which dehydrated her little body so severely that her weight dropped 15 percent in the twenty-four hours that preceded her cardiac arrest. That's like a two-hundred-pound man losing thirty pounds in a single day. Nobody knows how such a clear warning sign of dehydration could possibly have been overlooked, but one way or another it was missed by every person who scanned Josie's chart that day; or if it was noted by anyone, he or she failed to act. Perhaps it rang an alarm bell in the mind of a nurse, but in the fiercely hierarchical social order of hospitals, a person near the bottom may sometimes hesitate to speak up. Allowing Josie to drink a liter of juice in one sitting also may have contributed to her death, by suddenly diluting the electrolytes in her blood. Even if her sudden intake of fluid played no role in her death, it was a sure sign she was extremely dehydrated.

The final straw was when the pain specialist ordered another dose of methadone, unaware that the child's body was already so weakened that even a low dose of the drug might be enough to stop her small heart. By the time Josie was revived, she had already suffered massive brain damage. She spent two days on life support, and then, as her parents held their daughter tenderly in their arms, she died.

Josie King was killed by a third-world condition, dehydration, in a first-world—indeed a first-class—American hospital. Yet it's impossible to fix blame on any single person or event in the string of tiny missteps that led to her death. Perhaps the most devastating error of all was that nobody paid sufficient attention to Sorrel King's observation that her daughter was desperately thirsty.

This chapter from Brownlee's *Overtreated* begins with a nightmarish account of how a simple misdiagnosis can result in a tragic death. At the very least, mistakes in practicing medicine can alter a patient's well-being. Our first excerpt, from *The Spirit Catches You and You Fall Down*, demonstrated how communication and cultural barriers first caused Lia to be misdiagnosed with pneumonia, but in Brownlee's account, even when a parent is in constant communication with medical staff, or when patients can speak for themselves, misdiagnoses or mistakes can still happen. Has a family member or a close friend, or have you ever been misdiagnosed with a minor or significant illness? How do we, as a society, come to terms with the mistakes that can be made in medical diagnoses and treatments? In starting out with this anecdote about health care, what does Brownlee gain from her audience?

This assignment will help you with Major Assignment 3: Explaining a Medical or Healthful Intervention. Find Fisher's study ("The Implications of Regional Variations in Medicare Spending," parts 1 and 2, *Annals of Internal Medicine* 138, no. 4 (2003): 273-298) as well as "Summaries for patients. The implications of regional variations in Medicare spending: health outcomes and satisfaction with care" and "Summaries for patients. The implications of regional variations in Medicare spending: the content, quality, and accessibility of care." Read the study and the patients' summaries. Discuss the differences you notice in how the study and its outcomes are explained.

Some argue that patients need "health advocates," skilled practitioners who can represent them to their physicians, nurses, and hospital staff in case of illness or surgery. Search online for the growing profession of health advocacy and think about what this relatively new career offers to patients, health care providers, and others.

Brownlee's research and interviews demonstrate that patients, their family members, and their healthcare team must keep careful records of what medications have been prescribed, what tests have been administered, what surgeries have been completed, and how the patient's vitals have changed. Imagine that a family member or friend is going to the hospital for a medical procedure. Write a list of the kinds of questions that you have for your doctor and nurse and the kinds of information that any doctor should know about your subject's health history.

MAJOR ASSIGNMENTS

MAJOR ASSIGNMENT #1:
WRITE A HEALTH MEMOIR

BACKGROUND

Anne Fadiman tells the story of Lia Lee's life through Lia's experience with the American medical establishment and with Hmong spiritual healing. Alternatively, instead of actively seeking to heal emotional wounds, Julia Hansen writes about how she used nicotine to cope with unpleasant memories and past actions. Both authors deploy vivid description and personal narrative to draw the reader into the world of their subjects.

ASSIGNMENT

Using tools such as vivid description and personal voice, write a health memoir—a short biographical essay that foregrounds your relationship to illness, health, and well-being. You may choose to focus on a particular health-related episode in your life, or to identify a pattern that runs through your life that connects your health experiences to your growth as a thinking, reflective human being. Share as much or as little as you wish in the story you tell, but try to give your readers a sense of who you are as an author.

QUESTIONS FOR RESEARCH, REFLECTION, AND INVENTION

1. Who is the audience for your biographical essay?

2. What do you want this audience to understand, learn, or experience from reading your essay?

3. What kinds of details can you include about the physical circumstances of your health episode, or what kind of story can you tell about your healthful or unhealthful life, to draw in your reader?

4. What and when do you remember thinking about your health? What helps you to remember? Are there things that you would rather forget?

5. What aspects of daily life affect or might affect your health? Do you make everyday decisions (such as what to eat) that indirectly or directly have consequences for your health?

ABOUT MEMOIRS

Memoirs are biographical essays in which authors also make arguments about issues of concern or in which they reflect upon the consequences and underpinnings of the events in their lives that they recount. Some authors, such as Julia Hansen in *A Life in Smoke*, deliberately and carefully construct themselves in print as a literary character or persona. Think of your memoir as your chance to present yourself as an author to an unknown reader, as a reflective thinker to your classmates and to persons who already know you well, or as a character in a true-life story. You might begin by writing down any memories you have about health care or illness to see whether any particular episodes stand out for you as vivid experiences that you could share with your readers. If you can recall no particular episodes or incidents that you could memorialize, think about your relationship to a specific area of health, such as nutrition, relationships, or habits. As you reflect on these aspects of your life, look at them in light of their connection to your physical and mental well-being.

MAJOR ASSIGNMENT #2:
ANALYZE AN ADVERTISEMENT FOR PRESCRIPTION MEDICATION

BACKGROUND

We use the cliché "the picture of health" to describe a person whom we consider well, whole, and happy in all respects. Yet we might disagree about what constitutes "the picture of health." The cover of Time magazine that featured a young mother breastfeeding her three-year-old son struck some readers as a bold assertion of the natural and healthy practice of extended breastfeeding, but others as a vulgar sexualization of the relationship between mother and child. We call this kind of argument "figurative logic," because it uses images, both visual and rhetorical, to engage consumers' emotions and senses directly rather than employing reasoning to appeal to readers' intellect. This assignment will help you evaluate and analyze the intellectual and emotional appeals, the reasoned and figurative logic, that advertisers use to persuade consumers to purchase health commodities.

ASSIGNMENT

Identify a print advertisement for a prescription medication. You can find this kind of advertisement in magazines such as *Men's Health, Prevention, WebMD, People, Essence,* or *AARP*; your instructor might have further suggestions. Look closely at the image you have chosen and write a thesis-driven essay about the figurative or hidden logic that the advertiser is employing to publicize or sell this drug.

QUESTIONS FOR RESEARCH, REFLECTION, AND INVENTION

1. Which persons read the magazine where you found this image, and what kind of medications might they take? What do you think is this audience's relationship to health and health care?

2. What objects and words are featured in this advertisement? What is the content or main point of this image?

3. Can you describe and analyze the composition of this image? What colors, lines, shapes, and arrangements does it use?

4. What kinds of details populate this image? Does it include an elaborate background, or a single item in the foreground, or a mixture of both?

5. Do you respond emotionally to this image? How? How do you feel after free-writing about the image?

6. How effective is this image in making you trust or mistrust the medication? What response do you think the magazine's intended audience might have?

ABOUT IMAGE ANALYSIS

Pictures or images work instantly and vividly. Images evoke strong emotions in viewers, which is why advertisers deploy them; pictures can also work by using a kind of short-hand to allude to general cultural assumptions and beliefs. Those who work with images, from art historians to advertisers to graphic designers, use visual terms to describe, analyze, and use particular characteristics in images, such as color, line, composition, background, and foreground; they also pay attention to the medium in which they create the artwork or advertisement. Don't forget that you will still find many of the same rhetorical qualities you have learned to seek out in print texts, such as tone, style, organization, and audience.

MAJOR ASSIGNMENT #3:
EXPLAINING A MEDICAL OR HEALTHFUL INTERVENTION

BACKGROUND

The Fray's song "How to Save a Life" and the Save a Life Campaign explain how to intervene to prevent a suicidal friend from killing himself. The Fray's lyrics explain the intervention indirectly, but traditional explanatory writing can explain complicated procedures or processes in such a way that those who know little to nothing about such procedures can understand them. A medical or healthful intervention includes but is not limited to particular medicines, surgeries, or treatments; an intervention might comprise a change in one's diet, behavior, exercise or activity, sleep hygiene, or even in one's reading and writing habits.

ASSIGNMENT

Identify a health or medical intervention (an operation, a therapy, an exercise, a food, a habit) discussed in this book about which you would like to know more. Conduct research on this intervention and make sure that you understand it thoroughly. Now write an essay or make a YouTube video in which you explain (and demonstrate, if appropriate) this therapy or health intervention to an audience that is unfamiliar with it.

QUESTIONS FOR RESEARCH, REFLECTION, AND INVENTION

- Your instructor will give you further guidelines about which resources you should consult for further reading and how much you should read in preparation for this assignment.

- Your process or procedure does not have to be complicated or extremely technical. Even interventions that might seem simple to you (such as engaging in a particular exercise, or preparing a certain food) will need careful explanation to persons who have not encountered those interventions before.

- Nonetheless, you will have to ask yourself the following questions as you work through your assignment:

  1. Do you understand the process or procedure thoroughly? Do you need to check out library books, watch videos, or interview experts in order to become competent in your process or procedure?

2. How can you make your readers care about your intervention? Can you show them how and why the therapy or intervention you describe makes a difference to health?

3. Can you demonstrate to your readers how this intervention fits into existing patterns or institutions concerned with health, illness, and well-being?

4. Will multimedia elements such as images, sound clips, or videos help to explain your intervention as clearly as possible to your audience? Or will such tools distract from the explanation?

5. What will your audience know, and what will you need to explain? How would you explain your intervention to a grandparent? To a child? To a space alien?

ABOUT EXPLANATORY WRITING

Explanatory writing (sometimes called process writing) does not make an argument, but instead tries to lay out as clearly as possible a series of events or instructions. You can find models of explanatory writing in newspapers, software manuals, how-to videos on YouTube, and product packaging.

As you write your account, imagine going through the process one step at a time. Do not try to include a point of view or opinion, although you will need to make your reader understand why you think this intervention is helpful.

MAJOR ASSIGNMENT #4:
SERVICE-LEARNING SOCIAL MEDIA CAMPAIGN

BACKGROUND

Several of the readings ("Weather and Language Lessons," "RU Healthy?" and "Preparedness 101: Zombie Apocalypse") in this book, as well as some of the invention and writing assignments (the Pink Ribbon campaign and the CDC's anti-smoking campaign) use social media to communicate ideas and connect to audiences. Each reading and assignment uses or analyzes different kinds of social media, depending on the subject and audience.

ASSIGNMENT

For this assignment, you will identify a client that needs help (for example, the Diabetes Association, Down Syndrome research, a global water organization, or a cancer society). Some instructors may want their classes to work specifically with campus or city organizations. You will then conduct research about this nonprofit organization and design a social media campaign.

For the first half of your project, you will investigate your client and the organization's current approach to social media, write up a synopsis of your findings, and describe your social networking marketing plan. Your synopsis will include a history of the organization that you are promoting, any current social media plan that the client has in place, a description of organizations that are similar to your client's foundation and what these organizations do for social media, and why your client needs a new social media campaign. You will then explain your campaign's objective(s), your social media choices, and your campaign's target audience. Your instructor will decide the length of the paper and how many sources you should incorporate in your paper.

For the second half of your project, you will design the social networking campaign for your nonprofit organization. Your campaign must have two different "mock" social media pages: a Facebook page, a Twitter page, a Tumblr, WordPress, a Web site, and so on, and a multimodal component that your group created. The multimodal component may be a video or music clip, an animated cartoon, a screencast, an online presentation, a voiceover script, etc. You will work as individuals or in groups, depending on your instructor's preference.

QUESTIONS FOR RESEARCH, REFLECTION, AND INVENTION

1. How does your client currently use social media? Does it have a Facebook or Twitter page? What kind of Web site does it have? Does its Web site link to any blogs or other pages?

2. What would you say are the most important ideas that your client wants to communicate? Are those points being communicated in an effective manner on the Internet?

3. Who is your client's target audience (age, gender, education level, etc.)? Is its current campaign working for that age group? Should it reach out to another type of audience? Could that be what your campaign is about?

4. The types of social media you choose depend on the message and the amount of information you want to communicate. If you want to use Facebook in preference to Twitter, or use both, how is this decision important to your campaign?

5. What video, audio, or other multimodal element would help add to your campaign?

ABOUT SERVICE-LEARNING SOCIAL MEDIA CAMPAIGNS

Many nonprofit organizations use social media (Facebook, Twitter, newsfeeds, YouTube, blogs, and more) to spread awareness about their causes and to share updates about fundraisers, events, and other important information. Many more organizations, however, do not have the funds to hire someone to maintain these sites, so you could very well find an organization that needs your help in order to plan a real campaign. Social media campaigns can have very different goals: you could generate awareness about the charity's work, encourage others to volunteer their time and efforts to support the organization, focus on the story of a few people who have benefitted from the charity or organization, or educate the public about the organization's cause. For this project, your instructor will probably want you to focus on two of these goals, with your main objective being to promote health education.

MAJOR ASSIGNMENT #5:
THE PERSUASIVE RESEARCH PAPER

BACKGROUND

Many of the readings discuss controversial treatments for illnesses, disorders, and diseases. Some writers, such as Shannon Brownlee and Aneurin Bevan, argue more for systemic social change in healthcare; whereas other writers, such as William J. Broad, Anne Enright, Hanna Rosin, Denise Kersten Wills, and Dan Hurley, present recent findings about a specific health belief or drug treatment and then discuss the ways in which this treatment can help or harm others. For this assignment, you will conduct research about a health issue and voice your opinion about possible solutions.

ASSIGNMENT

Write a persuasive essay to convince someone to try or not to try treating a disease, disorder, or illness with a specific kind of medication or therapy. For instance, you might want to argue for the benefits of canine therapy for war veterans, to propose that health care plans should cover gym membership fees for all participants, or to encourage or discourage someone from seeking treatment for an illness or disorder.

QUESTIONS FOR RESEARCH, REFLECTION, AND INVENTION

* Your instructor will help you decide how much research and how many sources are appropriate for this assignment.

1. What are the main points that you would like to argue?
2. What and how much evidence or research do you need in order to support these points?
3. What are the counter-arguments to your claim? How will you argue against these conflicting claims? Will you need to make a compromise between two sides in order to come up with a good solution for the controversy?
4. Who is your audience for this essay?
5. In which magazine, Web site, or other medium do you hope to publish your essay in order to persuade your audience?

ABOUT PERSUASIVE WRITING

Writing an effective persuasive paper for your audience will require you to incorporate all three kinds of persuasion: ethical (ethos), logical (logos), and emotional (pathos). It is important for you to not rely too much on emotional arguments to persuade your readers because while emotional arguments can be powerful, they can encourage your audience to question your credibility if you have no facts (logic) or authority (credentials and ethics) to support your argument. It is therefore important to create a balance of support.

FILMOGRAPHY

DOCUMENTARIES

Exposés of the Medical, Agribusiness, and Pharmaceutical Industries, from Cradle to Grave

Google Baby (2009)

Surrogacy is big business, often outsourced to India, where American and Israeli couples can employ surrogates at a fraction of what it would cost at home. Israeli filmmaker Zippi Brand Frank follows entrepreneur Dr. Naina Patel in her clinic and investigates the extent to which childbearing has become a "commodity," as Frank comments.

The Alzheimer's Project (2009)

This series of four HBO films, made in collaboration with the National Institute for Health, draws attention to the ravages of Alzheimer's disease by publicizing the struggles of seven individual patients; advances in research; and the experiences of children, grandchildren, and caregivers of sufferers.

The Business of Being Born (2008)

This documentary uncovers the profit motive that underlines present-day obstetrics at all levels, and argues that both maternal and child health suffer in America because physicians fear crippling malpractice suits and because insurance companies profit from unnecessary interventions. The film includes wondrous and moving footage of live, natural home births.

Generation Rx (2008)

This well-meaning documentary asks whether parents are over medicating their children.

Food, Inc. (2008)

Director Rob Kenner, with the assistance of *The Omnivore's Dilemma* author Michael Pollan and *Fast Food Nation* author Eric Schlosser, divulges little-known information about America's food industry. Covering everything from the soybean industry and contaminated meat to animal cruelty and fast food companies and more, Kenner seeks to motivate his viewers to buy local, contact their congressman, and rethink their connection with the food that they eat.

Sicko (2007)

Controversial filmmaker Michael Moore compares the US health care system in 2007 with its counterparts in Canada, France, and the UK—and not to our credit.

Super Size Me (2004)

Morgan Spurlock consumed only food from McDonald's for thirty days and chronicled the deterioration of his health in this Sundance-award-winning film.

Sound and Fury (2000)

This moving documentary discusses the then-new technology of cochlear implants and two brothers in the Deaf community who disagree profoundly on how or whether they should insert the implants in their children.

The Lost Children of Rockdale County (2000)

A documentary that shocked the country, this film traces the origins of an outbreak of syphilis in a wealthy, upper-middle-class suburb of Atlanta during the 1990s. Researchers discovered that white children as young as middle-school age were engaging in risky sexual practices without the knowledge of their parents, many of whom provided money, expensive and fashionable clothing, and (in one case) a self-contained apartment for their teenage children—but not what these young people really needed: supervision by loving and mature adults.

NON-STANDARD THERAPIES GOOD, BAD, AND UGLY

Fat, Sick, and Nearly Dead (2010)

Morbidly obese, disease-ridden Joe Cross goes on an all-juice diet to lose weight and sets off on a road trip to convert others to his way of life.

Fat Head (2009)

Comedian Tom Naughton responds to *Super Size Me* by going on a diet of French fries—and losing weight on it!

Crazy Sexy Cancer (2007)

Actress Kris Carr, diagnosed with a rare vascular cancer, filmed a video diary of her quest for alternative therapies to supplement the treatment of her traditional oncologist.

The Split Horn (2001); *Between Two Worlds* (1984).

The first of these two documentaries about the Hmong (both directed by Taggart Siegel), *Between Two Worlds*, features the anthropologist Dwight Conquergood (from *The Spirit Catches You and You Fall Down*) as he undergoes a shamanic healing ceremony.

FEATURE FILMS

Medical Disaster Fantasies, Conspiracy Theories, and Dilemmas

Contagion (2011)

Steven Soderbergh directs an all-star cast in this medical thriller about an imagined worldwide viral pandemic.

Never Let Me Go (2010)

Kazuo Ishiguro's beautiful novel, adapted for the screen, poignantly begins as a seeming coming-of-age story before it develops into a mysterious dystopian fantasy in which cloned children are harvested for their organs.

Juno (2007)

A witty sixteen-year-old girl becomes pregnant. After considering abortion, she decides to give the baby up for adoption instead. Her family, quasi ex-boyfriend, and the child's adoptive parents all seek to comfort and support her, as Juno faces the psychological and physical changes that occur during her nine-month pregnancy. In turn, the adoptive parents also uncover truths about their marriage and their separate aspirations.

The Insider (1999)

Russell Crowe plays chemist Jeffrey Wigand, who blew the whistle on Big Tobacco's conspiracy to make cigarettes more addictive to consumers and to hide its knowledge of tobacco's unhealthy side effects.

Gattaca (1997)

Ethan Hawke and Uma Thurman star in this beautifully shot and prescient science fiction film set in a future where potential parents choose the traits that their offspring will inherit and so-called "naturals," conceived without engineering, suffer discrimination on the basis of their imperfect DNA.

Coma (1978)

This adaptation of a medical thriller by Robin Cook imagines a conspiracy of rogue doctors who induce comas in young, healthy persons after giving them anesthesia for elective surgery. An idealistic young surgeon investigating the mysterious coma of her best friend discovers them stored in suspended animation for a nefarious and profitable purpose (in a famous scene, we see bodies hanging on long wires from a high-ceilinged warehouse).

The Andromeda Strain (1971)

Scientists discover a terrible disease originating from outer space. Can they save humanity before the aliens detonate a massive bomb?

Young persons dying young, and older persons trying not to die at all

My Sister's Keeper (2009)

Sisters Anna and Kate literally owe their lives to each other: Anna, the younger, was conceived in vitro so that she would be able to donate blood and organs to Kate, who suffers from leukemia. Anna, however, begins to resist medical interventions that will compromise her own health and her future life.

The Bucket List (2007)

Two terminally ill men (played by Jack Nicholson and Morgan Freeman) resolve to fulfill their life's ambitions before they "kick the bucket."

Death Becomes Her (2002)

In this satire, Meryl Streep and Goldie Hawn seek the fountain of youth.

Wit (2001)

Emma Thompson's award-winning performance in this HBO movie wrenchingly portrays the brilliant but cold professor of Renaissance literature, Vivan Bearing, who when diagnosed with ovarian cancer must face her own mortality, the violence of chemotherapy, and the inadequacy of intellectual life to comfort or palliate extreme human suffering.

The Best Little Girl in the World (1981)

This television movie (adapted from Stephen Levenkron's 1978 novel) stars Jennifer Jason Leigh as Casey, a shy and high-achieving teenager who secretly spirals into anorexia when she takes up ballet.

Cocoon (1985)

Ron Howard's film uses retirement communities in Florida to explore issues surrounding longevity, resources, and medical ethics. The "cocoons" in question belong to an alien species that has hidden them for safe-keeping in a Florida pool that consequently rejuvenates the elderly persons who enter it.

Ordinary People (1980)

The first film directed by Robert Redford, *Ordinary People* portrays the toll taken on a reserved, upper-middle class white family by the death of the oldest son in a boating accident and the attempted suicide of his younger brother.

Love Story (1971)

Based on Erich Segal's best-selling novel, the heart-tugging "weepie" *Love Story* made famous the aphorism "Love means never having to say you're sorry." The film recounts the love affair of Jenny, a spirited working-class Italian-American woman (Ali McGraw), and Oliver, the preppy scion of wealthy WASP Harvard graduates (Robert Redford). Jenny and Oliver meet in the Radcliffe library and marry young, but their happiness is cut short when Jenny develops a terminal illness.

The Heart is a Lonely Hunter (1968)

Carson McCullers' now-classic novel came to the screen in an adaptation starring Alan Arkin as John Singer, a deaf-mute man who befriends several troubled persons in his small town, but whose own problems escape the notice of those around him.

Dark Victory (1939)

Bette Davis, in a signature role, plays a young woman in love with the physician who is hiding from her the fact that she is dying of an inoperable brain cancer.

TRANSCENDING DISABILITIES, MENTAL AND PHYSICAL

The King's Speech (2010)

Sweeping the Academy Awards, this film narrates the struggle of reluctant monarch George VI to conquer his stammer, with the aid of a determined (and profane) speech therapist.

The Black Balloon (2008)

In addition to the usual sibling tensions, two brothers share the challenge that one must attend to the other's autism.

The Diving-Bell and the Butterfly (2007)

This feature film dramatizes the true experiences of editor Jean-Dominique Bauby, paralyzed after a sudden stroke and rendered unable to communicate except by blinking his left eye. Nonetheless Bauby wrote and published a memoir, only to die just days after his book came out in 1997.

Rent (2005)

Based on the award-winning Broadway musical (itself an adaptation of Puccini's opera *La Bohème*), *Rent* chronicles the solidarity and struggles of artists, musicians, and drag queens in New York's East Village, in particular, the toll of AIDS, HIV, and drug use.

A Beautiful Mind (2001)

Russell Crowe stars as Nobel-prize-winning economist—and schizophrenic—John Nash in this fictionalized account of the scholar's life.

Girl, Interrupted (1999)

Susanna Kaysen's 1993 memoir about her incarceration in a mental hospital during the 1960s inspired this film starring Angelina Jolie.

Shine (1996)

Geoffrey Rush stars as David Helfgott, a promising pianist whose career is cut short by episodes of mental breakdown and illness.

Forrest Gump (1994)

Tom Hanks won an Academy Award for his portrayal of a developmentally disabled man who unknowingly attends some of the most important historical events in twentieth century history.

What's Eating Gilbert Grape (1993)

Johnny Depp plays the eponymous hero who must care for his autistic younger brother (Leonardo DiCaprio) in a poverty-stricken household.

Scent of A Woman (1992)

Al Pacino plays a blind, alcoholic, and retired military man who is contemplating suicide until his teenage caregiver (Chris O'Donnell) both saves and is saved by him.

My Left Foot (1989)

In a role that won him an Academy Award, Daniel Day-Lewis portrays Christy Brown, an artist and writer with cerebral palsy who can work only with his left foot.

Rain Man (1988)

Dustin Hoffman plays Raymond, an adult man with autism, and Tom Cruise plays the selfish younger brother (Charlie) who is unaware of Ray's existence until the sudden death of their father. The pair bond in an unlikely way when Charlie kidnaps Ray from the institution that has been his home in order to seek custody—and his father's fat inheritance.

Children of a Lesser God (1986)

Deaf actress Marlee Matlin won an Academy Award for her performance as a woman who resists learning to speak, even when coached by a charismatic teacher (William Hurt).

One Flew Over the Cuckoo's Nest (1975)

Milos Forman's Academy-Award-winning film dramatized the inhumane and humiliating treatment of many mental patients through its portrayal of the rigid and sadistic Nurse Mildred Ratched (Louise Fletcher).

Freaks (1932)

Tod Browning's shocking film about circus and sideshow performers—still upsetting today—tries to represent the human qualities of persons with disabilities but, limited by its historical era, offensively stereotypes its actors (real-life carnival performers) nonetheless.

TV SHOWS AND TV SPECIALS

Scripted Fiction: Sexy Doctors, Crazy Doctors, Funny Doctors—and Patients

The Big C (2010–)

Kathy (Laura Linney), a history teacher and devoted mother, is diagnosed with terminal cancer. Upon hearing her diagnosis, Kathy determines not to tell her family; instead, she orders a pool to be built in her backyard. Refusing to give the big "C" power to control her fate, Kathy, a once-reserved housewife, becomes outspoken, suddenly realizing that life is not about being perfect.

Nurse Jackie (2009–)

Edie Falco plays a witty, lively, and compassionate, but prescription-drug-addicted nurse.

Grey's Anatomy (2005–)

This Seattle-set series concentrates on the personal (and sexual) life of Dr. Meredith Grey.

House, M.D. (2004–2012)

In 2012 the successful and critically-acclaimed show *House, M.D.* ended its eight-season run. The lead character (played completely straight by British comedian Hugh Laurie with a pitch-perfect American accent) runs the fictional Diagnostic Medicine unit at Princeton-Plainsboro Hospital with overbearing, abrasive genius and the catchphrase "Everybody lies." The series based the physician House on Arthur Conan Doyle's fictional detective Sherlock Holmes: the characters had in common intellectual brilliance, an addiction to drugs, a devoted male friend, and an interest in music.

Nip/Tuck (2003–2010)

The fictional plastic-surgery practice of McNamara/Troy forms the center of this melodramatic serial.

Scrubs (2001–2010)

Narrated by medical student, then intern, then resident, J.D. (Zach Braff), this unusual show combined medical drama with comedy, and often featured musical or fantasy interludes.

E.R. (1994–2009)

This award-winning, long-running, fast-paced, and innovative medical drama gave George Clooney, among others, his start, and popularized techniques such as hand-held camera work in mainstream television.

St. Elsewhere (1982–1988)

Movie star Denzel Washington was featured in this six-Emmy-award-winning show about a challenged urban hospital and its dedicated doctors.

Dr. Kildare (1961–1966)

Starring a character (invented by Max Brand) who had previously featured in films from the 1930s and 1940s, the eponymous heart-throb Dr. Kildare (Richard Chamberlain) ushered in the now-popular genre of medical drama for the first time on television.

UNSCRIPTED, EDITED REALITY SHOWS

Heavy (2011–)

Morbidly obese persons are dieted and sent to fitness camp for six months.

Hoarders (2009–)

Psychologists are undecided whether hoarding (the uncontrollable collection of objects) forms part of obsessive-compulsive disorder or whether it is a distinct disorder; the subjects of this show hoard objects to such an extent that they are about to lose their homes or families.

Intervention (2005–)

Addicts of all kinds receive interventions and are convinced into going to treatment centers. The addicts' treatment and recovery are, sadly, sometimes not as successful as the intervention.

The Biggest Loser (2004–)

This competition rewards contestants for losing weight through extreme measures, such as strenuous workouts with militant personal trainers and drastically reduced-calorie diets, but the show also attempts to modify contestants' long-term behavior in more realistic ways.

Extreme Makeover (2002–2007)

Volunteers agree to extensive changes in their physical appearance, including cosmetic surgery, in this graphic show, which over time proved slightly too gruesome for television audiences.

WORKS CITED

Almasi, Elizabeth A., Randall Stafford, Richard Kravitz and Peter Mansfield, "What are the Public Health Effects of Direct-to-Consumer-Advertising?" PLOS Med 3(3): e145. Web.

Bevan, Aneurin. House of Commons Debates, vol. 422, cols. 43–142 43, 30 April 1946. Web.

Broad, William J. "How Yoga Can Wreck Your Body." *The New York Times*. 2012. January 5. Web.

Brownlee, Shannon. *Overtreated*. New York: Bloomsbury, 2007. "The Most Dangerous Place." 43–71. Print.

Chandaria, Kartik. "Weather and Language Lessons." Doctors Without Borders Blog, November 15, 2011. Web.

Dodd, Lamar. "Surgeons III." Pen-and-ink Sketch. Georgia Museum of Art, Athens, GA.

Ehrenreich, Barbara. *Bright-sided: How the Relentless Promotion of Positive Thinking Has Undermined America*. New York: Metropolitan Books, 2009. 21–27. Print.

Enright, Anne. "My Milk: On Becoming a Mother." *London Review of Books*. 22.19 (2000): 34–35. Print.

Fadiman, Anne. *The Spirit Catches You and You Fall Down: A Hmong Child, Her American Doctors, and the Collision of Two Cultures*. New York: Farrar, Straus, and Giroux, 1997. 20–31, 291–292. Print.

Feiler, Bruce. "What to Say to Someone Who's Sick: You Look Great and Other Lies." *The New York Times*. June 10, 2011. Web.

The Fray. "How to Save a Life." *How to Save a Life*. Sony, 2005.

Freedman, David H. "How to Fix the Obesity Crisis." *Scientific American*. Feb 2011. Vol. 304.2. 40–47. Print.

Gabbard, Dwight Christopher. "A Life Beyond Reason." *The Chronicle of Higher Education*. The Chronicle of Higher Education, 7 Nov. 2010. Web.

Gilbert, Daniel. *Stumbling Upon Happiness*. New York: Vintage, 2005. 165–188. Print.

Grady, Denise. "An Immune System Trained to Kill Cancer." *New York Times*. September 12, 2011. D1. Print.

Hansen, Julia. *A Life in Smoke*. New York: Free Press, 2006. 1–8, 48–56, 61–67. Print.

Houston, Katy. *Sweetness Follows*. Nashville, TN: Favorite Recipes Press, 2013. 82.

Hurley, Dan. "A Drug for Down Syndrome." *The New York Times Magazine*. 2011. Web.

Khan, Ali S. "Preparedness 101: Zombie Apocalypse." May 16th, 2011. Web.

Krisberg, Kim. "RU Healthy? Public Health Efforts Take On Text Messaging." *The Nation's Health*. 2009. 1, 16. Print.

The NAMES Project AIDS Memorial Quilt. http://www.aidsquilt.org/. Web.

Nestle, Marion. *What to Eat*. New York: North Point Press, 2006. 46–55.

Pinsky, Drew and Todd Gold. *Cracked: Putting Broken Lives Together Again: A Doctor's Story*. New York: ReganBooks, 2003. 53–65. Print.

Rosin, Hanna. "The Case Against Breast-Feeding." *The Atlantic*. May 2009. Web.

Schoeller, Martin. Time Magazine Cover, May 21, 2012, "Are You Mom Enough?" Web and Print.

Wills, Denise Kersten. "Healing Life's Traumas." *Yoga Journal*. Cruz Bay Publishing, 2012. Web.